Listening to the Word of God

A Tribute to Dr. Boyce W. Blackwelder

Edited by
Dr. Barry L. Callen

Published by
Anderson University
and
Warner Press
Anderson, Indiana

All scripture passages, unless otherwise indicated, are from the King James Version ©1972 by Thomas Nelson or the Revised Standard Version ©1972 by Thomas Nelson.

Copyright ©1990 by Warner Press, Inc.
ISBN 0-87162-516-4   Stock #D5800
All Rights Reserved
Printed in the United States of America
Warner Press, Inc.

Arlo F. Newell, Editor in Chief
Dan Harman, Book Editor
Barry L. Callen, Editor
Cover by Larry Lawson

IN GRATEFUL DEDICATION

Over several decades Dr. Boyce Blackwelder was a prophetic person who heard God's Word, interpreted it with care, and then conveyed it with clarity and courage to the minds and hearts of thousands of needy persons. This large body of grateful persons is represented by two brothers, Roland and Jack Anderson. They received personal benefit from this prophetic ministry and provided generous assistance without which this present volume would not have been possible.

Barry L. Callen
Anderson University

When my husband of 33 years heard the summons to lay aside the Gospel Torch, I was confident others would receive the call to pick it up and carry it on.

I am indeed grateful for this book, written in his honor, and deeply appreciate each one who has contributed to its publication.

My prayer is that it will have far-reaching results in challenging young men and women to follow the servanthood role of the Master and find fulfillment in a comprehensive study of the Word of God.

                    Lela Blackwelder Allen
                    October 4, 1989

Library of
KENNETH A. FAIRBANKS

Table of Contents

Chapters   Page

    Introduction   xi

Section I: Remembering the Man

1. Boyce W. Blackwelder: The Man, His Ministry, His Scholarship .... Barry L. Callen   1
2. Perspectives On Biblical Studies and Seminary Education.................. Boyce W. Blackwelder   19

Section II: Interpreting the Word

3. Equal Access to Grace in Ministry: Women and Men .... James R. Christoph   41
4. The Prophets: Divine Word or Human Words? .... George Kufeldt   57
5. Characterization and Reader Construction of Characters in the Gospels .... Frederick W. Burnett   69
6. Holy Spirit as Empowerer for Ministry in Luke-Acts....................... John E. Stanley   91
7. The Significance of the Differing Audiences in Galatians and Romans .... Lynn Spencer Spaulding   103
8. *Teleios* as "Mature," "Complete," or "Brought to Completion" in the Pauline Writings... Gene Miller   121
9. Babylon and the New Jerusalem: Interpreting the Book of Revelation .... Kenneth E. Jones   133
10. Ministerial Authority in Biblical Perspective ....James Earl Massey   153

    Bibliography 163

Introduction

An Historic Occasion

The school year 1990-1991 marks the fortieth anniversary of the founding of the School of Theology of Anderson University. The School of Theology serves as the seminary of the Church of God (Anderson, Indiana) and as a professional graduate school of the University, preparing persons for informed and inspired leadership in the church.

This volume is one important way for the University and the church to celebrate and profit from this historic occasion. The School of Theology is pleased to record and honor in this volume the ministry, scholarship, and memory of Dr. Boyce W. Blackwelder. Found in the pages that follow is an overview of the ministerial and academic life and perspectives of this gifted servant of God who devoted his final thirteen years to the teaching ministry of the School of Theology. Found also are several essays of original biblical scholarship prepared in his honor by a select group of his former students and teaching colleagues. These significant persons, now scholars and church leaders themselves, all were touched directly by the work of Dr. Blackwelder and are pleased in this small way to carry forward the task he loved so much, that of listening carefully to what the Word of God has to say.

Dr. Blackwelder served the seminary and its students as Professor of New Testament from 1963 until his death in 1976. May his love of teaching, his caring for persons, and his disciplined listening for the in-depth meanings in the Word of God characterize the seminary and its students for generations yet to come.

Vital Church Questions Addressed

A basic assumption in what follows is that the Bible is authoritative for the contemporary Christian. That authority, however, cannot play its proper role in today's church life unless we as readers of the Bible take an acceptable stance toward it. We must be willing to commit ourselves to set aside all encumbrances that would obstruct our hearing of that Word, including our personal and church traditions that would predetermine for us the supposed meaning of that Word. Biblical scholarship as evidenced in this volume seeks to honor biblical authority by engaging in honest listening to what the Word itself has to say on a range of subjects vital to church life today.

Chapter Previews

The decades of disciplined listening done by Dr. Blackwelder and the recent listening and subsequent writing done by these his grateful students and colleagues provide some significant messages for the hearing of today's Christian church.

After the introductory chapter by Barry L. Callen highlighting Dr. Blackwelder's life of ministry and scholarship, a previously unpublished paper follows in chapter two in which Dr. Blackwelder defines his own perspectives on biblical studies and seminary education. As illustrations of how such formative and enduring views can and should be applied for the benefit of today's church, a series of insightful essays then appear by contemporary biblical scholars committed to seminary education and the authority of the revealed Word when it is heard with care.

In chapter three James R. Christoph returns to the creation stories in Genesis. Despite what too often has been claimed by others, he explains his hearing that God's will for creation is equal access to grace in ministry for women and men. Genuine dignity, equality, and opportunity is assumed as God's intention in creation and in the body of Christ, the church, without regard to gender.

George Kufeldt addresses in chapter four crucial concerns related to "prophetic preaching." When so much on television and radio today excites, confuses, and sometimes embarrasses sincere Christians, it is important to consider this presentation of the biblical approach to the nature and role of God's true prophets. How can we hear God's Word and not merely human words seeking our attention and dollars?

Chapter five represents the extensive effort of Fredrick W. Burnett to explore the process of characterization as an avenue for better understanding the persons introduced in the Gospels. Although classical scholarship and much of the contemporary world of biblical criticism have tended to view "persons" mainly as types, as literary devises instead of pivotal and necessarily real individuals, Burnett raises important questions and suggests a rather different point of view. He concludes that "personal" aspects of characters in the Gospels, such as Peter and especially Jesus, may well have played a role in early Christianity greater than many form and redaction critics have been prepared to admit.

Since the transforming Christian message came right into the harsh realities of this world with a commission to bring good news and hope, in chapter six John E. Stanley seeks clarity on a unique empowerment designed to make the Christian mission possible. What was the nature and role of the ministry of the Holy Spirit in Luke-Acts? Utilizing a literary approach to the exegetical task, he concludes that the calling, gifting, and empowering work of the Holy Spirit was and very much is essential to accomplishing the mission of the church in any age.

Lynn Spencer Spaulding explores in chapter seven the significant differences between Romans and Galatians and clarifies the cruciality of understanding those differences for the integrity of the interpretive process. Only in knowing and accounting carefully for the distinctiveness of the original author and intended reading audience of each book can their vital messages be heard properly today.

"Perfection" in the Christian life is a concept often misunderstood and often the source of great frustration as one seeks to be all that God intends. Gene Miller uses chapter eight to make clear the subtle range of meanings of the Greek words in the New Testament that address this central goal of a Christian's walk with God. It offers needed assistance in determining what being mature citizens of the kingdom of God means.

Kenneth F. Jones reviews in chapter nine the range of traditional ways the Book of Relevation has been interpreted over the centuries. Recognizing that in this final book of the Bible is a vital message for the contemporary church, he suggests an approach to interpreting very unusual and difficult texts in a way that enables both appropriate exegesis and current application. Somehow this book must be saved from obscurity and also rescued from arbitrary interpretations if ever it is to be heard as an authentic and enduring word from God.

In the final chapter, James Earl Massey addresses the whole issue of ministerial authority in biblical perspective. The man or woman who receives God's call to ministry and listens with care to the revealed Word of God is a person with sacred responsibility to be fulfilled, not one with privileged rights to be forced upon others. Those persons being ministered to are intended to comprise a consenting community that recognizes and willingly receives the ministry. Ministerial authority is found in the minister's spirit of sacrificial service in the context of the community of believers. Though the world and even some ego-laden ministers fail to understand, success in Christian ministry is to be measured by the sign of the cross.

These ten biblical scholars have sought in a disciplined way to employ their scholarship as humble servants of God. In tribute to Dr. Blackwelder, beloved mentor, colleague and friend, these fresh explorations into the meaning of God's Word have been prepared. I hope that they may be of assistance as the church of today seeks to hear again the voice of God speaking to the lives of its members and to the desperate needs of its times.

Barry L. Callen
Anderson University
April 1990

BARRY L. CALLEN

B.A., Geneva College; M.Div., Anderson University School of Theology; M.Th., Asbury Theological Seminary; D.Rel., Chicago Theological Seminary; Ed.D., Indiana University.

University Professor of Christian Studies, Corporate Secretary, Special Assistant to the President, Anderson University (Anderson, Indiana). Former student, dean, and teaching colleague of Dr. Boyce W. Blackwelder.

Chapter 1

Boyce Watson Blackwelder: The Man, His Ministry, His Scholarship

by Barry L. Callen

Boyce Watson Blackwelder was a humble man with strong Christian convictions. He was a dedicated and thorough biblical scholar who labored tirelessly to understand the meaning of God's revelation and then communicate that meaning effectively to others. This present volume seeks to remember and honor this special servant of God and to carry on his labors by presenting the current work of a series of his select students and close colleagues.

From Weaving Cloth to Interpreting the Word

Boyce W. Blackwelder was born on February 3, 1913 in Concord, North Carolina. His parents, Charles and Martha McInnis Blackwelder, were both natives of North Carolina. Each migrated to Concord from rural settings. Charles was the ninth of thirteen children in a family that raised its own food, carded cotton and wool, spun yarn and wove cloth for the family's needs. His family moved to Concord when he was a lad. Eventually he found employment in the Cannon Textile Mills Company where he was a weaver of black cloth and then supervisor until his retirement at age sixty-nine.

Martha, on arrival in Concord, also went to work as a weaver in the same company as Charles. After meeting and marrying, they built a good life together. Little did they know in those early years that one day their son Boyce also would become a skilled weaver. For him, however, it would not be the meticulous handling of cotton or wool, but of Hebrew and Greek words that Boyce would come to believe form the fabric of nothing less than a sure presentation of God's revelation to humankind.

Young Boyce was full of initiative despite being rather shy. After his graduation from Concord High School in 1930 he joined his parents as a weaver of cloth at Cannon Textile. However, for Boyce the future lay not in that mill, but in a little white church building down the street from the Blackwelder residence. It was a congregation of the Church of God (Anderson, Indiana) pastored by Rev. Brady O. Privett. People said of Brother Privett that when he preached "words fell from his lips like bullets from a machine gun." Some of those words were to penetrate Boyce's life very deeply indeed.

The Blackwelder family had attended the Trinity Reformed Church ever since Charles and Martha had married. But Brother Privett began to change that through attracting Boyce to the Church of God. Privett had organized a small band to play in the services at his church and in the street meetings he held occasionally in the area. Boyce, who had played trumpet in his high school band, heard them practicing down the street. His interest and initiative took over. With his mother's permission, he took his trumpet to the church, joined the band, and became acquainted with the joyous worship and clear teachings of those saintly people. Soon his own sense of guilt for sin weighed heavily on him. On July 15, 1931, he knelt at an altar and his guilt was transformed into the wonder of forgiveness and new life in Christ. His life was significantly and forever changed.

Boyce was bold in his new spiritual experience. He quickly sought santification, what he understood as full commitment to and divine empowerment for whatever God had planned for him. That August, wanting to be faithful to Bible instruction, he was baptized in Pharr's Mill Pond wearing a new white suit. Indeed, many things were new besides the suit. He began to teach a Sunday School class, speak in midweek services, and help conduct cottage prayer meetings and evangelistic services. Both he and others soon recognized that he was called and committed to a life of active ministry. Accordingly, he was ordained to the ministry by the North Carolina Ministerial Assembly of the Church of God on December 30, 1931. He prayed earnestly for his own family, and soon, under the direct influence of his own preaching, both his mother and father and his sisters Margie and Nellie were converted to dedicated and fruitful Christian lives.

The time had now come for some serious preparation for this life of ministry. With exposure to issues of the *Gospel Trumpet*, national periodical of the Church of God, and books by Herbert M. Riggle, a well-known pioneer preacher and prolific writer, young Boyce became convinced that attending Anderson College and Theological Seminary (now Anderson University) in Indiana was God's will for him. He gained admission, bought a suitcase for ninety-eight cents, packed what little he had, boarded a train, and for the first time left North Carolina pursuing a vision that was in his heart.

Once in Anderson he found his way to the campus and was welcomed by President John Morrison. Boyce immediately wanted to know how to find Brother Riggle and was directed across the street to the Gospel Trumpet Company to meet personally the man whom later he would learn to call "Dad." Mrs. Minnie Riggle was serving as pastor of the small Arrow Heights Church of God on the west side of Anderson. The Riggles invited Boyce to attend church with them and then come on home for dinner. This began what were to become important personal and professional relationships for the future.

Boyce began attending Arrow Heights regularly, teaching and even preaching occasionally as he continued his studies at the college and supported himself in those difficult financial times with whatever work could be found. Convinced that God had called and would provide somehow, he was relentless in pursuing what was necessary to continue on, including carrying a sign over his shoulders to advertise meals at a restaurant in exchange for his own noon meal and any leftover donuts (which he would take back to campus where hungry friends usually were waiting!). His vision kept him encouraged; he was to prepare to spread the Word of God without thought of pay or personal sacrifice.

Pastoral Ministry

Boyce was committed simultaneously to serious Christian discipleship and biblical scholarship. The Arrow Heights congregation became a long-term focus of his growing pastoral and teaching skills. The Riggles left Anderson in 1933 and, with their encouragement, the church called Boyce to provide new leadership, interim at first, but coming to involve almost twelve years. He had become a pastor while a student and only a teen-ager, walking and then riding a bicycle across the city from the campus to fulfill his pastoral duties. He couldn't afford to purchase his first car until 1940. Despite such limitations, the church grew to about five hundred persons, its large mortgage was burned in 1939, the Church of God's most prominent evangelists came for special meetings, and additional property was purchased to allow more expansion. Boyce married Alice Lela Smith in July 1943 and their son Charles was born in September 1944. By that time all of the church's properties were debt free and a building fund was growing. Those were remarkable years of inspired leadership by a young man who, at the same time, was investing much of himself in serious academic study.

The Arrow Heights people were always gracious to their gifted, zealous young minister-student, and always he remained a serious student. On the Anderson campus across town from the church, for instance, Dr. Otto F. Linn, as Boyce later reported with deep gratitude, "first introduced me to the riches of New Testament Greek." While pastoring, Boyce earned from Anderson College and Theological Seminary a Bachelor of Arts degree in 1936 and a Bachelor of Divinity degree in 1938 and from the School of Religion of Butler University in nearby Indianapolis a Master of Arts degree in 1944. He wrote for the B. D. a thesis titled "The New Testament Standard of Christian Unity," exploring and reaffirming a key aspect of the teaching of his Church of God tradition. He concluded, for instance, that:

> Sanctification augments unity. The reception of the Holy Spirit as a second work of divine grace in entire sanctification cleanses the regenerate heart from inherent sin which in the final analysis is the root of division, thus removing the cause of disunity. And simultaneously the purified soul is filled with divine love and grace which seals the unity already established. It is evident that Christian unity is more than an intellectual doctrine—it is an experience in the Holy Spirit (106).

Then at Butler his extensive linguistic abilities in both Greek and Hebrew became evident, eventuating in an M.A. thesis titled "An Investigation of the Phrase 'Day of Yahweh' in the Prophets of the Old Testament."

There he met and was influenced deeply by persons like Dr. Toyozo Nakarai. His world was growing and focusing more and more in intensive biblical studies. Dean Kirschner of Butler's School of Religion was reported by President Robert H. Reardon of Anderson College many years later to have inquired about the whereabouts of Boyce Blackwelder and to have observed: "I have taught all of my life and he is one of the two most dedicated and most brilliant New Testament scholars I ever have had in my classes."

Boyce's scholarly attitudes were very evident and, in his mind and heart, fully compatible with his orthodox Christian commitments, including his clear commitment to the cruciality of the "subjective" Christian experiences of regeneration and sanctification. He concluded the Preface to his Butler thesis, for instance, with sentences worth careful note by Christian scholars who are tempted to intellectual arrogance or by Christian laypersons who are tempted to make their personal spiritual experiences the sole measure of all things.

> We realize that we have done little more than indicate something of the circumstances in which the prophets lived, and have outlined but briefly a few features of their thought. We trust that other workers will discover truths which we have overlooked. Thought can live if it is free to change. Old

ideas are being dispelled constantly by the appearing of new facts. We reserve the right to reconsider our position when new evidence warrants that we do so. The chasm between truth and individualistic or subjective interpretation of truth is sometimes wide. We have tried to be as objective as possible" (ii).

The call to pastor remained clear to Boyce, but the call to continue formal education now seemed equally clear. An opportunity for both came in the form of a call from the Belden Avenue Church of God in Chicago. Boyce assumed pastoral responsibilities there in December 1944 with the church understanding and supporting his desire to continue his education at the doctoral level. Thus, in 1946-47 he studied part-time for two quarters in the Divinity School of the University of Chicago and then in 1947 enrolled in the Th.D. program at Northern Baptist Theological Seminary. His circle of scholarly friends broadened as he joined the Society of Biblical Literature in 1951 and received the Th.D. degree in May 1951 after having written a dissertation titled "The Causal Use of Prepositions in the Greek New Testament." Dr. Julius R. Mantey, co-author with H. E. Dana of the widely used *A Manual Grammar of the Greek New Testament* (Macmillan, 1927), had supervised this major research and writing project. This dissertation, many of the implications of which would appear in Boyce's later books, came to the following conclusion:

The data observed has led to the conclusion that most of the Greek prepositions in the Hellenistic vernacular were used causally. This use was one of the consistent idioms of Koine Greek. A recognition of this important aspect of syntax is an invaluable aid in the translation of prepositions. In fact, controversies which have raged over certain problem passages in the New Testament are resolved in many instances by an awareness of the possibility of a causal translation for prepositions (145-146).

The Writing Ministry

Finally the educational foundation had been laid. In the coming years there would be built on that foundation, in addition to continued pastoring, sizable ministry structures of informed preaching, inspiring teaching, and extensive writing. At no time in this long process would Boyce ever permit his sometimes exhausting scholarly pursuits to isolate him from the practical demands of church and family life or to dull his vibrant love for the wonder and relevance of God's truth. During the Chicago years, for instance, the Belden Avenue church was served faithfully. Daughter Dorothea was born in 1949. Boyce, now rather well-known across the Church of God, spoke with increasing frequency in camp meetings and ministers' meetings. His articles began appearing with regularity in the *Gospel Trumpet* (he had exchanged the trumpet which had drawn him into the church fellowship back in Concord for a typewriter that would serve so well that particular fellowship and the wider church generally). When the doctoral degree was completed, there was a new freedom to accept new pastoral calls, first to the Park Place Church of God, Connersville, Indiana in 1951, where daughter Rhoda was born, and then to the Pine Avenue First Church of God, Erie, Pennsylvania in 1953.

During 1958, in the midst of the many activities of a growing family and a growing church in Erie, Dr. Blackwelder's first book was completed. After the Gospel Trumpet Company (Warner Press) had released *Light from the Greek New Testament*, Charles E. Brown, beloved historian of the Church of God and former editor in chief of the church's publishing company, released a glowing review in the August 16, 1958 issue of the *Gospel Trumpet*. He said the book "solves more problems and explains more puzzling passages than a whole cartload of commentaries" and, furthermore, the solutions "are not the snap judgments of an illiterate dogmatist but the carefully worked out insights of a sound scholar and a spiritual minister of Christ." A foreword was included in the book by Boyce's mentor and friend Julius Mantey of Chicago. Mantey judged this new book "a notable contribution toward making the marvelous truths in the New Testament more relevant and understandable to people with little or no knowledge of Greek." Many ministers readily came to agree. As late as 1976, near the time of Boyce's unexpected death, Baker Book House reprinted this book in an attractive paperback edition.

Dr. Blackwelder was indebted consciously to A. T. Robertson's *A Grammar of the Greek New Testament in the Light of Historical Research* (1914), which he called a "monumental work," and then, of course, to the subsequent work of Julius Mantey and his associates. Boyce, continuing this interpretive tradition, saw considerable meaning in the vocabulary and grammar of the Greek text of the New Testament. He made his own assumptions plain in *Light from the Greek New Testament*:

> A knowledge of grammar and syntax is a fundamental requisite for sound interpretation. A person cannot be a theologian unless he is first a grammarian. That is to say, basically exegesis is grammatical (30).

Consequently, Boyce's attention turned quickly to the development of his own original translations of individual New Testament books. The School of Theology of Boyce's alma mater in Anderson invited him to be its sixth Alumni Lecturer in November 1960. He chose the topic "Interpreting the First Epistle of John." This campus involvement was a first step toward what by 1963 would be a major change in Boyce's ministerial focus. In the meantime, the books *Toward Understanding Paul* (1961) and *Toward Understanding Romans* (1962) appeared, the latter including an original "exegetical" translation of the text of the book of Romans.

A Time To Teach

On August 25, 1963, Dr. Boyce Blackwelder preached his final two sermons in the Erie church which he called "this beloved congregation." Some thirty years of pastoral ministry were coming to an end. He announced to the church that he had been challenged by the opportunity of service in the Department of New Testament at the School of Theology of Anderson College (University). He had received this invitation very humbly and prayerfully, having made plain to President Robert Reardon and Dean Gene Newberry, "You must promise, you must covenant, that you will pray for me because it is an awesome responsibility." And so, on September 1, 1963, Boyce joined this faculty as an Associate Professor of Bible.

Faculty colleagues respected his credentials and extensive pastoral experience but had concern about how he would relate during the sixties when even the innovative teachers occasionally were "sawn and quartered" by some free thinking students. After all, his reputation had him pictured in at least a few minds as quite conservative theologically, pulpit oriented professionally, a man with his mind already made up on most things, and his strong views justified by his readiness to give detailed explanation of every word and grammatical construction in any related biblical passage, the authority beyond dispute. But, as senior colleague Dr. John W. V. Smith later observed, "Boyce's eagerness to be a good teacher and to be a participating team [member] on the faculty were immediately apparent."

Boyce delivered his inaugural address to the seminary community that October. He confessed again feeling a deep sense of inadequacy but made clear nevertheless that "we are convinced of the trustworthiness of the Scriptures . . . and we believe that, in submission to the authority of God's Word and in reliance upon the power of his Spirit, we can go forward with confidence toward the fulfillment of our mission." He then proceeded to identify "five basic imperatives," namely:

1. Our task is to reiterate the objectivity and abiding relevance of the New Testament;
2. Our task is to apply the results of linguistic research to the interpretation of the text of the New Testament;

3. Our task is to relate the work of the Department of New Testament to the other fields of study within the seminary curriculum;
4. Our task is to train faithful ministers who in turn will transmit to others the message of the New Testament;
5. Our task is to exemplify the ethical principles of the New Testament.

What followed this inauguration were thirteen busy and fruitful years of teaching, learning, growing, preaching, and publishing. *Toward Understanding Thessalonians* was published in 1965, followed by *Letters From Paul: An Exegetical Translation* in 1971. He then started similar preparation for an original translation of the four Gospels. At his death in 1976 he had completed Matthew, Mark, and Luke and had extensive notes on John. His wife Lela and former Greek student Dr. Gene Miller did the final editing of these materials so that *The Four Gospels: An Exegetical Translation* could be released in 1980. In the meantime (1976) Baker Book House had decided to reprint in paperback edition Boyce's first book *Light from the Greek New Testament* (1958).

Boyce was an avid reader of scholarly journals. His professional growth was stimulated further by his opportunities as a visiting scholar at Union Theological Seminary in New York City (summer 1966) and Harvard University Divinity School (sabbatical leave, fall 1969). Likely his most fulfilling experience was the intense six-week Middle East seminar in Cyprus, Lebanon, Jordan, and Israel in which he participated with his Anderson religion faculty colleagues during the summer of 1968. Enabled by a faculty development grant from the Lilly Endowment, Inc., nearly all major archaeological sites relevant to biblical studies were visited, often with interpretative lectures on-site by scholars of international reputation.

During the 1975-76 school year the decision was made that Dr. Blackwelder's years of dedicated teaching and writing and exemplary professional growth should be recognized by his being promoted to the rank of Full Professor, effective September 1, 1976. Boyce felt genuinely honored and fulfilled by this news, reflecting back on the sense of inadequacy with which he had begun his faculty tenure in 1963 and also seeing with gratitude the fruition of the faith he had expressed in his inaugural address—"In reliance upon the power of his Spirit we can go forward with confidence toward the fulfillment of our mission."

Boyce spent half of January 1976 in a preaching campaign in the island nation of Barbados. Following semester two of that school year he devoted the summer to preaching in a variety of settings in

Alabama, Tennessee, Oklahoma, Kansas, Texas, and Ohio. On August 23, 1976, while sleeping in a motel in St. Clairsville, Ohio, he unexpectedly and quietly completed his earthly ministry and was promoted well beyond the rank of Full Professor. His mission was fulfilled. He died "with his boots on," having preached twice the previous day and with his Greek New Testament and several other books lying on a table next to the bed.

A Continuing Legacy

In his own judgment one of Dr. Boyce Blackwelder's most significant life experiences was his opportunity from 1942-1944 to be a student of Dr. Toyozo Nakarai at Butler University's School of Religion in Indianapolis. He admired Dr. Nakarai as an "eminent scholar" because of his distinguishing qualities of depth of insight, wide range of knowledge (especially in the field of Hebrew and cognate languages), kind and noble spirit, respect for the opinions of other persons, and his constant "Christo-centric" life. Such qualities, however, were more than recognized and admired. Boyce Blackwelder lived them himself. He once prayed that "God will raise up in each future generation persons of the exacting scholarship, spiritual devotion, and radiant faith of His servant, Dr. Toyozo Nakarai." Certainly he dedicated himself to being an agent of God in helping with such raising up—and he himself was an outstanding example of the prayer fulfilled.

Several scholars now raised up are contributors to this present volume. I am grateful to be one of that number and always I will remember many stimulating hours in Dr. Blackwelder's classes at Anderson University's School of Theology. I remember his passion for precision, his saying that "a scholar is a person who is careful with the facts and whose opinion on a subject is no better than his information on that subject." I remember the paradox of his teaching style, both his gentle and humble simplicity and his tendency to forget that he was in a small classroom rather than a camp meeting tabernacle, his voice booming his insights with convincing notes of authority and finality. I remember that he remained a student himself, persistent in his own quest for truth. I remember how he cared for me as an individual student. I remember the seeds he sought to plant in the minds and hearts of his students: discipline, a love for God's Word, a respect for the pulpit and the pastorate, a loyalty to the high calling of God in Christ Jesus, our Lord. I remember Boyce, my teacher, and I praise God for my memories!

Dr. Gene Miller, another former student of Boyce and current Associate Professor of New Testament at the School of Theology, recalls the most outstanding and influential quality of Dr. Blackwelder as the blending of capable, professional scholarship and dedicated churchmanship. It was a rich wedding of Christian scholarship, spiritual dedication, and unflagging loyalty to the church.

Another current biblical scholar on the Anderson campus and former student of Boyce, Dr. Fredrick W. Burnett, has put a similar perception in a somewhat different way. He recalls two foci as the heart of Dr. Blackwelder's legacy, foci that no one of us can afford to ignore. One was his great love of the biblical text and his devotion to analyzing minutely every possible semantic implication of the original languages. "It was Dr. Blackwelder who helped instill in me the desire to spend time in rigorous study of the text. He was able to show me the beauty of the biblical text in its own language." The other was his unwillingness to pursue the meaning of the biblical text in isolation from its exposition. "It mattered greatly to him that the results of biblical scholarship were accessible to the church. It seemed that all of his scholarship and energy were directed to the goal of allowing the biblical text to be the authoritative guide for the church's proclamation of the gospel."

In 1958 Boyce began his first and best-known book, *Light from the Greek New Testament,* with these words: "The study of language is a most fascinating and enlightening adventure. This is true especially when considering the words of divine revelation. The student who discovers something of the infinite richness they contain is rewarded for all his strenuous efforts." Certainly Dr. Blackwelder's own conduct as a teacher reflected such an adventure and offered such a reward.

The annual faculty report to the dean of the School of Theology dated May 1, 1976, turned out to be Dr. Blackwelder's last. As with most activities, he took this annual reporting obligation seriously and put thoughtful substance into it. He concluded this particular one by sharing what he identified as "one of the most significant paragraphs I have read in a long time." In an Advent sermon titled "Advent . . . in an Atomic Age" preached in 1959 and quoted in the Union Theological Seminary News (New York: March, 1976, 6), Reinhold Niebuhr had declared and Boyce affirmed:

Nothing worth doing is completed in our lifetime; therefore we must be saved by hope. Nothing true or beautiful or good makes complete sense in any immediate context of history; therefore, we must be saved by faith. Nothing we do, however virtuous, can be accomplished alone; therefore, we are saved by love. No virtuous act is quite as virtuous from the standpoint of our friend or foe as from our standpoint. Therefore, we must be saved by the final form of love which is forgiveness.

Boyce commented on the continuing challenge of these words. "These aspects of the Christian faith are forever before us to give direction to our activities, clarity to our thinking, relevance to our aims, and spiritual quality to our lives. I would like to approximate them, motivated by the Holy Spirit who led Paul to write, 'I do not mean that I have already reached [my highest aims], or have already been made complete, but I keep pressing onward to lay hold of [the purpose] for which Christ Jesus laid hold of me' " (Philippians 3:12).

In matters of the Christian faith, Boyce was most careful to distinguish between the words "apprehend" and "comprehend." To him "apprehend" meant following after, grasping partially, enjoying a foretaste, still anticipating anxiously the revelation of the whole. "Comprehend" meant having achieved full understanding, having finally conquered the obstacles of our doubt and ignorance and finiteness. He was careful to share with students that he himself "apprehended" the good news of Christ with real joy, but that one day both he and his faithful students would have the privilege of "comprehending," no longer seeing dimly in a frosted mirror, but face to face.

Suddenly, on August 23, 1976, Dr. Blackwelder's comprehension was complete. After a series of public events in which large numbers of family, friends, students, ministerial and scholarly colleagues remembered, mourned and yet celebrated with a deep sense of thanksgiving, burial took place in Concord, North Carolina, where this good man's earthly journey had begun. The task now remains for us to follow his example and continue our own journeys of serious scholarship and obedient faith.

The legacies of Boyce Watson Blackwelder have taken several forms. Most importantly, he probably would judge, is that today scores of his students are in pastorates taking the Word of God seriously, seeking to interpret it with care and relevance for the people. In addition, in 1974 the General Assembly of the Church of God (Anderson, Indiana) directed that a national fund be raised annually in the church to assist the church's ministerial students seeking graduate-level preparation at the church's seminary, the School of Theology of Anderson University. At Dr. Blackwelder's death it seemed appropriate to all that this fund bear his name. To date well in excess of one million dollars have gone to the direct support of seminary students through the "Boyce W. Blackwelder Seminary Tuition Fund."

Following a chronological and bibliographic overview of the life and work of Dr. Blackwelder, this volume is comprised of a series of original essays prepared by a select group of Boyce's students and teaching colleagues, all persons who wish to honor his memory and carry on the central passions of his life. The viewpoints expressed in these essays may not always agree fully with each other or be in full accord with related viewpoints expressed by Dr. Blackwelder in his various writings. But that is the nature of honest and creative scholarship, something in which Dr. Blackwelder believed and to which he humbly gave his life.

Chronological Overview
Life, Ministry, and, Scholarship of Boyce Watson Blackwelder

The following are selected highlights only. Dr. Blackwelder, for instance, also was featured lecturer or preacher at numerous camp meetings and ministers' meetings over the years.

1913—February 3	Birth, Concord, North Carolina
1930—January 27	High School Graduation, Concord High School, Concord, North Carolina
1931—July 15	Christian Conversion
1931—December 30	Ordination to Christian Ministry, by the North Carolina Ministerial Assembly of the Church of God
1932—September	Journeyed to Anderson College and Theological Seminary in Indiana to begin ministerial studies
1933—August 1	Assumed the pastorate, Arrow Heights Church of God, Anderson, Indiana (through October 29, 1944)
1936—June 12	Bachelor of Arts graduate, Anderson College and Theological Seminary
1938—June 10	Bachelor of Divinity graduate, Anderson College and Theological Seminary
1943—July 19	Married Alice Lela Smith, Auburn, Indiana
1944—June 5	Master of Arts graduate, Butler University, Indianapolis, Indiana. Major, Semitics. Awarded the Temple Brotherhood Prize in the study of Hebrew.
1944—September 5	Son Charles born
1944—November 5	Assumed the pastorate, Belden Avenue Church of God, Chicago, Illinois (through October 28, 1951)
1944—December 19	Elected to Phi Kappa Phi honor society, Butler University chapter.
1946-47	Graduate Study, University of Chicago Divinity School

Boyce W. Blackwelder: The Man, His Ministry, His Scholarship

1947—September	Enrolled in the Doctor of Theology program, Northern Baptist Theological Seminary
1949—March 22	Daughter Dorothea born
1951—May 21	Th.D. graduate, Northern Baptist Theological Seminary. Major, New Testament Greek.
1951	Became member, Society of Biblical Literature
1951—November 1	Assumed the pastorate, Park Place Church of God, Connersville, Indiana (through November 29, 1953)
1953—January 9	Daughter Rhoda born
1953—December 1	Assumed the pastorate, Pine Avenue First Church of God, Erie, Pennsylvania (through August 25, 1963)
1958	Publication of *Light from the Greek New Testament*
1960—November 18	Alumni Lecturer, Anderson School of Theology, Anderson, Indiana
1961	Publication of *Toward Understanding Paul*
1962	Publication of *Toward Understanding Romans*
1963—September 1	Joined the faculty of Anderson School of Theology as Associate Professor of Bible
1963—October 4	Delivered inaugural address upon assuming the chair of New Testament of Anderson School of Theology
1964	Elected to membership, International Theta Phi Beta honor society, Christian Theological Seminary, Indianapolis
1965	Publication of *Toward Understanding Thessalonians*
1968—Summer	Visiting Scholar, Union Theological Seminary, New York City
1968—Summer	Participant, Middle East Seminar in Cyprus, Lebanon, Israel, and Jordan, with religion colleagues from Anderson College and the School of Theology, sponsored by Lilly Endowment, Inc., Indianapolis, Indiana
1969—Fall	Semester Visiting Scholar, Harvard University Divinity School
1971	Publication of *Letters from Paul: An Exegetical Translation*

1976—January	Preaching campaign in Barbados, West Indies, including the national camp meeting of the Church of God and an ecumenical holiness evangelistic campaign
1976—Spring	Promoted to Full Professor of Bible, Anderson School of Theology (to be effective September, 1976)
1976	Baker Book House reprint in paperback edition of the 1958 book, *Light from the Greek New Testament*
1976—August 23	Died, St. Clarisville, Ohio
1976—August 25	Memorial Service, Park Place Church of God, Anderson, Indiana; officiating ministers were J. Hershel Caudill, Keith Huttenlocker, Robert H. Reardon
1976—August 27	Memorial service and burial, Concord, North Carolina
1976—September 23	Memorial remembrance in Anderson School of Theology faculty meeting
1976—October 23	Memorial service, Anderson School of Theology Chapel; launching of the Boyce W. Blackwelder Seminary Tuition Fund
1979	Publication of the *New King James Bible* (Dr. Blackwelder had been a contributing scholar in this project)
1980	Publication of *The Four Gospels: An Exegetical Translation* (text edited by Dr. Gene Miller)

Selected Bibliography of Writings
Boyce Watson Blackwelder

Compiled by Barry L. Callen
Note: The following is limited to the chronological listing, by publication categories, of the writings of Dr. Blackwelder. In addition, many sermons and lectures also were influential means of his communications to various publics.

Theses and Dissertations

1938 "The New Testament Standard of Christian Unity," Bachelor of Divinity Thesis, Anderson College and Theological Seminary, Anderson, Indiana, 1938.

1944 "An Investigation of the Phrase 'Day of Yahweh' in the Prophets of the Old Testament," Master of Arts Thesis, Butler University, Indianapolis, Indiana, 1944.

1951 "The Causal Use of Prepositions in the Greek New Testament," Doctor of Theology Dissertation, Northern Baptist Theological Seminary, Chicago, Illinois, 1951.

Books

1958 *Light from the Greek New Testament* (Anderson, Indiana: Gospel Trumpet Company, 1958). Reprinted in paperback edition by Baker Book House, 1976.
1961 *Toward Understanding Paul* (Anderson, Indiana: Gospel Trumpet Company, 1961).
1962 *Toward Understanding Romans* (Anderson, Indiana: Gospel Trumpet Company, 1952).
1965 *Toward Understanding Thessalonians* (Anderson, Indiana: Warner Press, 1965).
1971 *Letters From Paul: An Exegetical Translation* (Anderson, Indiana: Warner Press, 1971).
1980 *The Four Gospels: An Exegetical Translation* (Anderson, Indiana: Warner Press, 1980). Published following the death of Dr. Blackwelder with the Greek text edited by Dr. Gene Miller.

Book Portions

1967 The chapter titled "The Baptism of the Holy Spirit" in *The Way to Christ and Other Messages* (Anderson, Indiana: Warner Press, 1967).
1974 The April 14-20 section of daily meditations titled "Resurrection Realities" in *The Upper Room Disciplines* (Nashville, TN: The Upper Room, 1973).
1979 The *New King James Bible* (Thomas Nelson Publishers, 1979). Published following the death of Dr. Blackwelder. He had been one of about one hundred scholars representing most of the English-speaking nations who had worked on this updating edition of the Authorized Version of the Bible (1611) over a seven year period. Dr. Blackwelder translated the book of Philippians and acted as consultant on a range of other passages.

Articles

"The Glorious Victory of the Risen Savior," *Gospel Trumpet*, April 15, 1933.
"What the Birth of Jesus Meant," *Gospel Trumpet*, December 23, 1933.
"Christian Preaching," *Gospel Trumpet*, October 27, 1934.
"The Wonderful Christ," *Gospel Trumpet*, December 21, 1935.

"The Incarnation," *Gospel Trumpet*, December 25, 1937.
"The Adequate Church," *Gospel Trumpet*, June 28, 1941.
"The Easter Imperative," *Gospel Trumpet*, March 31, 1945.
"Greek Words for Love," *Christian Vanguard*, Part I—Fourth Quarter, 1949, Part II—First Quarter, 1950, Part III—Second Quarter, 1950, Part IV—Fourth Quarter, 1950.
"What Is Christian Unity?" *Gospel Trumpet*, March 3, 1951.
"Church Government," *Gospel Trumpet*, October 13, 1951.
"Why Go to Church?" *Gospel Trumpet*, September 6, 1952.
"The Quality of the Preacher's Work," *Gospel Trumpet*, November 15, 1952.
"The Names of God in Genesis: Part I," *Gospel Trumpet*, December 6, 1952.
"The Names of God in Genesis: Part II," *Gospel Trumpet*, December 13, 1952.
"The Relevance of Christian Experience to the Problem of Unity," *Gospel Trumpet*, May 30, 1953.
"How To Be Saved," *Gospel Trumpet*, September 17, 1955.
"The Baptism of the Holy Spirit," *Gospel Trumpet*, May 19, 1956.
"Christmas Meanings," *Gospel Trumpet*, December 26, 1958.
"Upon This Rock," *Vital Christianity*, January 20, 1963.
"Binding and Loosing," *Vital Christianity*, February 3, 1963.
"The Keys of the Kingdom," *Vital Christianity*, February 10, 1963.
"New Testament Glossolalia," *Vital Christianity*, February 24, 1963.
"The Glossolalia at Pentecost," *Vital Christianity*, March 10, 1963.
"Paul's Attitude Toward Glossolalia," *Vital Christianity*, March 24, 1963.
"The Post-Resurrection Appearances," *Vital Christianity*, June 16, 1963.
"Christ the Logos," *Vital Christianity*, July 7, 1963.
"The Gifts of the Spirit: Part I," *Vital Christianity*, August 4, 1963.
"The Gifts of the Spirit: Part II," *Vital Christianity*, August 11, 1963.
"The Gifts of the Spirit: Part III," *Vital Christianity*, August 18, 1963.
"Faith and Eternal Life," *Vital Christianity*, September 29, 1963.
"Regret and Repentance," *Vital Christianity*, November, 17, 1963.
"The Nature of True Holiness: Part I," *Vital Christianity*, May 23, 1965.
"The Nature of True Holiness: Part II," *Vital Christianity*, May 23, 1965.

"Christian Unity in the Prayer of Jesus," *Vital Christianity*, April 10, 1966.

"Jesus Christ the Son of God: Part I," *Vital Christianity* December 10, 1972.

"Jesus Christ the Son of God: Part II," *Vital Christianity*, December 24, 1972.

"Thirty Errors of Modern Tongues Advocates," *Vital Christianity*, May 26, 1974.

"Thirty Errors of Modern Tongues Advocates," (corrected reprint after Dr. Blackwelder's death), *Vital Christianity*, August 9, 1981.

Unpublished Papers

1960 "Interpreting the First Epistle of John," sixth annual Alumni Lectureship, Anderson School of Theology, November 18, 1960.

1963 "The Gifts of the Spirit," read before the General Ministerial Assembly of the Church of God, Anderson, Indiana, June 21, 1963.

1963 "The Task of the Department of New Testament," Inaugural address of Dr. Blackwelder upon being inducted into the chair of New Testament at Anderson School of Theology, October 4, 1963.

1964 "Holiness in Doctrine and Practice," delivered to the Tradewinds Discussion Group, Anderson, Indiana, February 6, 1964.

1965 "The Implications of Rudolph Bultmann for Biblical Study," delivered to the Tradewinds Discussion Group, Anderson, Indiana, February 4, 1965.

1968 "A Summary Look at the Field of New Testament," delivered to the faculty of Anderson School of Theology, November 19, 1968.

1969 "A Perspective on Theological Education," delivered at Anderson School of Theology, September 5, 1969.

1975 "Annual Faculty Report," Anderson School of Theology, May 1, 1975, containing major sections titled "A Perspective on Theological Education," "The Character of Graduate Study," and "The Task of the Department of New Testament."

BOYCE W. BLACKWELDER

B.A., B.D., Anderson University; M.A., Butler University; Th.D., Northern Baptist Theological Seminary.

This previously unpublished essay was submitted by Dr. Blackwelder on May 1, 1975 as a portion of his faculty annual report to the dean of Anderson University School of Theology. His wish then was to state in this way some assumptions basic to his work as biblical scholar and seminary teacher. Although initially addressed to the seminary administration, the key insights of this essay are worthy now of careful review by a much wider audience.

Chapter 2

Perspectives On Biblical Studies and Seminary Education

by Boyce W. Blackwelder

The age in which we live is a most challenging one for teachers and students, especially for those of us who are involved in the deeper concerns of theological education. We are called upon to serve in a period characterized by momentous problems. Vast national and international crises recur without cessation. Intricate social and religious enigmas confront us. But, on the other hand, a significant heritage is ours and immense resources are available to us.

How shall we react, and more importantly, how shall we act as servants of God in these days in which the Christian ministry and church so often come under sharp criticism? We do well to remember that, in the midst of the many changes that are taking place in our culture, there is a timelessness about basic human experiences, and that it is to these experiences that the gospel speaks. It is our conviction that the New Testament sets forth a message that is as vital in the twentieth century as it was in the first.

A Perspective on Theological Education

Before looking at the more specific responsibilities of one department of seminary endeavor, let me say a word about the general perspective from which we view theological education in our time. Thus we focus attention upon three considerations.

The Theological Student

It is assumed that the theological student has a personal call from God. This is not to say that it can be explained or defined, but it is to say that there is an awareness of having been set apart for a unique work; that there are deep convictions that hold one; that there is a definite and abiding concern for the spiritual well-being of the present generation; that one's experience is something like that of Amos who spoke on the basis of "Thus saith the Lord" (Amos 1:3, 6, 9, etc.); or like that of Isaiah who "heard the voice of the

Lord saying, Whom shall I send, and who will go for us? Then said I, Here am I, send me" (Isaiah 6:8); or like that of Paul who declared that the responsibility of proclaiming the gospel had been committed to him (cf. Ephesians 3:2-9). Without such a conviction, I doubt that the student will find the sustaining interest and the depth of dedication that the ministry requires (cf. 2 Timothy 4:7).

It is assumed that the student is committed to the service of God; that this commitment is the preeminent concern to which everything else in life is subservient.

It is assumed that the student is a person of moral and spiritual integrity; that it may be said, "There was a man sent from God" (John 1:6). Of first importance is the person; preaching is secondary. We must be women and men of God before we can be spokespersons for God. We have all heard the adage, "It takes twenty years to prepare a sermon because it takes twenty years to prepare a life."

It is assumed that the theological student is a man or woman of personal devotion. We wish to learn and to think as individuals. We should also remember to pray as individuals. Each student and minister must build his or her own devotional life. This is a responsibilitiy that cannot be delegated—it cannot be done by proxy. Christianity is primarily a matter of *being* rather than a matter of doing. We can never do what we ought to do until we are what we ought to be. No person is any stronger outwardly than he or she is inwardly; and inner strength is maintained by a consistent prayer life.

It is assumed that a call to Christian service involves a call to prepare for such service; that consequently the student is here to listen, to learn, and to engage in research, to participate in dialogue, and to realize the maximum potential of the years of education.

There is no mechanical way of getting hold of truth. We must be careful about the nurturing of our thinking. The person who is reluctant to be exposed to thorough, consistent study will never apprehend the message in depth. Emotional excitement cannot be substituted for diligent study. The right sort of criticism is necessary. Absolute honesty is required. We are to apprehend truth actively, not passively accept it. The student personally should discover answers that may be found only through his or her own personal alertness and willingness to learn. Otherwise, latent thinking power is not developed.

It is assumed that the theological student is acquainted with the discipline that the Christian calling demands. In a sense, the ministry is what one makes of it—how one responds to opportunities and how one responds to difficult situations. We are exhorted to "endure hardness, as good soldiers of Jesus Christ" (2 Timothy 2:3). Proper habits of diligent inquiry, once formed, will, in the years to come, yield rich dividends to the preacher and to those who come under the influence of her or his ministry.

The Theological Institution

The basic purpose of theological education is to prepare men and women for leadership in the church, which is God's instrument for the evangelization of the world. With this purpose in view, there are several accomplishments which the church may expect of our endeavor:

1. Theological education may be expected to present legitimate reasons for the hope that is within us (cf. 1 Peter 3:15). If the seminary does not send forth persons who have an adequate awareness of what the gospel is, the seminary has not performed its intended function. The role of the theological institution, through its various departments, is to stimulate the student to an intensity of thought that will enable discernment of the deeper implications of truth and development of reasonable assurance of the substantial foundation on which the Christian faith rests.

2. Theological education may be expected to lead the student into an understanding of the nature and function of the church. The idea that the church is a group of quaint pietists, sitting in comfortable pews, isolated from the heart-cries of the world, is not the biblical concept. According to the New Testament, the first congregations were composed of radiant believers who were united through devotion to Christ the Savior and who realized both the individual and the social implications of the gospel. They were alert, concerned individuals who shared material goods with persons in need (Acts 2:41-47). Even in the face of persecution, they "went everywhere preaching the word" (Acts 8:4) with such enthusiasm that the great cities of the Roman Empire were influenced by their message (cf. Acts 17:6, 18:8, 19:10). Thus the early disciples set a precedent for the church for all time. In congregations that approximate this prototype, it is easy to see "where the action is."

3. Theological education may be expected to impart at least a general knowledge of the nature of human beings and of the environment in which ministers are called to serve. It would be a grave mistake to send graduates into a society that is criss-crossed with various kinds of tensions, personal maladjustments, ideological conflicts, and political ambiguities, without having imparted to the graduates some insight into the underlying causes of such exigencies and how the gospel can help to alleviate individual and community needs. The minister must have some understanding of the personality problems that neither psychology, nor sociology, nor political science, nor material and temporal benefits can solve without the dynamic of the gospel of Christ.

4. Theological education may be expected to produce scholars. Every field is involved, but just now I am thinking especially of Old and New Testament. The important manuscript and archaeological discoveries of the twentieth century have stimulated a renewed interest in the Bible, both with regard to its original texts and their meaning and to its contemporary relevance and authority. In order to pursue these findings and their implications for the Christian faith, philological specialists are needed. My hope is that the seminary will challenge students whose particular interests will center in biblical studies—in the historical background, languages, canonical history, and translation. The message of the Bible must be made available in the thought and expression of every generation, and translations adequate for today and tomorrow involve problems of philology and exegesis that can be handled only by persons equipped to work in these technical areas.

This is not to say that every theologue will become a skilled linguist or a textual scholar, but it is to say that from time to time—at least in every generation—there will come forth persons with unusual acumen and interest in biblical and cognate languages who will give themselves to extensive, penetrating studies in exegesis and exposition, so that coming generations may be enriched through the contributions of devoted men like Tischendorf, J. B. Lightfoot, B. F. Westcott, F. J. A. Hort, H. C. G. Moule, Robert Dick Wilson, A. T. Robertson, and Edward J. Young. In the encouragement and training of such persons, theological education is called upon to make one of its most vital contributions.

5. Theological education may be expected to assist in the spiritual preparation of students. Every servant of God will understand that the power of faith and trust is indispensable and that there are times when inward strength is the only resource. As I have already noted, spiritual development is primarily a matter of individual responsibility, but at the same time a seminary community should be characterized by an atmosphere that is conducive to both intellectual and spiritual progress. There is wisdom in the dictum, "Scholarship and sanctity must walk hand in hand."

The Theological Method

Although the Christian ministry is varied and should not be thought of exclusively as preaching, doubtless it reaches its highest expression in the proclamation of God's Word. Therefore, it follows that one of the most important considerations of the minister must be the proper use of the Scriptures. Paul exhorts Timothy to handle aright the word of truth (2 Timothy 2:15). The right use of God's Word presupposes its correct interpretation. Whether preaching is textual or topical or expository, it rests ultimately upon the speaker's hermeneutics, the interpretation of Scripture.

By what method or methods are we to interpret the Bible today? How much of our hermeneutical heritage is vital for the present task? The contemporary concern with historiography has affected profoundly modern trends in biblical studies. What is the connection between the New Testament kerygma and historical fact? How is the church's faith in and proclamation of the Christ connected with the historical person of Jesus of Nazareth and his message?

To state the challenge another way, the chief responsibility of the church is the evangelization of the world. This is to be done, of course, through the preaching of the gospel. We are to confront humankind with the saving implications of the atonement of Jesus Christ. But as we seek to bring the power of the Christian faith to bear upon human thought and action, immediately we face the problem of hermeneutics. By what method are we to interpret the New Testament? The basic question posed by hermeneutics is twofold: How can the biblical passages be understood in the light of the background out of which they came and how can we interpret their meaning in the present cultural context?

The building of a methodology of interpretation is a gradual process, requiring years of serious thought. Although the student comes to appreciate the scholarly contributions of the past, there should not be mere acquiescence to old concepts. Conclusions should be reached after arduous wrestling of mind and soul.

There is no single, all-inclusive interpretive method, no one complete approach. Different perspectives yield various insights; and in a given instance, one kind of perspective may be more fruitful than another. I believe that today we need a methodological procedure, or an insight, that will enable us to appropriate the merits of various discriminative procedures that scholars have found to be helpful in the interpretation of the Old and New Testaments. However, my conviction is that there are certain principles or guidelines to which we must hold as new ideas are tried and tested. I mention three of these guidelines.

1. **The Grammatical-Historical Approach.** The Bible is humankind's most valuable treasure of all the ancient documents, spanning, if we may assume that written records dating back to the time of Abraham eventually were incorporated into the Pentateuch, approximately twenty-one hundred years of history and literary activity. The modern interpreter has the task of ascertaining what the writer of a given book or passage originally intended to transmit. Therefore, any information that clarifies social situation, allusions, idiomatic expressions, or in any way provides contemporary comment on a writer's meaning or purpose is an important aid to interpretation.

The grammatical-historical approach may be defined briefly as the method required by the laws of grammar and the facts of history. This method implies that all Scripture is to be interpreted in the light of its natural literary form. It does not mean that the Bible is to be understood with an unbending literalism, but it does imply that interpretation must not disregard the literary and historical contexts. Of prime importance is some awareness of the *Sitz im Leben* (situation in life) out of which an event arose or was recorded. This is a most valuable aid toward ascertaining the meaning that the literature had for the original authors and for the first recipients. The grammatical-historical method is a basic safeguard against imposing philosophical or theological presuppositions upon the text. This approach seeks to reconcile seeming discrepancies and difficulties on the basis of careful exegesis. It takes into account all the pertinent advances in Hebrew and Greek syntax, biblical history, geography, and archaeololgy as such significant new data become available.

2. **The Christological Principle.** Here we emphasize the affirmation that Jesus the Christ is the main theme of the Scriptures. This truth, which is reflected directly in the New Testament and indirectly in the Old Testament, gives theological meaning and unity to the Bible. In this context, all interpretation serves the purpose of finding Christ or delineating his redemptive work.

This is not to say that only those passages that witness specifically to Christ are binding. There have been various ethical emphases in revelation. Certainly, God has spoken in the past through the prophets, and God's work had immediate application and validity to the original hearers. Nevertheless, we believe that the motif of expectation and fulfillment is meaningless apart from the Christological framework.

This principle has its greatest import in the realm of doctrine. For example, the deepest meanings of sin and atonement treated in the Old Testament find their most profound answer in the New Testament. The ultimate significance of history is unfolded only from the standpoint of its consummation in Jesus Christ.

3. **The Experiential Response.** By this we mean that a person cannot grasp the deeper implications of the biblical message if the Scriptures are read in a manner detached from the insights that come through Christian experience. In other words, the Bible should be studied with concern and engagement of the self—from the standpoint of personal involvement so that its message confronts one quite personally. Professor Porter stated:

> The interpreter must have a congeniality, a personal relationship to the issues directly or indirectly exposed in the text.

Alexander Campbell proposed that the interpreter "must

come within the understanding distance." The disturbing awareness of a Thou who confronts us as both demand and promise is the precondition of our understanding of the Bible (Porter 1964, 294).

We believe that the truth set forth in the Scriptures is not a set of doctrines to be apprehended only in a cognitive way, but that it is the declaration of vital realities to be appropriated by faith and obedience; that the interpreter is both a reader and an auditor, both a spectator and a participant. As the sacred text is studied, the message must awaken a response so that there is dialogue between the Speaker and the listener. Unless such a relationship is established, the student will be a pursuer standing on the outside looking for ideas rather than a partaker living on the inside, walking with the Master.

The interpreter of the New Testament, then, must realize that the history is, in a very real sense, the story of *his or her own life*; that he or she is involved in *all* who have sinned and fallen short of God's requirements (cf. Romans 3:23); that also *he or she* is included in the world for whose salvation God gave his unique Son (cf. John 3:16); and that *he or she* is the recipient of the grace that is extended to every person who places trust in the Savior (cf. Ephesians 2:8).

The experiential response means that the expositor must be within the community of believers if the Book of books is to be interpreted adequately. This emphasis reflects, I think, something of Kierkegaard's insight when he indicated that it is impossible to know the meaning of life speculatively. The Danish philosopher and theologian wrote, "Truth has always had many loud preachers, but the question is whether a man is willing in the deepest sense to recognize truth, to let it permeate his whole being, to assume all the consequences of it" (Kierkegaard 1966, 47).

So, without the experience of the committed, the Scriptures may appear to be a book of morals and traditions rather than a medium of confrontation. Doctrine, apart from personal involvement, leads to barren intellectualism. On the other hand, involvement apart from biblical doctrine leads to nebulous mysticism.

Commitment is not to be sought apart from reasonable assurance of the reality of the facts and events upon which the believer's trust is based. It is hardly possible to expect actual involvement in the Christian life by a person who denies the basic features of the New Testament message.

We hold that at the heart of the Christian faith certain facts must be retained as historically valid, although it is impossible to reproduce them like certain other scientific data; that without them

Christianity would crumble to the level of a mere ethical system and to existential despair. We believe that where these basic facts are retained, the God of truth speaks by the Holy Spirit through them to impart grace and meaning to human existence.

Because of its importance, its antiquity, and its vastness, the biblical field offers many challenges for research. I believe that the hermeneutical principles that I have mentioned above will point us toward a balanced methodology and impart a sense of direction as we endeavor to follow truth into the future.

The Character of Graduate Study

As I see it, graduate study has three basic purposes. Allow me to state them briefly.

1. To direct the student toward a comprehensive mastery of the substantial results of past and present scholarship within a chosen field of inquiry.

2. To aid the student in developing a capacity for individual research. Learning involves maintaining a proper balance between faculty supervision and student initiative. The principle of maximum challenge rather than the idea of minimum requirements should be emphasized. That is to say, the focus of concern should be upon achieving an internal level of competence, not merely upon completing certain external units of work. For example, the highest goal should not be for a student to read a certain number of books, but to become a competent scholar who can function independently at the research level.

The student in the biblical field should aspire to conduct investigations in the primary sources. The attainment of an intimate acquaintance with these sources, along with the exercise of a critical research function, gives a qualitatively distinctive dimension to graduate education.

An ample bibliography is available to supplement the study of the New Testament and students are expected to read widely in secondary sources. Nevertheless, the foremost emphasis should be given to an intensive study of the New Testament literature itself. Secondary studies should be tested in the light of a careful examination of the biblical text. The biblical text, in turn, should be interrogated from the standpoint of significant perspectives and hypotheses discovered in the secondary readings.

A grasp of the hermeneutical process will include efforts both to understand the original meaning of the New Testament documents in the light of the New Testament world and to relate this meaning to the present world situation.

3. To open vistas that will challenge the student to ongoing

scholastic development after the completion of the formal education. While graduate study is comprehensive in scope, it is not intended to be terminal in character. Rather, the entire range of study should be designed to launch the student on a lifetime of deepening scholarship, enabling pursuit in depth of many of the areas that can only be introduced within the limits of a formal degree program. Therefore, the primary emphasis during a seminary education should be on the development of methodological skills and on a critical assessment of enduring issues, rather than upon acquaintance with a quantity of information gained from extensive reading.

The Task of the Department of New Testament

What is our task in the New Testament field? What are the chief concerns that should engage our attention? What are the ultimate goals toward which we should strive?

The church has charged its theological seminaries with an objective that occupied a large part of Jesus' earthly ministry: preparing disciples to proclaim the Good News of the kingdom of God and to teach and edify Christian believers. Accordingly, we wish to concentrate our efforts upon a deeper understanding of the gospel and its implications for every aspect of faith and life.

The scholars who today take a stand upon the Bible as the Word of God may seem to be caught between the rigid theology of ecclesiastical tradition on the one hand and extreme historical skepticism on the other. Nevertheless we are convinced of the trustworthiness of the Scriptures and of the preeminence and uniqueness of Christianity, and we believe that, in submission to the authority of God's Word and in reliance upon the power of God's Spirit, we can go forward with confidence toward the fulfillment of our mission.

The overarching responsibility of this department is to delineate the central message of the New Testament: Jesus Christ the Incarnate Word who was manifested in history for the salvation of humankind. The message is apprehended in depth through acquaintance with the New Testament writings, because this literature is the record of the Christ-event and the interpretation of its significance.

Within the framework of this major imperative I see a seven-fold responsibility.

1. **Our task is to reiterate the objectivity and abiding relevance of the New Testament.**

The Christian realistic world-view begins with the postulate of special revelation. It holds that God exists and that we know of God's existence because God has made himself known to us. The heart of the revelation is to be found in Jesus Christ, the incarnate

Word, who came in human flesh to save sinners. The authentic record of the divine disclosure is to be found in the Hebrew-Christian Scriptures, the written Word, which is regarded as revelatory literature—God's word in human language. Although human instrumentality was involved in its production, the Bible is not to be thought of as a human achievement, but as the work of the Holy Spirit. It is a message that was given from an order beyond the realm of natural experience.

In contradistinction to rationalistic and empirical philosophies, which assume that a sufficient world-view can be formulated by human speculation alone, Christian realistic philosophy maintains that an adequate view is possible only on the basis of objective disclosure. The Christian world-view seeks to integrate the facts of existence in the light of the purpose of God as set forth in Scripture.

If objection be raised to the Christian starting point, we may reply that all philosophical systems begin with presuppositions of some kind, so that there is no valid argument for rejecting the hypothesis that a world-view may be constructed on the postulate of supernatural disclosure, especially in view of the rich spiritual background of the Judaeo-Christian heritage.

The Christian approach believes that all truth has its source in God, but it does not assert that all areas of truth are fully treated in the revelation set forth in the Scriptures. Apparently many fields of knowledge have been left for us to investigate and develop by our own God-given abilities. Researchers have discovered, within the limits of scientific methodology, a great deal about the structure and laws of temporal existence. We are indebted to the scientists, many of whom think within the Christian frame of reference, for every contribution that they have made to human knowledge and cultural advancement.

Philosophers, with their attempts to achieve an overall interpretation of the universe or to clarify meanings and relationships, often have stimulated thinking and rendered a helpful service to religion by exposing superstition and fanaticism. The Christian realist is grateful for all this, but insists that the significance of scientific and philosophical discovery can be apprehended only in relation to the truth that God's Word makes known concerning human nature and destiny. Beyond the domain of natural categories, we have received an objective, authoritative revelation. The disclosure that was made through the patriarchs, through the prophets, and in its fullness through the Lord Jesus Christ, is the ultimate basis, content, and standard of the truth. The message of the gospel is self-authenticating, for the truth that was objectively revealed may be subjectively apprehended by faith. That is to say, the person who approaches God, with humility and trust in Christ as prior conditions, will experience the self-evidencing reality of salvation. Truth as transforming power will enter the consciousness. This is the epistemology that Jesus expresses in John 7:17 and 8:31-32.

Often we hear the question asked, Is the Bible relevant to the twentieth century? Viewed from a superficial standpoint, modern persons seem far removed from the world of the biblical writers. With our complex society, what have we in common with the simple culture of nomads and primitive workers of the soil? Has not technological progress made the Bible an outmoded, prescientific document?

It is true that the Bible is a collection of ancient compositions, written in times outwardly much unlike our own; but this consideration is incidental. What is basic to an understanding of the Bible is the recognition that, in essential being, humanity has not changed with the passing of the centuries. Character and fundamental needs are the same as they have been ever since the beginning of recorded history. As Carl F. H. Henry once put it, "It is precisely to man *as man* that the message of the Bible is addressed—and modern man is still *man*" (Henry 1960, 20). As the record of God's timeless concern for humankind, the Scriptures embrace the entire course of history and set us in the context of the divine purpose.

What about the relevance of the New Testament and of the Bible as a whole, viewed from the receding horizons of the space age? Heretofore human activity has been confined to one body in space—this earth. We have known relatively little about the vast universe of which we are an infinitesimal part. What science knows has been learned from the examination of one category of material, that of earth, and from one realm of life, that of earth. We have learned something about the earth's gravitation, magnetic fields, trapped radiation, atmosphere, and magnetosphere. In our lifetime brave persons have gone forth to explore the material of the moon. Perhaps, in later flights, astronauts may explore the surface of Mars and compare its material with that of Earth; and it is possible that future space explorations may achieve the most exciting endeavor of all, the discovery of extra terrestrial life.

What can we say about the theological implications of these possibilities? According to the biblical concept, God is eternal and infinite; hence God is not limited by any aspects of time and space. In relation to the universe, God is both transcendent and immanent. Therefore, nothing in the observed or yet unobserved creation is outside God's sovereignty.

The prologue of the Fourth Gospel introduces the preexistent Logos who is identified with the incarnate Christ (John 1:1-18). At the creation of all things, the Logos was already present. He was in intimate, reciprocal communion with the Father (*pros ton theon*, face to face with God, 1:1b), and in essential being (denoted by the anarthrous predicate, *theos* 1:1c) the Logos was *God*. Three times in his opening verse John uses the verb *en*, *was*, the durative imperfect, which points back indefinitely beyond the beginning of the time-space sequence and shows that in all eternity the Logos *was*—characterized by timeless, unchanging existence.

Paul and the author of the Epistle to the Hebrews also emphasize the preexistence of the Son of God (cf. Col. 1:16-19; Heb. 1:2-3). Thus the New Testament shows the cosmic outreach of our Lord. He who was before time and space came into the world to save us, and in the fulfillment of his ultimate purpose he will receive us into the consummate glory that is to be realized beyond history.

2. **Our task is to apply the results of linguistic research to the interpretation of the text of the New Testament.**

Basically exegesis is grammatical. Of course, much more is involved, but it is all built upon a linguistic foundation. Consequently grammatical study is a requisite of the first magnitude for every person who would apprehend and communicate the greater depths of the Christian faith.

The literature of the New Testament has a tremendous interest for the sincere inquirer because of the message that it discloses. Each part of speech—every phrase and word—calls for minute investigation where so much is at stake.

It is not possible to render the total thought of one language into another language. The central ideas can be expressed, but a certain untranslatable residue always remains. If we are to grasp the full force of the truth of the New Testament, we must study it in the language in which it was written originally. The person who knows best what the devices and idioms of speech meant to the writers who used them is the one who can best gain access to the message that those authors sought to convey. When opinions of interpreters have differed widely, it often has been because a knowledge of grammatical principles was lacking. Without the guidance of sound hermeneutics, the caprice of subjectivism may take over and give rise to strange dogmas and vain notions. Scholarship means, among other things, being careful with the data with which we work.

Modern scholarship has exploded the once-popular view that the language of the New Testament was a peculiar kind of Greek, a religious dialect alone adequate for the expression of revealed truth. The term "Biblical Greek" was used by grammarians in the past to designate the type of Greek found in the Septuagint and in the New Testament. Because of the content and interest, there is a sense in which one may continue to use the designation "Biblical Greek." But now it is well established that the New Testament books were written in the vernacular of the Koine period—in the Greek commonly spoken throughout the Graeco-Roman world. This gives a note of reality and vividness to these documents that is not usually present in formal literary style.

The New Testament is not the only testimony to the character of the Koine. Hence the scientific method is to study the language of the New Testament as a part of a greater whole, not as an isolated phenomenon. The other monuments of that interesting age that are important sources of illumination on New Testament vocabulary and syntax are the papyri, the ostraca, the inscriptions, the Septuagint, and the literary Koine (Leonard, 1989). The literary Koine is represented by the writings of Polybius, Plutarch, Lucian, Philo, Josephus, Dionysius of Halicarnassus, Diodorus Siculus and others.

Since the turn of the twentieth century, New Testament philology has undergone thorough reconstruction in the light of the evidence made available by the science of antiquities. The texts preserved on stone, papyrus, and on fragments of pottery that have been unearthed by the thousands present biblical scholars with a veritable storehouse of information. These fascinating memorials of the Imperial Period represent the ordinary language of the people of the Mediterranean world, the type of speech in which the gospel message was recorded. They are exceedingly valuable for the linguistic study of the New Testament, both because of the wide range of their literary quality and because of their exhibition of the typical Koine.

The real beginning of the application of scientific method to the language of the New Testament was the work of G. B. Winer, whose *A Grammar of the Idiom of the New Testament* in 1822 inaugurated a new epoch in New Testament grammatical approach. A definite contribution was W. D. Whitney's *Sanskrit Grammar* in 1875, and there are many other distinguished names of the new era, among them Moulton, Milligan, Deissmann, W. M. Ramsay, Grenfell, Hunt, and A. T. Robertson. Robertson's monumental work, *A Grammar of the Greek New Testament in the Light of Historical Research* (1914), sums up the progress of the century and applies the new principles at salient points to the interpretation of the New Testament.

In addition to Hellenistic culture, the major factor, there were other elements in the background of the language of the New Testament. There was the influence of the Hebrew Old Testament and of the Septuagint. Furthermore, inasmuch as the New Testament writers were Jews (with the exception of Luke who was probably a Greek) and bilinguists, it is logical to expect some reflections of Aramaic, the native vernacular of Palestine. The Hebraisms and Aramaisms in the Greek New Testament are far less than was once supposed. Dana and Mantey* refer to examples in Matthew 19:5; Luke 1:34, 42; 20:12. The voluminous papyrus records, to which we have referred, illustrate much of the New Testament vocabulary and syntax and make it clear that many expressions once called Hebraisms were actually idioms of the Koine, which was spoken widely in the Graeco-Roman world.

There are traces of Latin influence in the Greek New Testament. This is to be anticipated since Rome, the prevailing political regime during the period in which the New Testament was written, was the center of Latin culture. The Roman Empire, in its many official relationships with the peoples under its control, naturally left reflections of Latin in the popular language of the early Christian period. But the Latinisms in the New Testament are few. "The number is small, even in comparison with the Hebraisms (Dana 1957, 14)." They are mostly judicial and military terms, and names of persons, offices, institutions, places, coins, articles of apparel, and the like.

Along with vocabulary and etymology, accurate interpretation must consider a number of other pertinent materials, including textual criticism, historical development of the terms, the authorship, occasion, and purpose of a composition, the characteristics of the writer, and the context of a given passage.

One should remember that grammars and dictionaries are not the authorities in a language. A language is determined by the people who speak and write it. The usage of the best educated persons determines the literary style of a language, while the people as a whole decide the vernacular. Lexicons and grammars only state, more or less correctly, the rules used by the people who express a language.

The function of a grammarian, then, is not to make the laws of language, but to learn and teach them. By diligent work he or she acquires the principles and viewpoint of a language and becomes familiar enough with it to interpret accurately its idioms.

The student should become acquainted with the related fields of the Koine, enabling exploration of the evidence supplied by the philological data of the Imperial Period, i.e., the papyri, ostraca, inscriptions, the Septuagint, and the literary Koine, all of which were written in the same general type of Greek as the New Testament and throw light on the meaning of the sacred text.

The student should realize the value of both the deductive and the inductive methods of research. Induction is exceedingly important for a person who is working in lexicography. It enables one to gain range and depth in an understanding of words, and to check on the possibilities and nuances of terms treated by dictionaries and grammars. Quite often it becomes possible to add substantially to existing information.

In summary, we might say that we wish to place in the hands of the student the linguistic tools that will enable a right handling of the New Testament, which include interpreting it lexically, syntactically, historically, contextually, logically, and analogically.

3. **Our task is to relate the work of the Department of New Testament to the other fields of study within the seminary curriculum, in order that students may develop appreciation for the total program of the seminary community.**

If the various theological disciplines are to be most effective, they should not be isolated from one another. The person who would achieve balance in viewpoint must not only choose for focus from among the various fields of research, but must appreciate the importance of related areas of knowledge. It would be a loss to consider as inapplicable any subject that might add to one's understanding of the nature and methods of a particularized study. Therefore, if the interpreter of the New Testament is to produce a maximum of results, he or she must carry on dialogue with the other theological disciplines and with the relevant nontheological fields. There should be a cultivated acquaintance with every realm of data that can provide significant insights into New Testament exegesis and exposition.

In a very real sense every department of the theological curriculum is an integral part of the whole. Each is nourished by the same basic roots. The study of New Testament history is continuous with the study of Old Testament history. Old Testament doctrine and New Testament doctrine are connected with Systematic Theology, with Church History, and with the History of Christian Doctrine and Apologetics. Also vitally related to Biblical Studies are Contemporary Theology, Philosophy, Philosophy of Religion, Ethics, Psychology of Religion, Christian Education, and Applied Theology. The perusal of the discourses of the prophets lays a groundwork for a study of the preaching of the apostles and New Testament evangelists; and biblical preaching provides criteria for an appraisal of preaching and evangelism in all subsequent periods.

The significance of the contribution of the various academic fields in the modern college and university to the exposition of the Scriptures can be seen when the student seeks to develop the specific techniques that constitute the science of interpretation. For example, grammatical interpretation cannot be achieved without an understanding of basic linguistics, both that of the original language of the text and that of the speech of the interpreter's own people.

Logical interpretation requires some knowledge of the science of inference. Historical interpretation presupposes some mastery of the techniques of historical investigation, and psychological interpretation calls for some acquaintance with the nature of human personality. The problems of metaphysics and the approaches that persons take toward a comprehensive interpretation of existence, enter into the background of the biblical interpreter's task. In these and many more related fields the universities help to provide the data that are essential for the students who are to work with the Holy Scriptures.

The integration of the seminary's work leads to a more complete apprehension of the Bible as a whole. A great many Christians seem to practice an almost total disregard for many portions of the Scriptures. A lack of understanding of the relation of the Old to the New Testament has led a number of laypersons and ministers to accept the false idea that the God of the Old Testament is different in character from the God who is revealed in the New Testament. A careful study will result in a proper acquaintance with the meaning and relationship of the biblical material.

One of the most fruitful compensations of Old Testament study is a better understanding of much of the vocabulary of the New Testament. Such prominent words as sin, repentance, holiness, atonement, covenant, kingdom, and a great many others have profound Old Testament backgrounds that we must know if we are to grasp the deeper implications of these terms. The Christ of the New Testament is the Messiah who was promised in the Old Testament. In fact the term *Christ* is derived from the Greek equivalent of the Hebrew term for *Messiah*. Jesus is also declared to be *Kurios, Lord. Kurios* is the Greek translation of the Tetragrammaton, the most significant designation among the Hebrew names for God. The Tetragrammaton is the term generally rendered *Yahweh*, which is the name for God in covenant relationship with his people (cf. Exod. 3:14). The more usual Hebrew appellation for Deity is *Adonai*, a term adopted by the Jews to avoid pronouncing the Tetragrammaton, which was regarded as too sacred for utterance.

The value of the Septuagint for our study can scarcely be overemphasized. Both historically and religiously its importance is many-sided. It is valuable alike to the textual scholar and to the expositor, and its many contributions are appreciated by students of both Old and the New Testaments. As the first translation of the Hebrew Old Testament into a foreign language, the Septuagint exerted an extensive influence. It released the great revealed truths concerning creation, sin, and the promise of a Redeemer from the relative isolation of the Hebrew-Jewish language and people and gave them universal impetus through the instrument of the *Koine*, which was the *lingua franca* of the Graeco-Roman world. The Septuagint was the Bible of early Christianity before the New Testament was written.

The Septuagint was used widely by the writers of the New Testament, the majority of their Old Testament quotations being borrowed from it. It was an expedient means for missionary work. The Old Latin, Egyptian, Ethiopic, Armenian, Slavonic, Gothic and other versions were made from it.

As a linguistic and theological bridgehead between the Hebrew of the Old Testament and the Greek of the New Testament, the Septuagint preserves meanings of Hebrew words that were current when the Septuagint translation was made, but which were later lost. Thus a number of New Testament expressions are to be understood in the light of the Hebrew terms that they represent in the Septuagint. Of course Christianity has poured new and more significant content into many words carried over from the Greek Old Testament and selected from the Koine in general.

4. **Our task is to train faithful ministers who in turn will transmit to others the message of the gospel.**

In 1 Corinthians 11:23 we notice Paul's *"parelabon. . . paredoka,"* and in 15:3 his *"paredoka . . . parelabon"* as he speaks of the solemn responsibility of receiving and passing on the doctrines of the gospel. This is the divinely ordained method of perpetuating Christianity in the world (cf. 2:2).

The noun *paradosis*, meaning *that which is handed over or handed down* (rendered "tradition" in English translations) is used by Paul in the singular in 2 Thessalonians 3:6, and in the plural in 2 Thessalonians 2:15 and 1 Corinthians 11:2. The collection of these doctrinal norms constitutes a *paratheke* or *deposit* of truth that is to be imparted to believers. *Paratheke* is used three times in the New Testament, all in the Pastoral Epistles (1 Tim. 6:20; 2 Tim. 1:12, 14), and in each instance with the verb *phulasso*, which means *to guard, watch, defend, preserve*. In the first and last instances, where it refers to ministerial responsibility, the aorist imperative, denoting urgency, is used.

There were two general areas of the theology of the early church. The first, denoted by the term *kerygma*, or *thing preached*, was the proclamation of God's acts for the salvation of humankind, and included the word about the incarnation, the cross, and the resurrection. The second area, denoted by the term *didache*, or *teaching*, was instructions dealing with the believer's continuing response to God, and with his or her relationship to other believers, and with the demands of holiness and Christian service.

In varying ways all the New Testament writers delineate the

significant themes that were universally proclaimed in the church of the first century. The duty of the contemporary seminary is to prepare persons to carry these truths to the present generation. Thus we remind the church of its original charter and mission.

> There is a vast body of knowledge waiting to meet much of the world's ignorance but there is need for a teacher to fill the person gap between the ignorance and the knowledge. There are great resources of healing opened by the advances of modern medicine but it takes the physician to step in and mediate the source of healing to the need for healing. There are profound therapeutic powers in human life waiting to bring wholeness to broken persons, but often it takes the counselor to step into the person gap and bring the encounter between the illness and the therapy. Is it then surprising that on the deepest level of all God has left room for this ministry of mediation? (Dana 1957, 15).

An awareness of the vital role of the human relationship in the work of the ministry calls not only for humility, but it urges us to seek the best possible preparation for this responsibility. Men and women who believe that their personal religious experience, plus a few carelessly acquired opinions about the Bible and homiletics, meet the requirements of the Christian ministry have a distorted view of nature of this high calling. It seems to me that total commitment to Christ includes the commitment to prepare—to learn, to develop, to be one's very best for God's service.

Every candidate for the ministry needs to reflect at considerable length upon the strenuous duties that will be required. Three years of graduate study in deepened consecration is not too much for the serious task of preaching the gospel. Ministers should know that for his own *purpose* Christ has selected them to serve his cause in a unique way. They should be persons who know the meaning of devotion to our Lord and who have enough knowledge of the Bible, the church, human personality and secular society to serve God effectively.

The minister is many things to many people, including being a preacher, a pastor, and an administrator of the work of a congregation. But the fact remains that the primary responsibility is the proclamation of God's Word. In order to carry out this duty, the minister must *know* the Word of God. In order to know it, it must be studied, and study requires intensive, consistent work.

The excellency is of God. God may use persons with little or no formal education; but God has much more to use in an educated ministry. It seems to me that God's most effective instrument is a person of faith who is at the same time a person of intellectual ability and practical efficiency. This goal requires a teaching program that is thorough in scholarship, wide in range, and intensive in focus.

5. **Our task is to indicate the vast potentialities of the New Testament so that students, after leaving the classroom, will have the equipment and abiding interest to continue study on their own initiative.**

6. **Our task is to reiterate the character of the Scriptures so that the minister will never forget that the divine commission is to "Preach the Word!"**

If we believe the Bible to be the record of God's timeless concern through Jesus Christ for the salvation of all humankind, it follows that the truths of Scripture are timeless, universally applicable, and always relevant. Although the Bible came through writers of long ago, it deals with the ultimate questions of existence and enunciates principles of experience and conduct that anticipate human needs in every period of history. Today we have the same basic problems, frustrations, and aspirations that characterized ancient peoples. Apart from the revelation recorded in the Scriptures we have no answer to our quest for meaningful existence.

7. **It is our task to exemplify the ethical principles of the New Testament.**

The Bible is a means to an end. All the activities that center around it should contribute to the enrichment of character. Thus our responsibility as a living example is a major one. We are not only to respect the text of the New Testament, interpret it correctly, and teach it carefully, but our conduct should reflect consistently the redemptive truth that it discloses. The Beatitudes are sublime utterances, but even more significant than the *Sermon* on the Mount is the *Man* on the Mount. What matters most is not what we say, but how we live. Our everyday behavior is the acid test of our religion. The gospel is God's word directed to the whole person—to a person's intellect, emotions, and will—and not to any one aspect of personality. The total person is involved in the development of Christian character.

A great deal of scholastic activity is oral. Schools operate largely in the realm of words. They exist to a certain extent by reading, writing, and talking. Classes are conducted, lectures are given, and a considerable amount of information is disseminated by means of discussion. This procedure is demanded by the very nature of the teaching-learning process. But there is a subtle danger in this situation: students may assume that life itself consists mostly of opinion and talk. Someone has said: "Seminaries cannot stop talking; if they did they would go out of business. But they can try to talk in ways that are closely related to responsibility." Perhaps we should ask ourselves quite often, Is the opinion expressed in the classroom mere words? Or does it prepare us to act meaningfully in obedience to Christ our Lord?

We are aware that there are definite limits to what can be conveyed by lecture and discussion in the field of religion and that truth can be taught far better by example than by precept. However earnestly we may try to define love, one act of silent forbearance, or one sympathetic deed, will picture it more clearly than a dozen descriptive phrases.

Thought is the vehicle that conveys much of what an educational institution has to give. It is necessary and right that there should be a constant emphasis upon clear and critical thinking. But as Christians, there should be no serious gap between our words and our deeds. Life cannot be lived merely by talking about it. A person who does not reflect obedience to Christ in human relationships is certainly unaware of the implications of the Christian ethic. A student who excels in courses of study, but whose character remains below par because of not learning that seminary is a place for ethical growth as well as for accumulating information, has not understood or has not responded to the highest summons.

Students who think seriously about the implications of their Christian belief and shoulder responsibilities in definite Christian witnessing come to a maturity of faith while they are still in the seminary. This kind of academic existence is capable of producing persons more adequately prepared for the ministry than graduates who emerge from a mere school of ideas.

In these days when the world needs so desperately to hear the gospel, and when trained workers are required to carry the message, we wish to serve more and more effectively through a growing mastery and use of the tools that God in his providence has provided for our generation. To this end we seek the guiding influence of the Holy Spirit as we resolve to maintain a personal willingness to hear God speak in and through the Holy Scriptures.

Notes

* There are two types of Koine: the literary Koine that is represented by extrabiblical literature, by most of the inscriptions, and by a few papyri; and the vernacular Koine which is represented by most of the papyri and ostraca, and by nearly all "Biblical Greek."

JAMES R. CHRISTOPH

B.A., Anderson University; M.A., Anderson University School of Theology; Doctoral candidate, Duke University.

Assistant Professor of Biblical Studies, Warner Southern College (Lake Wales, Florida). Former student of Dr. Boyce W. Blackwelder.

Chapter 3

Equal Access to Grace in Ministry: Women and Men

by James R. Christoph

The Church of God Reformation Movement, among many other Christian groups, clearly has affirmed active roles for women in public ministry.[1] This position has been demonstrated in practices like the open admission of women to ordination. Such understanding, however, has been challenged within Christendom by such widely diverse elements as the Roman Catholic Church and the Southern Baptist Convention. Dr. Boyce Blackwelder, nevertheless, maintained the position of open access of women to serve the kingdom of God:

> According to the general context of the New Testament, women are free to pray, witness, exhort, and preach, inasmuch as there is no distinction between men and women regarding salvation and the graces and gifts of the Holy Spirit, (Gal. 3: 28) (Blackwelder 55-56).

The question of the role of women in society and the church has stimulated much new research and debate. These investigations have heightened concerns about the methods of the reading of the Bible and applications in church practice. Two camps are easily identified. On the one side of this debate are the traditional views categorized as patriarchal. These views maintain that men were created to rule and women were created to follow. The patriarchal focus is established upon the claim that God in the Bible gives the human race universal, timeless, and specific gender roles. A prime example of this view is "The Danvers Statement"[2] that recently appeared in *Christianity Today* (January 1989).

On the other side are the editors of *Vital Christianity* and its writers who recently devoted an entire issue (May 1989) to showing acceptance of women in leadership roles. The same theme also had been discussed with approval in the *Center for Pastoral Studies' Centering on Ministry* (Anderson University's School of Theology: Winter 1980). Current research has directed attention to a reevaluation of the biblical sources themselves. To this task we shall now turn.

Where To Begin

This discussion will proceed by accepting the pattern of some continuity and movement of thought between the Old and New Testaments.[3] In choosing this pattern, this study presumes that use of Old Testament concepts and theology is proper to assist interpretation of the New Testament. At the same time, I also assume that New Testament teaching can and should influence the understanding of the intent and structure of the Old Testament message.

The fundamental problem of where to start the interpretation task has been recognized from ancient times in both Christian and Jewish circles. Robert C. Dentan wrote:

> The Christians of the first century, like the rabbis, were aware of the diversity of the authorship of the Old Testament books, and Jesus at any rate was aware of the different levels of value within the Old Testament and was willing to quote one part against another (Mark 10:5-7).[4]

What is commendable about Dentan's observation is that he takes seriously the idea that Jesus must have recognized the differing inherent values of individual texts of Scripture. This is a decision that must precede the citation of a given text in attempting to answer a question about any specific practice. An individual interpreter must determine what text has sufficient inherent value to serve as a substantial authoritative starting point. The sections of Scripture cited in the debate about divorce, for instance, are all elements of the most central division of the Hebrew Bible. Jesus answers the policy question by choosing two texts from the opening chapters of Genesis to repudiate the practice of divorce permitted by alternate claims of "Mosaic" legislation in Deuteronomy. The view espoused by Jesus (understood through Mark) presumably suggests the Genesis texts to have revealed the equal value of persons of both genders, "male and female." Thus the destruction of the marriage bond of "one flesh" through divorce by either male or female constitutes adultery against his or her spouse. This idea within the first century setting could well be identified as revolutionary.

The corrective use of Genesis (Gen. 1:27; 5:2; 2:24) in this manner functions like a step of the hermeneutical process presented by John Bright in the James A. Gray Lectures at the Divinity School of Duke University. Bright claims that the preacher must preach only Christian sermons from the Old Testament: "That is to say, the text must be interpreted in full recognition of Christ as the crown and norm of revelation" (Bright 197-98).

The procedure that Bright suggests calls for the interpreter to perceive the verdict of the New Testament upon the theological concerns underlying the precise meaning of any text in the Old Testament (Bright 211-12). The use of the Genesis texts in Dentan's illustration is comparable. Scholarship unquestionably recognizes Jesus' affirmation of persons independent of social status, nationality, or gender.[5] Jesus introduces a startling standard on the basis of an allusion to Genesis 1:27 (or 5:2) in Mark 10:6. Jesus' own concern for persons, male and female, might be understood as providing an opportunity to see anew a concern for persons, both male and female, within these Genesis creation texts. This concern, when joined to a text of the Eden story (Gen. 2:24) presenting the idea of marriage as a "one flesh" creation (Mark 10:7-8), would deny the usual Rabbinic patriarchal understanding. The teaching presented by Mark specifically rejects the existence of two in the marriage bond. The Rabbinic view of leader (male) and follower (female) is thus corrected by the emphasis upon the creation of the one flesh relationship.

Bright's verdict step demands that the interpreter evaluate the message of any text of the Old Testament on the basis of corresponding New Testament teaching. Does this example of Jesus ratify, modify, or abrogate the claims of Genesis? If, as it is claimed, the Genesis texts present the traditional Rabbinic viewpoint and thus teach patriarchal orders for society and family, these conceptions still would need to be reconsidered with respect to Jesus' ministry and teaching and the remainder of the New Testament. Bright's verdict step thus offers a reliable procedure to avoid the introduction of possible distortion from Old Testament teaching and practices deemed substandard to the teachings of the gospel.

The Genesis creation stories therefore need to undergo a careful reexamination in the light of the Jesus who employs citations from these accounts in a fundamentally different way and with dramatically different results from traditional conventions. This examination should proceed with full awareness of the shifts of meaning introduced by gender preconceptions.

Two Creation Stories

The opening chapters of the book of Genesis present the reader with two distinct accounts of origins. Each story reflects its own particular perspective, purpose, and style of development.

The first story (Gen. 1:1-2:4a) reverberates with stately refrains and cadences. It emphasizes the powerful word of the one God over chaos and indeterminate matter. The scope of its heralding is no less than the vastness of the whole of the universe. The second narrative (Gen. 2:4b-25) by contrast unfolds the mysterious beginnings of the human family in the finite limits of the paradise of Eden. Its effect is accomplished in several scenes through a rapid pace of literary brush strokes revealing the tender concern of Yahweh God for this earthling fashioned from clay. The story climaxes with the intervention of divine care to introduce Yahweh's solution for loneliness by the establishing of community in relationship and unabashed trust.

Westermann reports that stories of what has been created appear in two forms:

> Two basic types may be distinguished: there are stories of the creation or origin of the whole and stories of the creation or origin of the one (i.e., of a particular thing). Generally speaking the creation of the whole (that is of the world and humankind) is the later form, and the creation of the one is the earlier form.[6]

Thus it may be observed that the two accounts that Genesis transmits offer examples of both types: the creation of the whole (Gen. 1:1-2:4a) and the origin of the one (Gen. 2:4b-25). The function or purpose of the story can help to explain the sharp contrast of focus and features of presentation. These unique elements may be further clarified if it would be possible to identify the community of ancient Israel responsible for the oral (possibly even written) transmission of these independent narratives.

After investigation of the characteristics of both, U. Cassuto has attempted to identify the locus of origin:

> The two traditions, the one dealing with the story of creation and the other with that of the garden of Eden, were of different types. The former, which treats of a more speculative subject, passed apparently through the circles of the "wise men". . . the philosophical groups who delved into the mystery of the world's existence. The latter, which is concerned with a simpler and more popular topic, remained nearer to the broad masses of the people and assumed a form more suited to them in its vivid portrayals (Cassuto 72).

The distinctive interests of these diverse populations can thus additionally help explain the difference in scope and the general overall stylistic variations as well.

Yet even after an initial confrontation with the multifold variety between these two accounts, a more fundamental question remains with respect to the question of the role of woman. Just how do these narratives compare in their treatment of the female gender of homo sapiens? Do the underlying theological premises correspond or do these stories present divergent viewpoints that cannot be reconciled? A careful inspection of these stories should provide helpful assistance for answering these questions.

Genesis 1:26-29

The first creation story presents the events of the sixth day in Genesis 1:24-31. The narrator, following the description of the origin of land creatures, abruptly introduces into the story a new form of speech. This new element of divine speech, "Let us make . . . ," has been interpreted variously. While Westermann suggests that its use here as a plural of deliberation is a sufficient explanation,[7] many other modern and ancient interpreters hold that the form reflects royal language of the heavenly court. In any case, this form draws attention to a significant change in the story due to its heightened concern for the creation of humankind. This inference is supported by the twofold use of "man" (*'adam*) in verses 26 and 27 and the threefold use of "create" (*bara'*) in verse 27. In this way, the account clearly emphasizes the more immediate activity of God with respect to humanity.

The word translated here as "man" must not be confused with the concept of gender as "man" or "male," for its use in the deliberative statement of verse 26 points to its function in the sense of genus. The phrase, "and let them have dominion. . . ," suggests the same meaning. Von Rad stated: "The Hebrew word *'adam'* ('man') is a collective and is therefore never used in the plural: it means literally 'mankind' (L. Koehler)" (Von Rad 55).

The most poignant indicator for emphasis in verse 27 is the change of literary form from prose to poetry. The text reads:

So God created/man in His own image, In the image of God/He created him; Male and female/He created them.[8]

Although there is much debate about the meaning of the image of God,[9] the Hebrew poetic parallelism clearly demonstrates that the female of the human species is created in possession of this same feature. She participates in the divine image in no grammatically, demonstrably different way in contrast to the male. Mary Hayter, when discussing the *Imago Dei*, says:

> Whatever it is correct to say about the creation of the male in the image and likeness of God applies to the female. Anything and everything that may be deduced from the text about "man," "mankind," "humanity," is relevant not simply to one half of the human race but to all men and women (Hayter 92).

Therefore any claims to variation of degree in bearing the divine image based upon gender distinctions should be rejected. Such readings overlook or ignore the plain reading of the text. The third line of this poetic refrain candidly recounts the creation of a plurality of persons, "them," in genders male and female.[10]

Some would object that the account given in chapter two indicates the priority of the man as male. At this precise point, the terminology and concepts that Paul himself cavalierly employs in the pivotal passage 1 Corinthians 11:2-16 unfortunately allows such an understanding.[11] An objection, reflecting this perspective, may be raised suggesting that the "him" of line two refers to the antecedent "man" in line one. Grammatically, however, the "him" of line two cannot refer to man as male for the category male is only first introduced in the following line. As already stated above, *'adam* does not mean male but humankind and it is used as a collective noun. Therefore the word *him* cannot carry any male gender connotations in this setting.

Recognition of the function of Hebrew poetic parallelism has also provided a useful approach for understanding the meaning of the *Imago Dei* with respect to the relationship between woman and man. Jewett observed that "according to this view, Genesis 1:27b ('male and female made he them') is an exposition of 1:27a ('in the image of God created he him') (Jewett 33)."

This view understands that "man" was created to live in community or in partnership. Westermann commented:

> A lone human being remains a complete human being in his lonesomeness. What is being said here is that a human being must be seen as one whose destiny it is to live in community; people have been created to live with each other.[12]

Thus man and woman are to live and work in partnership as a representation of the smallest unit of community. At this point, if one is disposed to find it, the first story fails to provide instruction in an alleged order of creation. If sexual distinction means difference in rank or function the story offers no hint. No hierarchical roles are formulated. No gender behaviors are suggested.

Ignoring this lack, the account continues with a divine blessing upon "them." Even more surprising, the orders to reproduce (*peru urabu*) and populate (*umil'u*) over earth, to subdue it (*ukibshuha*), and have dominion (*uradu*) over the animal kingdom are given in the plural form (Hayter 89). This clearly suggests that both male and female are included in the divine plan of action. This conclusion, however, should be no surprise, for it simply follows the specified intent of the deliberative statement in verse 26, "and let them have dominion" (*weyirdu*).

The reading of image in Genesis 1:27 has been interpreted theologically as a reflection of the trinitarian relationship in the Godhead. This view takes the divine community of the trinity as the *apriori* of human community. Scanzoni and Hardesty, for example, discuss the image and likeness of God by saying:

> We believe that the image of God is not only rationality but "relationality." All persons, male and female, are created by

God with rational self-awareness, and also with the capacity for self-transcendence. The fellowship of husband and wife, of parents and child, and even the fellowship within the church reflect the dynamic mutuality and reciprocity of the Trinity, which agreed, "Let us make man in our image."[13]

Formulating the idea in this way suggests that the relationship of the sexes mirrors the affairs of Diety. As the dogma of the trinity would hold to some idea of divine equality of the persons of the Godhead, so some idea of human equality between the persons of the human family must be recognized. This equality of persons would naturally extend to equality between the genders. How far this correspondence between the divine and the human should be traced is an important question. Should the conception be understood from the view of being only or also entertain the ideas of a mutuality of function discussed in such trinitarian dogma?[14] However these questions may eventually be decided, the idea of sexuality in the Godhead should be denied cautiously (Jewett 43; Hayter 37-41).

Genesis 2:18-25

The second creation story focuses upon the origin of human social matters. It ignores the explanation of the appearance of the cosmos as a whole, unlike the first account in Genesis 1. Its story line only touches upon broader elements as a backdrop to establish the time setting for the unfolding of its theme. The narrative (Gen. 2:4b-25) in its extant form is composed of four paragraphs,[15] the last of which is the subject of this paper.

In this division of the story, tension mounts as Yahweh God declares his creature alone and his solution is announced (Gen. 2:18). Next, the unexpected happens; the creator fashions some animals to bring to his garden resident. Tension or humor or both increases when the earthling encounters the animals to name them, but still a solution to the problem of being alone is not discovered. Then, at the climax of the account, the narrative reveals the divine creation of the woman (Gen. 2:21-22). Thus the intent of the story is to show the divine plan of creating persons in social interaction and not the making of an ideal of one who is alone.

The verse that introduces this section expresses the first negative evaluation in the book of Genesis (2:18). Solitary existence is judged by Yahweh God as not good or, from the divine solution, incomplete. Man (*àdam*) is human only in relation to an other like oneself. Members of the animal kingdom cannot suffice. Thus the earthling needs another person with whom to relate. The story reveals that Yahweh God knows how to subdue the state of loneliness. The divine solution is the creation of the ideal opposite, the same but different—not a clone copy but a mirror image. The answer is the divine creation of the *èzer kenegdo* (Gen. 2:18, 20).

This person, woefully misunderstood as a "helpmate" (misread from "help meet" in the KJV), has been the frequent subject of much commentary study. It is now almost conventional in current sources to recognize the use of the word *èzer* ("help") to describe Deity in the Old Testament.[16] This modern scholarly intent is plain: to substitute a more respectful meaning and reject a traditional reading connoting servant (if not slave) or assistant in precreation (Hayter 101-2). What has not been presented in the contemporary literature is an exhaustive look at the use of the root of *èzer* throughout the Hebrew Bible to ascertain its broader scope of use. This chapter shall now offer such an examination.

The Use of the Root '*Z-R in the Hebrew Bible*

Extensive investigation of the actual use of Hebrew words is easily facilitated with the assistance of the exhaustive Hebrew concordance composed by Mandelkern (1896). Only four times (counting the two in Gen. 2) out of the twenty-two appearances of the masculine noun *èzer* is the word used in description of human beings. The predominant use characterizes Deity as "help" (Ex. 18:4; Dt. 33:7, 26, 29) or recognizes God as the source who provides it (Ps. 20:2; 89:19; 121:1, 2).

The two uses shown outside Genesis are revealing. The word appears in Isaiah 30:5 with respect to the royal staff of Pharaoh who were attempting to establish an alliance with Judah. The prophet, however, mocks their ability to be a help. Yet aside from the question of effectiveness, an ally would not be subservient but equal. Yet here human help is scorned.

The second example is used in Ezekiel 12:14 to describe the doom about to fall upon Zedekiah's staff, (literally "his help") and military guard. Those who function as the king's helpers here, like above, do not labor in what could be characterized as subservient roles. These two examples both show a use comparable to that of royal counselors or advisors. Advisors provide the help of their counsel to the king. The king in actuality plays the subordinate role of the one who receives aid. The helper who gives help functions in the superior position. This inquiry thus confirms the claim of Jewett: "The word for "help" in Genesis 2:18, 20 (*èr*) is never used elsewhere to designate a subordinate (Jewett 124)."

The uses in the Hebrew Bible of two other feminine nouns *èzrat* (2) and *èzratah* (3) both translated "help" are strictly limited to the description of Deity. The word *èzrat* is found in parallel to contrast the success of human "deliverance" (Ps. 60:11) with the divine. The word *èzratah* is used in parallelism with "deliver" showing divine

Equal Access to Grace in Ministry: Women and Men

help as delivering (Ps. 44:26). No appearances used to describe the activity of humans occur.

The third Hebrew noun, *èzrah*, also feminine in form, is found more frequently. Ten examples are employed in divine description. Several of these are found in parallelism with "deliver" or "deliverance" (Ps. 38:22; 40:14, 17; 70:2). This word, in contrast to other nouns, is employed more often in examples of human help. Nine examples are identified. The most common use is in expressions indicating assistance of allies, military and political (Judg. 5:23, Isa. 10:3; 20:6; 31:1; Nah. 3:9; Jer. 37:7; Lam. 4:17). A late use in 2 Chronicles 28:21 considers the effect of tribute before an enemy. Its use in legal matters (Job 31:21, twice) recognizes the unfair advantage of one disputant having legal counsel and the destitute opponent (an orphan) presumably without.

Nevertheless, the primary use of *èzrah* denotes a meaning like ally, someone or some force of equal rank. The use in Job introduces a clear legal connotation. The attorney helps the litigant. No one should claim that the attorney (helper) occupies a position of inferior rank. Rather the superior standing of the legal advisor assists the one contracting his or her aid thus to argue the case in court. The one who receives assistance stands in a lower position.

The appearance of verbal forms including participles are much more frequent in the Hebrew Bible. Some forty examples are employed with respect to Deity or deities while thirty-three appearances of verbal forms describe human activity. Various verbal roots are used in parallelism with other verbs like "save," "deliver," and numerous other verbs of divine help.

The predominant use with respect to human activity again concerns the function of persons or nations as an ally. Several can be cited: the tribes beyond the Jordan (Josh. 1:14), the coalition of Adoni-Zedek (Josh. 10:4), Joshua to the Gibeonites (Josh. 10:6), Horam to Lachish (Josh. 10:33), and the Syrians to Hadadezer (2 Sam. 8:5). Several examples of verbal forms reveal a use with a function of "advocate." The righteous king assists the oppressed who have no one to defend them (Ps. 72:2). Job's counselors may thus sarcastically be described in their dealing with his predicament (Job 26:2). Their arguments, however, contrast with Job's arguing a case in the gate on behalf of the poor and orphan (Job 29:7, 12). The just act of Job corresponds to the care of God (Ps. 10:14). The "advocate" use in these texts represents the *qal* participle.

Two late uses suggest a function related to the royal staff. King Uzziah receives aid through the invention of military weapons (2 Chron. 26:15); while Hezekiah is helped by the diverting of the city water supplies (2 Chron. 32:3).[17] In both of these cases the reigning king and inhabitants of Jerusalem receive benefit through the expertise of the king's staff. Though the royal staff are subjects of the king, these two examples do not characterize the functions of a subordinate but, as stated earlier, represent one who gives assistance from a superior position as royal counselor or advisor.

The root `-z-r` in the whole of the Hebrew Bible does not reflect the connotation of servant; even subordinate functions cannot be cited. Since the subject of the majority of all occurrences is used with respect to God, the suggestion that *èzer* means the help of one in some inferior position must be rejected. To cavalierly read the word *èzer* with respect to woman, the divine solution of the earthling's loneliness, as a subordinate assistant is wholly arbitrary if not dishonest. The reason the Rabbinic tradition depends so strongly upon inference of order in chapter two of Genesis should be obvious. Paul himself never suggests such "helper" ideas even when he employs the Rabbinic order inference. The word *èzer* thus does not connote someone of inferior rank. Rather, evidence cited by Cassuto from Bereshith Rabba[18] confirms the Rabbinic awareness of the biblical lexical function of *èzer*: "She was given him for an adviser (Cassuto 133)."

Yahweh God's Solution

Hayter considers that inferences from the phrase *èzer kenegdo* have been employed as the most prevalent argument for the subordination of women. The inferences thus drawn suggest:

> ... the case that woman was created solely for the sake of the man, to serve him, more or less as a bondslave serves a master. The spoken or implied corollary of this is that on her own woman has little worth or value; she is fit *solely for assisting man in the establishment of a home and family* (emphasis added).[19]

The evidence, however, of the general use of the word *èzer* suggests the opposite. The woman, if an *èzer* functions as an advisor or a person of superior rank. Yet Hayter rightly objects to this as an inaccurate characterization. The reason is that *èzer* appears in the Genesis phrase with *kenegdo*. This results in an important adjustment to the usual meaning of the word *èzer*. Hayter thus objects to the meaning of women as superior to man that some persons suggest:

> This supposition is illegitimate, however, since *'ezer* is here modified by "fit for him," *kenegdo,* with its connotations of "counterpart," "corresponding to," "alongside of." *Kenegdo* tempers the hint of superiority with ideas of mutuality and equality (Hayter 102).

The story next narrates that Yahweh God forms the animals and presents them to God's creature (Gen. 2:19). Cassuto considers that the divine purpose for the naming of the animals by the earthling was to assist God's creature with a personal awareness of his difference from the animals. The *àdam* first needed to develop a consciousness of what could not solve his loneliness problem. Cassuto thus wrote:

> It would seem that the text intends to tell us only that the Lord God wished to engender in the heart of the man a desire for a helper *who should correspond to him exactly* (Cassuto 128, emphasis added).

The earthling, however, does not find a suitable partner (Gen. 2:20). Therefore the crisis must be solved by Yahweh God; the earthling only serves to be a source for building material in the divine plan. The first creature plays no active role (Gen. 2:21). The woman is not created from the earth directly but indirectly through the "raw" flesh of the *àdam*. Yahweh God then introduces the woman to the man, now acknowledged male for the first time, and the man exclaims his approval of the divine initiative. The man thus recognizes a suitable partner. The divine good is for the man not to be alone. The goal of the story, the community of man and woman, is then achieved.[20]

Much is written about the so-called naming of woman by the man (Gen. 2:23). This interest involves the commonly argued conception of authority of the name-giver over the named thing or person.[21] Nevertheless, Westermann rejects such speculations.[22] But even if such notions were valid, a detailed comparison of passages where naming is clearly intended would show that all the necessary Hebrew elements are not included.[23]

In Genesis 2:23 the narrator interrupts the account to offer a comment about marriage suggested by the meaning of the story just presented. The conclusion clearly reflects conditions external to the story, "a man leaves his father and his mother," for only two live in the garden as the next verse makes plain. The major surprise, however, of his comment is the form of the marriage practice: the man leaves his home and is joined to another. This practice surely could not have been the custom of the writer's day with roots in a patriarchal society. What is the reader to make of this? Could it be that the story has been misunderstood? Jewett wrote:

> If the implication which the rabbis drew, that the woman is subject to the man because she was taken from the man, is intended by the narrative, then why does not Genesis 2:24 read: "Therefore shall a *woman* leave her father and mother and cleave unto her *husband,* and they shall become one flesh?" (Jewett 127, emphasis added).

The comment of the narrator may well be a key. If Jewett's suspicion is correct, and his conclusion of traditional Rabbinic misinterpretation cannot be overlooked, then the narrator's comment introduces a startling observation. The second story of creation thus appears to present the same message as that of Genesis 1. Both express the divine intention for humans, male and female, to live in partnership. Westermann arrived at the same conclusion:

> There is no essential difference between the creation of humans in 1:26 and Gen. 2; the person is also created by God as his counterpart in Gen. 2 so that something can happen between creator and creature. The difference is that Gen. 2 expresses it in story form and not in conceptual terms (Westermann 157).

The story closes with the man and woman living in the free expression of trust where nakedness is no concern (Gen. 2:25). Now the story can conclude with "it was very good" (Gen. 1:31).

Conclusion

The accounts of the origins of humankind and the human family (Gen. 1:26-29 and 2:18-25) offer ideas that have implications for the equal access to grace of men and women in ministry. These implications are pertinent to the current debate about women's roles in the church since many ideas are founded on these accounts.

All persons of both genders equally participate in the *Imago Dei*. The number of arguments offered in the past should make no difference to this claim. Therefore, no gender, be it male (as has been customary) or female, can present itself as the one ideal form of God's representative to stand in the place of God. Thus no reader can infer correctly the presence of any gender barriers upon the fulfilling of a pastoral or priestly role.

The creation account offers no evidence for the possession of a difference of degree in reflecting the divine image with respect to gender. The text offers no hint of any "divine order of creation," a supposed universally valid rule for the functioning of men and women in public or private settings. Subordination of either gender does not reflect the divine intention. Rather, God's desire was and is mutuality and community—in a word, equality, of all persons.

The message of the gospel proclaims the introduction of a new creation in Christ. Therefore, what has been understood to have been lost through humankind's unrighteousness can and will be restored through the grace given in Christ Jesus.[24] Harmony and unity were lost to self-seeking and blame but sexual differences continued. The original creation-harmony of community and mutuality can and is being restored in the community identified as the body of Christ. No one should distinguish between the grace offered to men and women with respect to entering this community of faith as well as in serving the body in leadership functions.

The image of God points to participation in community and partnership—"relationality." The story understands the existence of the sexes as God-given from the beginning and designed for social interaction. The focus of the second account is essentially the same. The highlight of the story is the divine creation of woman and the man's ready recognition and acceptance of Yahweh God's solution to human loneliness. The view of an independent, self-sufficient male gender has no foundation in the first account and is even candidly denied in the second narrative: "It is not good for the man to be alone" (Gen. 2:18).

Ministry can thus be understood in terms of community and partnership of both genders. The first account presents humankind as male and female jointly called to fulfill the divine mandates without specific gender distinctions. In the same manner, in the new creation, no reader should find limits or distinctions for employment in the body of Christ with respect to gender, but a message of service grounded in community and partnership.

Endnotes

1. Consider F. G. Smith 1914, 252-265; C. W. Naylor 1918, 5-6; C. E. Brown 1939, 5, 13; John Stanley 1975, 2, 6; Sharon Sawyer 1976, 1, 2, 7; Marie Strong 1978, 4-6; Sharon C. Pearson 1989, 32-36.

2. See announcement: "Council on Biblical Manhood and Womanhood, The Danvers Statement" 1989, 40-41. This confessional statement affirms that "some governing and teaching roles within the church are restricted to men." The list of council members reveals a virtual who's who of conservative fundamentalist scholars.

3. This relationship may be understood within one of four patterns: (1) no continuity, a position rejected by the early church; (2) continuity, with the flow of ideas from the New into the Old Testament; (3) continuity, with the flow of ideas from the Old into the New Testament; and (4) continuity, with movement of thought in both directions. See Gerhard F. Hasel 1975, 105-127. For additional discussion the reader may consult John Bright 1967, 58-160.

4. Robert C. Dentan 1951, 154. See also Paul K. Jewett 1975, 136-137.

5. Note the insights of Charles Caldwell Ryrie 1958, 26-31. See especially the discussion about how Jesus' teaching contradicts the accepted Rabbinic understanding. Mary Hayter 1987, 113. Hayter makes reference to "disorder" as the result of sin with respect to the parallel text in Matthew 19:8.

6. Claus Westermann 1984, 22-23. Westermann's introductory section concerning the form and function of creation stories is extensive.

7. Westermann 1984, 145. The trinitarian allusion is now widely contested.

8. Cassuto 1961, 53. See his comments on the poetic form, 57. Westermann also notes shift from prose to poetry (1984, 160).

9. See Westermann for extensive bibliography and summary of options (1984, 147-156).

10. This poetic declaration of the divine creation of two sexes simultaneously thus introduces difficult questions for theories of an original androgynous or hermaphrodite order of being. See Cassuto 1961, 57-58; Hayter 1987, 97; Von Rad 1961, 58.

11. The use of the Greek word *aner* with or without the article in 1 Corinthians 11:3, 4, 7, 8, 9, 11, 12, and 14 should be considered as imprecise. The concepts thus introduced do not faithfully represent the meaning of the Hebrew text in Genesis 1 or 2 because Paul is not offering an argument that begins with the Genesis text. The positions taken integrating male and female, especially in verses 7 to 9, rather are derived from a perspective of Rabbinic tradition. See Jewett 1975, 53-57, 112-110; Letha Scanzoni and Nancy Hardesty 1974, 28. An argument established upon the understanding of the Hebrew text would have been more effectively served by the Greek word *anthropos*. The Septuagint is only slightly more effective in rendering the Hebrew. The Septuagint translator demonstrates a disposition toward substituting the proper name "Adam" in place of rendering "the man" in Genesis 2.

12. Westermann 1984, 160. Westermann reads this same meaning for the story of Genesis 2, "There is no essential difference between the creation of humans in 1:25 and Genesis 2" (160). See his other comments (194, 232) on the purpose of the second account.

13. Scanzoni and Hardesty 1974, 23-24. Jewett 1975, 33-40, 43-49 presents several pages of select excerpts of Karl Barth in addition to a valuable critique of the excesses of Barth's theological language. Westermann discusses Barth in his excursus on the treatment of Genesis 1:26-27: section 5. The person as God's counterpart, 150-151.

14. I am not convinced that this line of argument is that helpful, and certain pitfalls should be recognized in its use. Particularly in its application to functional concerns, the argument can be made that while divine equality of being must be maintained, divine roles in the economy of redemption appear at least with respect to some functions to be divided up among the persons of the Godhead. The functions suggest positions of superiority and inferiority, concepts that must be held in tension with the claim for equality. Thus only the Son became incarnate or the Spirit witnesses to and glorifies the Son. A similar problem with respect to the roles of women and men is discussed by Jewett 1975, 85, 111.

15. Following the RSV, 1973: Gen. 2:4b-9, 10-14, 15-17, and 18-25.

16. Westermann 1984, 232, says: "Genesis 2 is unique among the creation myths of the whole of the Ancient Near East in its appreciation of the meaning of woman, i.e., that human existence is a partnership of man and woman."

17. Hayter 1987, 102; Jewett 1975, 124-125; Westermann 1984, 227. See especially *Archaeology Review* 9 (1983) who links this word to the root *g-z-r* "to be strong."

18. Allusion to the marvelous engineering task involved in war preparations including the construction of the Siloam tunnel (2 Kings 20:20).

19. The Bereshith Rabba is a playful homiletic commentary on Genesis. The citation is 20:11.

20. Hayter 1987, 101. Hayter presents five inferences derived from Genesis 2 that have been employed to argue the inferiority of the woman (96-102).

21. Westerman 1984, 226-233; Cassuto 1961, 133; Von Rad 1961, 82-83. Westermann observes: "It is significant that we in our present state of civilization agree with what Genesis 2 says about the relationship of man and woman" (322). Genesis 20:11 is the citation.

22. Westerman 1984, 228-229, 232; Cassuto 1961, 130, 136; Von Rad 1961, 80-82.

23. Compare Gen. 2:20; 3:20; and 5:2. In these three examples the specific naming phase includes a form of *qara'* ("call") and a form of *shem* ("name"). See Hayter 1987, 100.

24. Although only the two creation accounts have been discussed, the importance of the rebellion story needs some comment. The story of the rebellion in Eden suggests that the root of humanity's problem is the race's constant attempt to abrogate the distinction between humankind and God, creature and Creator. Thus the subjugated status of the woman outside the garden is the result of human rebellion against the biblical divine order of creation and the consequent disorder introduced into the human family. The inferior status of woman in the patriarchal society of the biblical writers was not the reflection of divine will but the consequence of human sin and pride.

GEORGE KUFLEDT

B.A., B.Th., Anderson University; M.Div., Anderson University School of Theology; Ph.D., Dropsie University.

Professor of Old Testament, Anderson University School of Theology (Anderson, Indiana). Longterm teaching colleague of Dr. Boyce W. Blackwelder.

Chapter 4
The Prophets: Divine Word or Human Words?
by George Kufeldt

Anyone who listens to what generally is billed as "prophetic preaching" on either television or radio could get the impression that the biblical canon of prophetic writings consists almost entirely of such passages as Ezekiel 38-39, Zechariah 12, the book of Daniel, and the book of Revelation. Such preaching also may mislead the listener into believing that the prophets were concerned only with predicting "the times or the seasons" (Acts 1:7), identifying nations who will try to destroy modern Israel, and naming "the antichrist."

A thoughtful and careful comparison of these sermons will reveal a wide range of interpretations of the specifics of the prophetic writings having to do with nations, events, and dates. In other words, it is clear that typical "prophetic preaching" usually takes the divine word as revealed to the biblical prophet and turns it into a human word that is forced to fit into a human scheme of interpretation that reflects the everchanging international scene.

Such an approach to biblical prophecy commits three basic errors. First, it tends to ignore the bulk of the prophetic writings. Second, it misunderstands and misinterprets the primary mission and message of the biblical prophet. Third, it confuses or ignores the distinctions between prophetism and apocalypticism.

Surely it is only reasonable to believe that preaching that is prophetic will reflect the emphases of the whole of the biblical prophets' message as they declared "thus says the Lord." This means that the preacher will recognize the difference between the messages of the prophet and that of the apocalyptist and will not use them indiscriminately to construct what may be a "logical" but nonetheless human system of eschatology. The construction of such a system of eschatology through proof-texting ignores what is a foundation stone of biblical interpretation: the biblical text must be interpreted in the light of its context. Whenever the context is ignored, it is all too easy to use the text for one's own purpose and to give it a meaning not intended by the originally inspired writer.

In order to remain true to the original intention and meaning of the divinely inspired word of the prophet and thus avoid making it a human word, it is necessary to review the life and work of the Old Testament prophet himself or herself. This essay will strive to do that by emphasizing and clarifying the prophet as a person, the prophet's purpose, and the prophet's proclamation.

The Prophet as a Person

The answer to the question, "What manner of a person is the prophet?"[1] is the basic clue to the total meaning of the prophet's life and work. Indeed, as Bruce Vawter has noted, "The classical prophet of the Old Testament was a prophet quite as much by what he was as by what he said" (Vawter 24. See also Heschel ix ff.). While it may be true to think and speak of the prophet as "God's spokesperson," this very truism may lead us into forgetting that "the prophet is a person, not a microphone" (Vawter x). Not only is he or she "endowed with a mission, with the power of a word not his own that accounts for his greatness—but also with temperament, concern, character, and individuality" (25). As a person, the prophet is not so much an instrument as a partner, an associate of God" (25). So keen was this sense of partnership with God that the prophet Amos confessed, perhaps a bit unwillingly: "Surely the Lord God does nothing, without revealing his secret to his servants the prophets. . . . The Lord God has spoken; who can but prophesy?" (Amos 3:7-8).

Clearly then, the prophet is an uncommon person. True, she or he has an unusual sensitivity to the cries and heartbreak of the common person, but this sensitivity stems from an uncommon relationship with God. This identity with God enables the prophet to understand the hurts of all of God's creatures. The prophet is not stirred by what is seen in the world as much as he or she is sensitized by the heartbreak of God that is shared personally. Consequently, "to the prophets even a minor injustice assumes cosmic proportions" (6). Sharing in God's awareness of humanity's sin, people's inhumanity to others, the prophet never became a partisan preacher. For the prophet, as with God, sin is sin, whether committed by the poor or the wealthy, the enslaved or the powerful, the apostate or the religionist, the outcast or royalty.

As one who stood "in the council of the Lord" (Jer. 23:18), the prophet could not avoid speaking the word of the Lord to the people "whether they hear or refuse to hear (Ezek. 2:5). Thus, the prophet did not debate the relative merits of a situation or problem, but rather began not with the problem but with the verdict, the judgment of God, which is really an extension of the moral character and holiness of God.[2] "This is the marvel of a prophet's work: in his words the invisible God becomes audible ... The authority of the prophet is in the Presence his words reveal" (Herschel 22).

It is inaccurate, then, to regard the prophet as simply a person with a divine message. Rather, the prophet is a person who not only has a divine call, but one who also has an unusual relationship with the divine, giving insight into the human predicament beyond that of other persons. This is the primary distinguishing mark between the true prophet and "the prophet who deals falsely."[3] This depth of divine insight that the prophet has because of his or her unique partnership with God leads to a primary concern with and involvement in the events and times in which the prophet lived. Admittedly there are predictive elements in the prophet's concerns and message, but even the foresight that she or he had grew out of the insight that the prophet had into the times in which he or she lived. The prophet never predicts events in isolation; the future is always determined by humankind's response in the present to God's word as revealed by the prophet.

The Purpose of the Prophet's Call

It has been said, and probably rightly, that "if Israel had lived up to God's Torah or Law, to what she knew, the prophets would not have had a job." The prophet's task was to call Israel back to God, to live as people under and within the covenant. They were reformers, calling the people of Israel to return to the ideals and standards set forth in the Torah, the keeping of which would have enabled Israel truly to have been God's special, unique people.

God's purpose in calling the prophets may be seen as being twofold in scope. First, it was to call Israel to repentance from sin, to turn from "harloting after strange gods," and to return to Yahweh. One of the words most frequently used by the prophets was the Hebrew word *shûv*, meaning "Return!" or "Repent!" This call might seem to be unnecessary in view of the flourishing cultic practices of the prophets' times. But this was just the problem—it was ritual without meaning, it was worship without God (at least the true God). To make matters worse, it was the official religious leaders, the priests, and the cultic prophets, who were leading the people in this ritual without meaning. Thus, the task fell to God's servants the prophets to call them from ritual without meaning to repentance and righteousness.

Second, the prophets were called to remind Israel that religious activity not supported by moral and ethical living is worse than no religion at all. Hand-in-hand with the religious leaders, the civil and economic leaders were trampling all the principles of right and decency into the ground, and were running roughshod over any and all who stood in their path so that they could gratify their lust for power and wealth. For them too the prophets had one primary word: "Repent and return" to the principles and ideals of the covenant, to the standards that must be obeyed if any society is to survive.

Because the nation's leaders generally had turned from God and had abused all that was right and righteous, the task fell to the prophets "to declare to Jacob his transgression and to Israel his sin" (Micah 3:8), to remind the people "that it is evil and bitter . . . to forsake . . . God" (Jer. 2:19). It was a call that no prophet relished (see Jer. 1; Isa. 6; Ezek. 2, 3), but in spite of little evidence of positive response to their work (see Jer. 25:3-7), these preachers of the divine word carried out their God-given mandate.

The Prophet's Proclamation

The message of the prophet cannot be separated from the prophetic mission. In many ways they are identical. Rather than examine each facet of the prophet's theology, the purpose of this essay will be served more specifically and effectively if at this point the prophet's proclamation is related to and seen against the exegetical principles that must be followed in order to understand the perennial meaning of the prophetic word.[4] In illustrating these exegetical principles, it will be necessary to show how they are commonly ignored or misused, resulting in the divinely inspired message of the prophet becoming reworked into a human system of eschatology.

The principle that underlies the message of every biblical prophet is the fact that the prophetic speaking was first and foremost to his or her own day and time. This means that generally he or she was a known person speaking to a known people within the framework of a known politico-religious situation, usually involving obvious economic problems or excesses. Not even an Amos, who spoke as an outsider to the Northern Kingdom, really violates this basic principle, since he seems to have been recognized quickly enough as a prophet of Yahweh (see Amos 7:10 ff.). Whatever else the prophet was vocationally, "the function of the prophet was first of all that of a preacher and teacher of the will of God" (Milton 3).

This principle is unmistakable in every prophetic call of which we have record. Amos (7:1-6, etc.) was called to warn the Israelites of his own generation (not a hundred years hence) that "the doom is ripe upon [God's] people Israel."[5] Isaiah (6:1-13) was called to pronounce judgment upon his own people whose sin (see Isa. 1, etc.) would not be ignored any longer by Yahweh.

Jeremiah (1:4-13; 20:7-18) was most reluctant to accept his prophetic mission because it required that he declare to his own people that God's watchful eye had not been closed to the terrible social and moral abuses that were rampant in the land, even at that moment (see Jer. 2, etc.).

Ezekiel was commissioned to confront his own people with their sin in spite of the fact that they were "a rebellious house" (see all of chapters 2 and 3) and so were constantly violating all they knew of God's will. Not only that, but his "acted parables" (Ezek 4 and 5, etc.) were a direct warning about the destruction that would come upon the people who themselves were watching his skits with only half interest, unless they repented and returned from their wicked ways.

As spokespersons to their own day, the prophets were primarily and predominantly concerned with preaching repentance and obedience to their own people.[6] The religious, moral, and social sin of their own people and their own day was the basis for their being called to be spokespersons for God and to call backslidden Israel to a sense of God's wrath and judgment. Thus, the abuses before the very eyes of Amos as he ministered in Bethel prompted him to show God's verdict: "I hate, I despise your feasts . . . your solemn assemblies. . . . Take away from me the noise of your [raucous] songs; . . . Woe to those who lie upon beds [inlaid with] ivory . . . but are not grieved over the ruin of Joseph!" (Amos 5:21, 23; 6:4, 6).

Almost every page of the prophetic writings is full of this indictment of the sins of the people of Israel and Judah and warnings of the soon-coming judgment of God unless they repented quickly. That they did not heed the message of the prophets is all too clear from the fact that Israel fell to the Assyrians in 722 BCE and that Judah was destroyed by Babylon in 587 BCE.

Since the prophet preached to the people and situations of his or her own day and time, it is necessary to understand the prophet's time in order to understand fully the resulting message. This means that we must understand the social, moral and even economic imagery and terms used by the prophets as they reflected the experience of the prophets and those among whom they worked. This includes taking the word of the prophet as it was intended, without interpreting it to fit some preconceived notion of either theology or history.

For example, when Amos, Hosea, Isaiah, and Micah all spoke of Assyria, they meant the great world power of their day by that name, and not Russia or China of our day. When Habakkuk spoke of the Chaldeans (1:6), why should these people be interpreted as being the Greeks, or worse, the Soviets? Habakkuk's message was a simple word of warning and comfort to his own people within the time-framework of the religious and political situation in which he lived and ministered. This does not mean, of course, that his message is "dated" or useful only for one particular situation. We must recognize that the Chaldeans had their day in history, but we can also see that every generation has its own "Chaldeans" who are still under God's sovereignty and that it is always true that "the just shall live by his faith" (Hab. 2:4). At the same time, we must not forget that Habakkuk was speaking to his time and people about the Chaldeans or Neo-Babylonians and not about either Russia or China in our time.

This is not to deny a predictive element in the prophetic message. It does mean, however, that the emphasis is placed on the primary focus of the prophetic word. That focus is the recognition of sin in all its forms and that God is still calling people and nations to repentance and obedience. Sin is a violation of the covenant relationship, and this violation, just as obedience to it, determines both the present and the future. It is not simply a matter of cause and effect, but rather a belief, based on historical experience, that God is always faithful to his covenant. As promise is part of the covenant, so also judgment is the consequence of covenant disobedience. But, the God who is faithful to this covenant can make judgment a means of redemption.

Thus, one might say that there are two kinds of predictions.[7] First there are those that are of events near at hand, usually involving judgment because of sin, violation of the covenant. Second are predictions of events in the undated future, which are usually promises of hope, restoration, and perhaps final consummation. These too are covenantal in basis and nature, and often transcend ordinary covenantal expectation. Indeed, the promised future hope is not limited by nationalistic expectations but becomes universal and spiritual in nature. This certainly is how the New Testament writers understood the failure of the old Israel to fully live up to its covenant with Yahweh. Only the coming of Christ as the unique seed of Abraham fulfilled God's promise. So now the divine purpose of this covenant was being revealed in the New Israel.[8]

Prophetic and Apocalyptic Writings

One of the greatest sources of misinterpretation of the prophets is the failure to see the differences between prophetic writings and apocalyptic writings. Most people recognize that sections such as Zechariah 9-14, the last half of the book of Daniel, and the book of Revelation are different from Amos, Hosea, Isaiah, and Jeremiah. These sections of Zechariah, Daniel and Revelation are apocalyptic in nature, and so they use highly symbolic language and thus are difficult to understand. This is true since the symbolism is unnatural and even weird as compared to the familiar, natural imagery used by Amos, Ezekiel, Jeremiah, and others.

The Prophets: Divine Word or Human Words?

To go into any full discussion of apocalypticism here is impossible.[9] The observation must suffice that while the prophets optimistically called the people of their own time back to God, leaving the ultimate choice in the people's hands, the apocalyptist usually wrote to people who were suffering persecution and who could be rescued only through the direct intervention of God. The apocalyptist wrote in symbols understood only by the persecuted while the prophet spoke and wrote plainly of God's judgment on sin and the choice of repentance that the people still had.

Adding to the confusion between and the misunderstanding of the basic meanings of prophetism and apocalypticism is the failure to recognize that the Old Testament concept of eschatology or the end-times is not the same as one finds in the New Testament. The fact is that the Old Testament has very little teaching (in fact, almost none) about concepts such as heaven, hell, life hereafter, resurrection, and a final judgment. The finding of such concepts in the Old Testament is a reading back into the Old Testament from the New Testament.

These ideas or beliefs actually developed in the intertestamental period, as evidenced by the many Jewish writings of that time. For example, it is clear from the gospels that the Pharisees accepted these ideas. Only two passages in the Old Testament, Daniel 12:2 and Isaiah 26:19, approach anything like a possible statement concerning resurrection and life hereafter. Both of these passages, however, are found within definite apocalyptic sections, and so must be interpreted in the light of that kind of context and the date when these passages were written. These verses most likely reflect the dream and hope of a time when the persecution of God's people (probably the Maccabean period, 168-165 BCE) will be over and when those who died for their faith during this persecution will be raised to enjoy life and freedom again on this earth in the restored Jewish community.

While we can assume that the people of the Old Testament must have had some hope of life beyond the present, they did not have the ultimate revelation through the resurrection of Christ that Christians have. The present life is all they had assurance about, and so they wanted to live as long as possible. All they really knew was that this life is all there is, and that when they died they would go to Sheol, the universal grave where all the dead ultimately go. So, when David said of his dead illegitimate son, "I shall go to him" (2 Samuel 12:23), he was referring to his own ultimate destiny in Sheol, and not to a glad reunion in heaven someday. For the Old Testament, whatever follows this life was a great mystery, which is still basically true for the Christian as well.

Without any clearly defined ideas and hopes about the world to come, the people of the Old Testament obviously had to place their emphasis on the here and now, on this world, the only world they knew. Thus, when Job says "I know that my [redeemer/vindicator] lives, and at the last he will stand upon the earth, and after my skin has been destroyed, yet from my flesh I shall see God" (Job 19:25-26), he is not looking to a better life in a world yet to come. Instead, he is looking for and expecting vindication in the here and now, where he lived, for his faithfulness in the midst of his suffering. He believed that God would again restore his health here, in this world, as, indeed, the ending of the story indicates (see Job 42).

In the same way, both the prophets and the apocalyptists looked toward the future within the limitations of their restricted understanding of that future. When they speak of destruction of the present wicked world order, evil nations, and then of God's activity in restoring his people, this restoration of God's people and their land must be seen in terms of this world, the place where they lived. They were not thinking and writing in terms of a detailed history of the events after a universal judgment and end-time scheme. They certainly idealized this hoped for restoration of God's people, but it was not a hope deferred to the world beyond time.

So, when Isaiah wrote about swords being turned into plowshares and universal peace (Isa. 2:2 ff.), he was dreaming about God's rulership becoming real in this world. He had no idea when this ideal would become real, whether in his lifetime or in some undated distant future. That future, however, would take place in this world and not in a world yet to come. It remained for Christian revelation to develop the ideas of a world beyond time, where the ideal would become fully realized.

It is most important to remember that the apocalyptist, just as the prophet, wrote for the benefit and encouragement of the people of his or her own time. This means, then, that the symbolism was understood by the original readers and that it had specific application for their own time. So, to think that the people and places referred to in Ezekiel 38-39, Daniel 7-12, or the book of Revelation, can be identified historically with specific people and places in our time is to misunderstand and to misuse the message of the apocalyptist. For example, who or what were Gog and Magog of Ezekiel 38-39? Whoever they represented to the original writer and readers, if indeed they were understood as specific persons or places or both (even Revelation 20:8 seems to understand them differently), the original writer certainly did not have modern communist Russia in mind. Thus, to interpret Meshech and Tubal (Ezek. 38:3) as the Soviet cities Moscow and Tobolsk, as some do today, is to violate completely valid exegetical principles and to open the door to even greater excesses and error. One must ask how these names will be interpreted in the future when Russia will have fallen, as it must inevitably.

The point is that while we cannot identify Gog and Magog with certainty, even in their original setting, anyone with a sense of apocalyptic recognizes that "they represent the concentrated enmity and fury of the kingdoms of the world against the Kingdom of God" (Milton 45-46). These need not always be political kingdoms, for the greatest enemies of the rulership of God often are the more subtle forces such as apathy, materialism, and respectability. Whatever and whoever the enemies of God's rulership may be, the message of apocalypticism says that God is still on the throne and he will triumph in the end. To use the biblical text to chart the course of historical events beforehand and to name the villains of history yet in the future is to turn the divinely inspired word into a human word. It is to center our attention on clever schemes and finite interpretations rather than on the one who is the beginning and the end and who is in control of all between.

The Perennial Proclamation of the Prophet

How then should we interpret the message of the biblical prophet in and through our teaching and preaching?

1. The prophet must be recognized as one who had a unique relationship with and understanding of God. The prophet was a partner with God.

2. The prophet must be understood and interpreted within the context and in the light of the times and situations within which he or she lived.

3. The prophet was first and foremost a preacher of repentance, one who saw all of life, whether spiritual, social, political or economic, in terms of the divine will and purpose.

4. The prophet was always a bold and courageous foe of evil no matter where it was found or who was guilty of it. The prophet sensed and portrayed God's wrath as no one else did or could.

5. The prophet was not a diviner of future events or one who scheduled the mighty acts of God on the human calendar. Whatever the prophet said about the future grew out of the alternatives with which God confronted humankind through the prophet in the midst of the human situation at that moment.

6. The prophet proclaimed both judgment and hope, the twin facets of God's redemptive love. The prophet knew that humankind cannot really understand or respond to God's redemptive love apart from a sense of God's wrath on sin.

7. The prophet proclaimed God's ultimate victory over sin and evil. This victory did not hinge on a human timetable of events. The prophet was convinced that the final victory of the rulership of God is an assured fact. In both the Old and the New Testaments this victory is described in terms of spiritual realities: "The kingdom

shall be the Lord's" (Obadiah 21). "The kingdom of the world has become the kingdom of our Lord and of his [Anointed One], and he shall reign for ever and ever" (Rev. 11:15).

The declaration of the divine Word of God is a terrible, awesome responsibility. Unfortunately, it is all too easy to see it through human eyes and within the framework of preconceived human notions and schemes of theology. Only as the interpreter uses tried and true, legitimate methods of study and interpretation will she or he proclaim the divine word and not merely a human word.

Endnotes

1. For a good discussion of this question, see Abraham J. Heschel's "What Manner of Man is the Prophet?" which is the first chapter of his thought-provoking work, *The Prophets*. Harper Torchbooks. (New York: Harper and Row, 1969).

2. Note, for example, that Isa. 1:18 is not a plea for repentance so much as it is an ironic or sarcastic indictment of Israel's attitude that religion consists only of cultic acts. The context of a passage (here Isa. 1:10-20) must always determine the meaning of it. For further discussion with examples of this important aspect of biblical interpretation and understanding, see my essay in the Robert H. Reardon *festschrift, Educating for Service*, edited by James E. Massey (Anderson, IN: Warner Press, 1984), 87-104.

3. This is the Old Testament term for our "false prophet" (Jer. 6:13; 8:10). See Jer. 23 for the classic description and indictment of the false prophet.

4. The reader is directed to John P. Milton's *Prophecy Interpreted*. (Minneapolis: Augsburg Publishing House, 1963), 3-52, for a detailed exploration of the pertinent principles of interpretation. Milton's entire work is heartily recommended to anyone in search of a responsible antidote to the widespread misinterpretation of the meanings of prophecy for our time. Of equal effectiveness in showing how the writings of the prophets should be interpreted is Dewey Beegle's *Prophecy and Prediction*. (Ann Arbor, MI: Pryor Pettengill, Publisher, 1978). Beegle minces no words in his critical appraisal of specific schools of so-called "prophetic preaching."

5. The reader should read this passage (as well as Jer. 1 and other examples of Hebrew word-play) in various modern versions such as Moffatt, Knox, the Jerusalem Bible, and the New English Bible in order to get the meanings carried by the original Hebrew. Unfortunately, neither the KJV or the RSV make any effort to reflect the Hebrew puns or word-plays.

6. Obadiah and Nahum were so concerned about the sins of Israel's enemies, Edom and Assyria, that they spoke no word of condemnation of the sin of their own people. But, in such short books, it would not be reasonable to expect the full spectrum of the prophetic message.

7. See Beegle, *Prediction and Prophecy*, pages 32-70, for a fuller discussion of this point. Note also Milton, *Prophecy Interpreted*, page 11 ff.

8. Some pertinent New Testament passages are Acts 3:25; Gal. 3:9-14; Eph. 1:1, etc.

9 Especially helpful for understanding apocalypticism and their relevance for any generation are the following paperback books: Paul Hanson, *Old Testament Apocalyptic* (Nashville: Abingdon Press, 1987); D. S. Russell, *Apocalyptic: Ancient and Modern (Philadelphia: Fortress Press, 1986);* George Murray, *Millenial Studies: A Search for Truth* (Grand Rapids, MI: Baker Book House, 1948).

FREDRICK W. BURNETT

B.A., Anderson University; M. Div., Anderson University School of Theology; D. Min., Vanderbilt Divinity School; M.A., Ph.D., Vanderbilt University.

Professor of Religion, Anderson University (Anderson, Indiana). Former student of Dr. Boyce W. Blackwelder.

Chapter 5

Characterization and Reader Construction of Characters in the Gospels

by Fred W. Burnett

Recent work on narrative criticism of the Gospels has emphasized plot and story, but very little has been done with characterization. This is due mostly to the disarray of the theoretical discussion about characterization in current literary criticism. The need for studies of characterization in the Gospels, however, is an urgent one, since it is being recognized that other areas of inquiry like Christology may depend partially upon the results (Keck 1986, 362-377).

In this chapter we will survey the issues that must be resolved in studying characterization in the Gospels. Three areas of debate are most pressing for Gospel critics: the debate in current literary-critical circles about characterization in fiction, the debate about the most appropriate genre with which to compare the Gospels, and the debate about characterization in both classical and Graeco-Roman literature. We will argue that any theory of characterization for the Gospels must consider both the textual indicators and the reading process. When the latter is taken into account, it becomes clear that characterization must be considered as a continuum on which even secondary characters may momentarily achieve "individuality." Although this chapter is primarily a survey of the theoretical issues and of their bearing on characterization in the Gospels, its thesis will be applied summarily to the character of Peter in the Gospel of Matthew.

The Literary-Critical Discussion

The current debate about characterization centers around the question of whether characters in *any* text are persons or words. Are characters individuals or personalities, in any sense of these words, which can transcend the text in which they exist, or are characters only functions of the text and its plot (Rimmon-Kenan 1983, 31-32). Robert Scholes, for example, cautions: "the greatest mistake we can make in dealing with characters in fiction is to insist on their 'reality.' *No character in a book is a real person* [italics added]. Not even if he is in a history book and is called Ulysses S. Grant" (Scholes 1968, 17). Scholes's position represents basically what Marvin Murdick calls the "purist" argument. Murdick contrasts this position with the "realist" position which maintains that characters do acquire an independence from the plots in which they occur and that they can be discussed apart from their literary contexts. Murdick himself chooses the purist position but with a caveat:

> Today [in contrast to the nineteenth-century] we know that fictional or dramatic characters are only more or less efficient patterns of words subordinate to larger patterns; but it remains a fact that legends can gather round Hamlet as they gather round historical figures (Murdick 1960-61, 213).

Murdick contends that both approaches have their problems. The purist critics have trouble reducing characters to plot functionaries in Chaucer, Shakespeare, and other great character writers, but the realists have trouble talking about characters as real persons with most dramatists and writers of allegory (211). Norman Holland states what the impasse is for critics:

> The old critics say we must think of dramatic characters as real people; the new critics say we must not. Logically, we cannot have it both ways, and logic comes down squarely against treating the characters as real (Holland 1975, 266).

The question for Holland is whether logic or experience is to govern the critic. He points out, for example, that psychoanalytic critics do in fact treat characters as real people. Thus, it *can* be done, but *should* it be done? (267-271).

Several critics, however, have decided that they can treat characters as both people and words. Seymour Chatman, for example, questions the Aristotelian primacy of plot over character for every narrative. He argues for an "open structuralist theory" of character as the only viable theory, i.e., a theory that should "treat characters as autonomous beings, not as mere plot functions" (Chatman 1978, 119; cf. 117-119, 132). Chatman then, steers a middle course between those who argue that all of the critic's attention should be focused upon the medium (the words or only the plot) or only upon the characters. He contends that both critical acts can be justified; they simply have different focuses. "Both character and event," he says, "are logically necessary to narrative; where chief interest falls is a matter of the changing tastes of authors and their publics" (113; cf. 136-137).

If character and action are interdependent, then subordination of one to the other depends upon (1) the type of narrative and (2) the focus of the reader-critic. Because of the latter, the hierarchy of plot/character is fluid and reversible. Rimmon-Kenan's conclusion is applicable here:

> The reversibility of hierarchies is characteristic not only of ordinary reading but also of literary criticism and theory. Hence it is legitimate to subordinate character to action when we study action but equally legitimate to subordinate action to character when the latter is the focus of our study (Rimmon-Kenan 36).

This is to say that "character" is a construct developed during the reading process. "Character," then, is an *effect* of reading. (Todorov 1980, 77). The reading process seems to be a process of naming connotations evoked in various ways by the text. As Barthes contends: "The same (or the signified connotation, strictly speaking) is a connotator of persons, places, objects, of which the signified is a *character*. Character is an adjective, an attribute, a predicate (for example: *unnatural, shadowy, star, composite, excessive, impious,* etc.)."[1] A character, then, is constructed by the reader from indicators that are distributed along the textual continuum. Traits are inferred by the reader from the indicators. The indicators themselves—discourse information (narrator's statements, statements of other characters, setting, and so forth) and the speech and action of the character—are what I mean by "characterization" (cf. Rimmon-Kenan 1983, 59 and Berlin 1983, 33-42).

To say that "character" is a construct developed during the reading process means, on the one hand, that character can be reduced to textuality. It can be dissolved into the segments of a closed text or the motifs from which it was constructed or both. The process of construction, in other words, can be reversed (Weinsheimer 1979, 195). On the other hand, character as an *effect* of the reading process can "transcend" the text. "Character" as a paradigm of attributive propositions can give the illusion of individuality or even personality to the reader. Whether or not transcendence of the text occurs will depend upon the indicators provided by the text and the reading conventions that are assumed for the narrative in question.

It is difficult to know what reading conventions are presupposed by the Gospels. The "death of character" in modern fiction, which is usually dated from D. H. Lawrence,[2] cannot be assumed as a reading convention for any literature before the nineteenth-century. The death of character is usually attributed to the dissolution of the view of the stable Self, but this, of course, cannot be taken as a reading convention of the Gospels (e.g., Macauley and Lanning 1964, 94-98). As Rimmon-Kenan poignantly asks: "Even if we grant the 'death' of character in contemporary literature, can we also retrospectively 'kill' him in nineteenth-century fiction?"[3] Theories of characterization drawn from modern narrative poetics can be applied to biblical texts only when the horizon of expectations for what constitutes a character in a particular text has been clarified (cf. Culpepper 1983, 105).

Characterization in Classical Literature

With regard to most literature even remotely related to the time of the Gospels, it is argued generally that characters were types rather than individuals in any sense, and that they seldom diverged from traits initially given in the narrative. The main difference between ancient and modern biographical literature, i.e., literature roughly before the rise of the novel in the eighteenth century, is that in the former, characterization and reading conventions understood the character to be typical, static, and immutable while in the latter character is individual, open to change, and developing (Gill 1983, 471; Macauley and Lanning 1964, 61 and Murdick 1960-61, 211). There is little doubt that particularly in classical writers, characters were presented as types, i.e., either as an ideal representation or as an example of the characteristics of a species or group (Korfmacher 1934, 85). The implications for reading a text with this understanding of characterization are stated clearly by Scholes and Kellogg:

> In every case, whenever we consider a character as a type, we are moving away from considering him as an individual character and moving toward considering him as part of some larger framework. This framework may be moral, theological, referable to some extra-literary scheme; or it may be referable to part of the narrative situation itself (Scholes and Kellogg 1968, 204).

Although this view of characterization has been extremely influential in biblical studies, several issues need to be raised.

First, in studying characters in biblical literature scholars have almost been forced to use understandings of characterization from the classical world. It has been pointed out many times that there is no comparable presentation in any Jewish literature to that of Jesus in the Gospels. The Talmud and Midrash have some biographical fragments, but these are within the framework of haggadic stories about rabbis from the Tannaitic and Amoraic Age. The stories show little interest in a connected, biographical narrative in which the sayings of the rabbis are to be understood (Vermes 1984, 20; Neusner 1984, 47). Qumran produced nothing biographical about the Teacher of Righteousness or about any members of the community. In apocryphal and pseudepigraphal literature there is little biographical writing, and what does exist only has the aim of contemporization of the material (cf. Ps.-Philo, *Jubilees*, and *Genesis Apocryphon*). Biography or autobiography in Jewish literature is attested only in Greek. In Philo (*Life of Moses*) the interest is in allegorical teaching about virtues, and in Josephus' *Vita* there is little to compare with the interests of the Evangelists. Even in the Hebrew Bible only the stories of David are related at any length, and it is questionable whether or not these stories are biographical in any sense.[4] Almost by default, then, biblical scholars have been forced to turn to the classical world for their understanding of characterization.[5] This is not to deny that the study of characterization in classical literature can be justified historically and philosophically (Stanton 1974, 118-119; Vermes 1984, 148 n. 28).[6] There are, however, problems with the use of this material, and this brings us to the second point about using typical characterization from this literature for understanding characterization in the Gospels.

Classical scholarship has usually made its understanding of types genre-specific. Kormacher, for example, concludes his study of classical type-characterization with this remark:

> The considerations here advanced will perhaps suffice to indicate that in comedy, tragedy, and epic at least the fixed type characters of rhetorical theory were subjected to modifications in accord with the *genre* in which they chanced to appear (Korfmacher 1934, 85).

The problem, of course, is that the Gospels, while they are closer to literary forms from the hellenistic world than to anything from Judaism, do not fit precisely any extant genre. *If* the aims of characterization were different for each genre, than using characterization from one genre (e.g., the encomium) or from several genre could be misleading when applied to the Gospels.[7] The debate continues, of course, not only about the genre of each Gospel but also about what constitutes a genre at all and about whether or not knowledge of a genre is important in any sense for interpretation.[8] Perhaps the study of characterization in the Gospels should be less genre-specific (cf. Stanton 1974, 118-119). In any case, one should proceed with caution before concluding that characterization in any Gospel is like characterization in the "classical or hellenistic world."

Biblical studies has inherited its emphasis upon the typical and the representative from the form critics, who, in turn, inherited their emphasis upon the typical from classicists. The typical and the conventional were enhanced in the study of biblical characterization by the repression of the individual and the personal. The latter emphases were seen as later and legendary.[9] For reading the Gospels this has meant that the Evangelists had little interest in Jesus' or any other Gospel personage's past. Guenther Bornkamm, for example, is correct when he says that the Evangelists in relating past history were proclaiming "who he is, not who he was . . . what belongs to the past in the history of Jesus should always be investigated and understood in relation to its significance for the present time today and the coming time of God's future" (1960, 17). It does seem to be the case that "the early Church did not allow the life of Jesus to become a thing of the past" (Marxsen 1968, 127-128), but does it follow that the Evangelists had little interest in the human character, or even in the "personality" of Jesus? The conclusion that they did not have such an interest has been tied to assertions that the Gospels are not biographies in any sense and are to be classified with *Kleinliteratur* ("folk-literature").[10] Both conclusions have recently come under attack (Stanton 1974; Shuler 1982; Talbert 1977), but the emphasis upon reading personages in the Gospels as types persists, probably because of the influence of both form criticism and arguments based upon classical literature.

However, and as a third point, some classicists have argued that it is an oversimplification and a distortion to argue that the main difference between ancient and modern characterization is that the former portrays the character as static and unidimensional. Christopher Gill, for example, points out that although this is one difference between ancient and modern characterization techniques, this conclusion "exaggerates the degree of difference in this respect." Gill contends that a more accurate way of stating the difference is "that between a character-centered and a personality-centered form of biography" (Gill 1983, 471). His concern is to show that ancient historiography and biography, though it does not highlight personality, does allow for and portray character development.

In this respect historiographers and biographers within both Greek and Roman philosophical schools recognized that a number of factors working in combination influenced the development or change of adult character or both. Gill, then, rejects the dichotomy between "nature" (*physis*) and "character" (*ēthos*). He contends that ancient historiographers no less than philosophers saw one's nature (*physis*) as one factor among many—upbringing, habitual training, education—in character-formation. What this means, of course, is that one's innate qualities (*physis*) do not necessarily determine the ethical character (*ēthos*) that one eventually develops (470-471).

Several other factors enter the discussion at this point. First, there is little extant evidence of any genre that could be called "biographical" apart from Plutarch's *Lives*. Much of the discussion about characterization, therefore, has concentrated upon Plutarch. Gill's discussion concludes that Plutarch does allow for and presents development of character,[11] and it does seem to be an overstatement to say that change and development of character were unknown in ancient historiography and biography (cf. Stanton 1974, 121). Does this mean, though, that development of character, without the presentation of a character's inward life or "personality," is primarily a plot formulation rather than a character formulation (cf. Scholes and Kellogg 1968, 168-169)? It does seem clear that the modern understanding that a character is to be understood *primarily* through his or her psychological development is not part of ancient characterization (Dihle 1956, 81; cf. Dihle 1983, 383, 411). But, does it also follow that ancient historiographers had no interest in the character as an *individual* since little inward life is presented?

Second, for ancient characterization in general one's character (*ēthos*) certainly seems to be revealed through one's action (*praxis*).[12] This indirect method of characterization seems to be the main method of the ancient world, and the Gospels are certainly no exception (Stanton 1974, 167; cf. Sternberg, 1985). The key question is: if the reader is to infer traits about a character from that personage's words and actions, do the reading conventions of the particular text under scrutiny allow the reader any room to construct the character's individuality? Several considerations lead one to answer this question affirmatively.

First, it does seem that an interest in the individual was apparent in the ancient world. It is true that the evidence for this kind of interest in the individual is primarily nonliterary, but is there any relation between the two, i.e., does the developing interest in nonliterary portraiture reflect a larger cultural code for the understanding of character in other media? G. Misener, for example, argues that individual portraiture of historical persons was attempted by Ion of Chios in the fifth-century BCE. At the same time, fifth-century drama masks began to move from the typical to an interest in facial expressions. Under Euripides' influence the masks became more realistic about the way the character *as an individual* was perceived by the audience. Misener believes that the portraitures and the drama masks of the fifth-century reflect a change from the typical to individuality. She also relates her discussion to the plastic arts and concludes: "A similar change from the typical and ideal to the individual begins to appear in plastic art toward the end of this period" (Misener 1924, 105). Misener extends her discussion to the Peripatetics, who practiced portraiture of legendary heroes, and to Plutarch, whom she considers the best extant representative of Peripatetic biography. She concludes that for Plutarch physical appearance and acts disclose one's inner character (108n.4, cf. Evans 1948, 189-217). If the move from the typical toward the individual in nonliterary portraiture did assume a larger cultural code of this sort, and semiotic study would support such a suggestion (see, e.g.,

Silverman 1983), this would have far-reaching ramifications for the study of ancient characterization—especially since many of the accepted conclusions have been based upon Plutarch's *Lives*.

What Misener has argued for the Greeks, Hanfmann has argued for the Romans. Roman portraiture was mostly typical, i.e., represented the virtues of a group, through the third and second centuries BCE. Individuation proceeded slowly until "interest in individual personality clearly becomes a paramount concern in the time of the late Republic (l00-30 BC)." It is important to note that Hanfmann attributes some of this development to the influence of hellenistic portraiture (1952, 454-455). Thus the developments in Roman and in Greek cultures are not isolated and idiosyncratic ones.[13]

A. S. Osley has traced what is known of Greek biography before Plutarch. Although he does not argue for a development from the typical to the individual, Osley does note that the Alexandrian librarians had enough data to compose biographical notes on authors for cataloguing books, that in Greek oratory very personal attacks were made on the private lives of opponents, and that funeral encomia seemed to be personal and individualistic. He also contends that at least two of Aristotle's pupils, Aristoxenus and Phanias, made personality a prominent part of their biographies. He is concerned with *how* biographies were written, but he concludes:

> With the break-up of Greek political life a unified conception of history was lost; interest was stirred no longer by the underlying meaning of contemporary events, but by the biographies of personalities (Osley 1946, 16-17).

Second, Greek tragedy has played an important role in the discussion of ancient characterization, especially as it relates to the Gospels (cf. Bilezikan 1977). The argument is usually made that tragic characters were for the most part typical and undeveloping. No less of an authority than H. D. F. Kitto can say that "Greek tragedy never interested itself . . . in the development of character" (1950, 24). That much does seem clear. What does not seem clear is: does Greek tragedy exclude all interest in the character as an individual?

Kitto himself apparently does not believe this to be the case. He points out that the structure of the Greek theater itself was a limiting factor on characterization:

> The Greek theatre, normally confined by its Chorus to one time and place, could not trace change or growth in character; what it could do was to reveal more and more of the depths of a character *already existing* [italics added] (169).

This tells one how tragedy presented character, but it does not tell how the audience "read" the character presented in one particular tragedy. Was the character in a particular tragedy to be read in light of prior tragedies about the same character so that the audience could perceive development or regression in the character? Or, if a character was being presented for the first time, would audience expectations include an intertextuality for subsequent tragedies about the same character? I am not really debating with Kitto because he neither raises nor answers these questions. He does, however, imply answers.

Kitto points out that the confines of time and space on characterization were accidental, not fundamental, in Greek tragedy. That is, to move the Chorus around the stage was physically very difficult (169 n.1). Kitto also acknowledges that in some tragedies the situation and plot were subservient to character, for example, in Sophocles' *Electra* (71-72, 337). Most importantly, Kitto confirms the point Misener makes about the individuation of tragic masks in Euripidean tragedies. In Euripides' later plays, especially in the stories about Electra and Orestes, Kitto sees characters "who are regarded purely as individuals, not in any degree as types, or tragic and exemplary embodiments of some universal passion" (258).

From modern views of characterization, which are interested in psychological description and change, indirect characterization in tragedy or in ancient biography and historiography appears to be simplistic. It appears to be minimal characterization, and thus one can easily argue from a modern point of view that characters were only types and symbols. How audiences and readers inferred characters from the words, deeds, and relationships, and by what larger codes, however, still seems to be an open question. The discussions of the interest in the individual in portraiture and in tragedy, and the limited number of extant sources for both tragedies and biographical writing, should make one think about the possibility that ancient audiences and readers constructed much fuller characters than is usually thought.

It is, for example, very difficult to transfer characters from one tragedy to another. Creon appears in Sophocles' *Antigone, Oedipus Tyrannus,* and *Oedipus at Colonus*. It seems impossible to imagine the docile and passive Creon of the *Antigone* as the same Creon who is active and tyrannical in *Oedipus Tyrannus* or the brazen liar in *Oedipus at Colonus*. There appears *to us* to be no consistent conception of Creon's character. However, does this mean that Creon must be confined to each particular play and that a "common critical error is the tendency to take these plays as some kind of trilogy?" (Beye 1975, 269; cf. 270-271). The lack of other sources about Creon and the modern distaste for minimal, indirect characterization may cause one to read these characters solely as types, when for ancient audiences oral traditions, discussions at home and at work about Creon, and so forth, may have contributed to Creon's change of character between plays.

Concerning the lack of sources (and the knowledge of the larger codes), the argument is usually put forth that both legendary and historical characters in tragedy had been "fixed" long before tragic poetry began. The poets had to deal with the fact that heroic personages were fixed and perhaps stereotyped in the audience's mind. At the same time, the evidence indicates that "if the persons of the heroic world are fixed, they are fluid as well, and their stories, in variants, can vary them" (Lattimore 1965, 58-59; cf. Brereton 1968, 26). Thus, there can be several Creons or Helens who may appear conflicting to us but to an ancient audience may be read as a change in the character of the individual.[14]

The indirect, minimal method of characterization is the problem. Beye recognizes the problem and leans toward interpreting the characters solely as types. He has to acknowledge, however, that one could also argue that "neither playwright nor audience needed extensive characterization, that the actions were natural and complex individual extensions of fully realized characters that peopled the minds of every member of the culture."[15] Thus, from what appears to us as a minimum of characterization may have been read in maximal terms by contemporary auditors and readers. Stanton capitalizes on this uncertainty for his discussion of Jesus in the Gospels:

> If the gospel traditions did intend to sketch out the character of Jesus of Nazareth, to show what sort of person he was, how would this have been accomplished? . . . the techniques of modern biographical writing were not those of the ancient world, where simple accounts of the actions, words and relationships of the subject were considered to provide at least as satisfactory a portrait as any character analysis or comment by the author. Hence there is no need to conclude that an investigation of the gospel traditions which finds somewhat similar "unsophisticated" methods in them, and which emphasizes the degree to which they reflect the character of Jesus, is based on presuppositions drawn from the modern world with its intense interest in personality and biography. The gospel traditions employ techniques of character portrayal which seem almost naive to the modern reader and which can be and have been overlooked by scholarly eyes. A very simple and brief account of a person's relationships with others can reveal a good deal about the person concerned; the synoptic traditions need not be elimi-

nated on account of their brevity. As long as such accounts referring to the same person cohere with one another, a few words can reveal a good deal about the character of the person concerned.[16]

To return to the question with which this discussion began, it does seem plausible that reading conventions which demanded that the reader infer character indirectly from words, deeds, and relationships could allow even for the typical character to fluctuate between type and individuality. If so, it would seem wise to understand characterization, for any biblical text at least, on a continuum. This would imply for narratives like the Gospels that the focus is upon the degree of characterization rather than on the type of characterization. Adele Berlin's suggestion is very helpful in this respect:

> One might think of them [degrees of characters] as points on a continuum: 1) the agent, about whom nothing is known except what is necessary for the plot; the agent is a function of the plot or part of the setting; 2) the type, who has a limited and stereotyped range of traits, and who represents the class of people with these traits; 3) the character, who has a broader range of traits (not all belonging to the same class of people), and about whom we know more than is necessary for the plot.[17]

Before these suggestions are applied to the example of Peter in Matthew, there are two other brief points that should be considered.

"Character" was defined above as a paradigm of attributive propositions constructed during the reading process from indicators along the textual continuum. It was also mentioned that character as effect may "transcend" the text at times, i.e., give the illusion of individuality. The reading process itself, as an imaginative process of filling gaps in the narrative, encourages the reader to develop individual images of textual indicators.[18] The indirect method of characterization encourages the illusion of individuality by demanding that the reader infer traits from words, deeds, relationships, and attributive propositions given in the text.

Chatman's discussion is helpful here. He defines a "trait" in terms of narrative criticism as "a narrative adjective out of the vernacular labeling a personal quality of a character, as it persists over part or whole of the story (its 'domain')" (1978, 125). Inference of such traits is crucial for classical narrative, Chatman says, because traits "contribute to that sense of the verisimilar consistency of characters" that is the cornerstone of classical narrative (122). But, *how* are traits named by the reader? The reader, of course, infers them from the contemporary trait code of the real world. The traits may not exist as actual verbal adjectives, but "clearly we must infer these traits to understand the narrative, and comprehending readers do so. Thus the traits exist at the story level: indeed, the whole discourse is expressly designed to prompt their emergence in the reader's consciousness" (125).

This suggests that a trait is only a convenient grouping by the reader of a plurality of unrelated textual indicators. A trait, then, is not "veridical" or "really there" but is a reader's construct. Gordon Allport, speaking of real persons rather than texts, has estimated that in English approximately eighteen thousand words designate traits, excluding hyphenated words and longer descriptive phrases. The mathematical possibilities for inferring traits from one's actions, words, or relationships seem almost endless. If one infers from traits that a personage is a certain "type," then the type, for Allport, exists only nominally, i.e., in the eye of the beholder. Allport, then, rejects the notion that clear-cut types exist (1967, 334-335). This is so not only because the type may be an idiosyncratic reconstruction which does not reside in the actual person alluded to, but also because "no trait theory can be sound unless it allows for, and accounts for, the variability of a person's conduct" (333). Traits (and types) usually designate what one perceives as the constant portion that allows the designated person to transcend the trait. In other words, whether observing real persons or reconstructing character from a narrative, indicators (acts or words) at different points in the continuum (a person's life or in a text) may cause the inferred pattern of traits to be restructured, thus giving the notion of variation or "individuality" (334).

Chatman builds upon Allport's discussion of inferring traits. Although he is content to leave the understanding of mechanisms to other theorists about how a reader's inference of traits issues in the notion of personality for fictional characters, Chatman is convinced that it happens (125-126). The refusal to acknowledge this process of trait construction with the consequent refusal to apply the notion of "personality" to characters is for Chatman "to deny an absolutely fundamental aesthetic experience."[19]

A character, then, is a paradigm of constructed traits that the reader attaches to a name (cf. Chatman 1978, 137). The proper name, especially in classical texts like the Gospels, becomes the crucial factor in the construction of character, but it also allows the character to transcend the text and creates the illusion of individuality or "personality" (cf. Kermode 1979, 77-78). Barthes is most succinct on this point:

> When identical semes traverse the same proper name several times and appear to settle upon it, a character is created. Thus, the character is a product of combinations: the combi-

nation is relatively stable (denoted by the recurrence of the semes) and more or less complex (involving more or less congruent, more or less contradictory figures); this complexity determines the character's "personality," which is just as much a combination as the odor of a dish or the bouquet of a wine. The proper name acts as a magnetic field for the semes; referring in fact to a body, it draws the semic configuration into an evolving (biographical) tense (Barthes 1974, 67-68).

Or, again: "What gives the illusion that the sum [of semes] is supplanted by a precious remainder (something like *individuality* . . .) is the Proper Name, the difference completed by what is *proper* to it. *The proper name enables the person to exist outside the semes* [italics added], whose sum nonetheless constitutes it entirely."[20]

One more factor which has not allowed biblical critics to argue that a typical character can at times fluctuate between the typical and the individual has been Forster's distinction between the flat and the round character. Even in Forster, however, there are hints that flat and round characters should be understood on a continuum rather than as mutually exclusive catetories (Rimmon-Kenan 1983, 40-42). The importance of this for a discussion of types is that Forster understands flat characters virtually as types in ancient literature (Forster 1927, 103-104). That Forster himself saw that "flat" and "round" were not mutually exclusive categories is shown in his discussion of Jane Austen's Lady Bertram.[21] Here a flat character fluctuates momentarily and becomes a round character because the narrator endows Lady Bertram with opinions. Forster comments that "these are strong words, and they used to worry me because I thought Jane Austen's moral sense was getting out of hand." He then asks of Austen: "has she [Austen] any right to agitate calm, consistent Lady Bertram?" (Forster 1927, 113; cf. 112).

G. C. Jones correctly notes that with this comment Forster acknowledges an important process of characterization, viz., that a flat character can be transformed momentarily into a round one. Forster, though, does not pursue this and chooses instead to explain the change in terms of the logic of the scene (Jones 1983, 121-122). The narrator's comments on Lady Bertram were not essential to the plot, and momentarily she was transformed into a round character with an inner life of possibly more than one trait.[22] The tendency of critics who have used Forster's distinctions on characters in biblical literature has been to say that because a character is flat and typical, any notion of roundness or individuality is excluded.[23] If these categories are seen as degrees of characterization, however, then characters who are typical can become round momentarily during the reading process. In other words, both the strategies of characterization in the text and the process of "readerly" construction of character need to be emphasized in biblical characterization.[24]

Summary

The current debate about characterization in fiction recognizes the textuality of "characters," but it also allows the reader-critic to focus upon character as textual segments or character as an effect, a reading construct, which can, depending upon the textual indicators, allow the reader-critic to speak of characters as "persons." It seems best to speak of degrees of characterization in biblical texts and to plot textual indicators on a continuum for any particular text from words at one pole to "persons" at the other pole. In the case of literature like the Gospels the continuum of actant (agent) to type to character is a useful scheme.

Reading conventions for character construction in ancient literature (and drama) preferred indirect characterization, and personages were for the most part typical and flat. There is, however, some indication that personages at times could be read as developing and approaching individuality. When the possibility of such reading conventions in ancient literature is coupled with the contemporary notion of reading as a process of nomination, particularly in "readerly" texts like the Gospels, it is certainly plausible that textual indicators in certain texts could allow for reader construction of a character as a "person." Even if a personage is a type (flat) in some texts, the indicators could allow for momentary transformation into a rounder character. I am convinced that this happens, for example, in the case of Peter in the Gospel of Matthew.

Peter in Matthew

Although this theoretical discussion can only be applied summarily to a reading of Peter in Matthew,[25] I agree with those who argue that in Matthew, Peter is predominately a type representing the characteristics of the disciples as a group.[26] This is evident primarily in his role as spokesperson for the group. There are, however, several textual indicators (techniques of characterization) that allow the reader to transform Peter momentarily into an individual who transcends his typical function as a member of the disciples.[27]

A primary technique of characterization that encourages the reader to construct the personage "Peter" as an individual is that Peter has at least two names: Simon (Barjona) and "Peter" (*ho Petros*). The names, of course, enable the reader to identify the semes as the same character, but having more than one name could be ambiguous and cause the reader to have more gaps to fill. Thus a character like Peter becomes more complex for the reader. This is true particularly when the names (or titles) seem to be interchangable (4:18; 10:2; 16:16, 17; cf. Weinsheimer 1979, 195). Furthermore, whether it is a name or a title, there is no closure for the reader concerning Peter. The reader does not know if Peter becomes the "Rock," as *ho Petros* implies, or even what this function means. This indeterminacy creates a gap and requires reader imagination to fill it. In this one sense, at least, Peter is an open-ended character, i.e., one who is not limited to actions only within the narrative world but is open to possible future actions as the "Rock" of the disciples (cf. Chatman 1978, 133). It is precisely this kind of textual indicator which helps to create the illusion that names refer to something independent of texts, and it helps to support the illusion of the nontextuality of characters. The text has a beginning and an ending, and is thus closed, but the reader is encouraged to speculate beyond the ending of the text. Unless the reading conventions encourage the reader to keep the text bounded, characters can be extended beyond the text and approach the status of historical persons.[28]

Another way in which the reader is encouraged to construct a character out of Peter is that the reader is given more knowledge about Peter than is necessary for the plot. From Matthew 8:14, for example, the reader learns that Peter has a house, is married or is a widower, and probably has relatives who live with him or nearby. Peter has a brother who, not incidentally, is always identified as *Peter's* brother (4:18; 10:2). The reader also knows that Peter is a fisherman (4:18). This is not much knowledge, but it is a higher degree of characterization than the "agent" usually has (cf. Berlin 1983, 32). These touches of privacy are unnecessary to the plot and are indicators, however minute, of "personhood" (cf. Lattimore 1965, 63).

Another textual indicator is whether or not a personage is given emotions and opinions. Fearlessness is given by Jesus as an important trait for discipleship (10:26, 28, 31), but fear caused by life-threatening circumstances characterizes both Peter and the disciples (14:26). There is little question that the reader is to infer fear not only for the disciples who flee at Jesus' arrest (26:56) but also for Peter's denial where the reader's focus is solely upon him (26:69-75). Peter also expresses strong opinions. He disagrees not only with Jesus, but by implication, with God as well (16:22; 26:33, 35).

Peter's emotions and opinions, however, usually represent the group of disciples. There are textual indicators, though, that allow the reader momentarily to see Peter as separate from the group. The main ones are where he contrasts his fidelity to Jesus with the group's fidelity (26:33) and his denial scene. Peter also has a scene alone with Jesus and he is the only disciple for whom Jesus works a miracle (14:28-32 cf. 17:27). Even though he is a secondary character, Peter gets knowledge that only the reader has, thus converging the discourses of reader, and character (16:16, cf. 1:1, 17, 18; 2:4, 11:2).

This is particularly important at Peter's recognition scene because the character now apparently sees himself as the narrator and reader have seen him all along (26:75).

Although most of the textual indicators mentioned above continue to characterize Peter as a type who is representative of discipleship, Peter's denial/recognition scene is where he is momentarily "rounded" for the reader. Peter's denial is not essential to the plot; it has nothing to do with Jesus' trial and fate.[29] The recognition of himself or herself by a secondary character *and* a whole scene of dialogue with other secondary characters is something almost unheard of in ancient literature. Auerbach, for example, is intrigued with this scene. He says that "the nature and the scene of the conflict . . . fall entirely outside the domain of classical antiquity" and the scene "fits into no antique genre." The use of direct discourse among such secondary characters, he feels, helps prove his point (1953, 42, 45-46). This scene encourages the reader to take an interest in the character or "personality" of Peter himself.[30]

Chatman proposes three criteria for distinguishing between mere "walk-ons" (agents) and characters. First, he asks if the existent is "human," i.e., does it stand out in any sense as a person? With touches of familial relationships and emotions and opinions, Peter does seem to meet this criterion. Second, does the existent have a name? The importance of the names for understanding Peter is quite evident. A related question is: does the existent appear independently in a scene? Peter does. Finally, to what degree does the existent affect the plot, and to what degree does the plot affect the existent? Peter functions mostly as a foil for Jesus' teachings, but there does seem to be an interest in him that is independent of the plot.

Chatman softens his own scheme by saying that "the above fail as criterial marks of character, but they seem relevant as features." He concludes, however, that the features are relevant to the reading process and should be placed on a continuum:

> Characterhood, in this view, would be a question of degree: a human being who is named, present and important is *more likely* to be a character (be he ever so minor) than an object that is named, present, and important, or a human being who is named, present, but unimportant, or whatever (1978, 141; cf. 139-140).

In terms of Chatman's approach, a sequential, diachronic reading of Peter suggests that Peter is a secondary character who functions as a type, but who, at the points noted on the textual continuum, approaches characterhood and even "personality."[31] If this is the case, it may mean that "personal" aspects of characters in the

Gospel narratives—especially the personality of Jesus—played a more important role in early Christian proclamation than form and redaction critics have been willing to admit.

Endnotes

1. Roland Barthes 1974, 190. James Garvey reaches a similar conclusion and says that character is reconstructed from "attributive propositions" 1978, 63. For Chatman also character, a paradigm of traits, is constructed by the reader out of narrative adjectives (1978, 125).
2. See McCarthy 1961, 173; Robie Macauley and George Lanning 1964, 61; and Murdick, 1961-62, 212.
3. Rimmon-Kenan 31. Chatman's caution, though in another context, is also to the point: "It would be a fundamental misconception to assume that there is only a difference of degree and not of kind between the simplest narrative—the folk tale or fairy tale—and modern fiction" (Chatman 1972, 78).
4. Stanton 1974, 126-131; Vermes, 1984, 20; cf. Klaus Koch 1969, 202-205. This is not to deny that the Hebrew Bible has highly complex *narratives*, but only to say that the concern does not seem to be with the individual character. It is usually argued, e.g., that the Patriarchal stories seem to deal with eponymous heroes even if the historicity of the individual Patriarchs is affirmed (see McKane 1979, 12, 16; D. B. Redford 1970, 1966-67. Any *literary* individuality is usually suppressed by the interpreter on the assumption that real, historical readers would not have individuality in any sense as part of their constructive repertoire. Meir Sternberg has rightly questioned this assumption, and much work remains to be done in this regard with narratives in the Hebrew Bible and in Jewish-Hellenistic narratives (253-255 passim).
5. Cf. Stanton 1974, 135. There are several reasons why characterization in classical literature became important for Gospel critics, even though the temporal gap is a wide one and it would have seemed more plausible for them to have studied characterization in hellenistic narratives. First, postclassical writings like the Gospels and the Greek novel have not been considered "true" literature by literary critics (Haegg 1985, 3-4). Second, there was a revival in the Roman Imperial period of classicism and Atticism. Hellenistic writers tried to follow Aristotle and his rules for characterization (Haegg 114). Third, the Greek novel originated only in the hellenistic period (Haegg xi), and it is not unusual for these writers to follow Aristotle on plot or characterization. If Graham Anderson is right, the temporal gap, though wide between hellenistic writers and classical ones, may be inconsequential for studying plot and character in hellenistic novels, since they were retellings of ancient plots in new contexts and attempted to follow Aristotle (*Ancient Fiction,* 1984, 19, 27, 88, 217). In this respect George A. Kennedy shows both the necessity of using classical rhetoric to interpret the Gospels and its relevance in the New Testament period generally, even for *"Kleinliteratur"* like the New Testament (1984, 1-33). As he says, "Classical rhetoric was one of the constraints under which New Testament writers worked" (160). Finally, once form-critics had accepted the conclusions given above and had taken the Homeric model as the one for understanding the oral development behind biblical literature, the emphasis upon the conventional and the typical in biblical characterization rather than the individual and the personal became the dominant view. It was supported

by appeal to typical characterization in classical literature (see Otto Eissfeldt 1965, 3-4 *passim*; Werner G. Kuemmel 1972, 82-83, 306; Charles H. Talbert 1977, 1-23; and Philip L. Shuler 1982, 1-23).

6. It is also necessary to turn to the Greeks by default because they were the only ones who structured a system of rhetoric and poetics that is extant. As Kennedy says: "In understanding how their [Jewish or Greek] rhetoric worked we have little choice but to employ the concepts and terms of the Greeks (1984, 10).

7. If the aims of biography and history, e.g., were carefully separated (Stanton 1974, 123), then even though the personages portrayed may be types, the emphases that the reader should infer from the *same* type could be quite different (cf. A. S. Osley 1946, 20).

8. For a review of the debate see Robert Guelich 1983, 183-219. He concludes: "Thus one looks in vain to the Graeco-Roman as to the Jewish literary world for a comparable literary analogy to the Gospels" (194). Stuart Miller has stated the problem that confronts any literary critic: "Genres, as everyone knows, do not really exist. Croce has rightly told us that each work of art is individual. Yet genre terms are inescapable if one is to talk about literature" (1967, 3).

9. See note 25 above. Also see James Muilenburg 1969, 1-18; Koch 1969, 11-16; and Rolf Knierim 1973, 435-467.

10. Probably the most quoted statement in this regard is Rudolf Bultmann's: "There is no historical-biographical interest in the Gospels, and that is why they have nothing to say about Jesus' human personality, his appearance and character, his origin, education and development; quite apart from the fact that they do not command the cultivated techniques of composition necessary for grand literature, nor let the personalities of their author appear" (1968, 372; cf. Conzelmann 1973, 15-16).

11. 473-480. Contrast D. A. Russell who argues that althought Plutarch does admit the possibility of change in one's *ēthos*, he seems not to allow for change in one's *physis*. This means, of course, that Plutarch's conception of characterization is probably the progressive revelation of innate qualities. Russell, however, rightly leaves the question open. It is not clear that Plutarch did not envision a change in one's *physis*, or at least the degeneration of it, and Russell acknowledges that in Plutarch *ethos* and *physis* are often blurred together (1976, 138-154, esp. 147 and n. 2). This semantic blurring is precisely one of the points upon which Gill seizes.

12. Russell 1976, 144; Stanton, 1974, 122, 125; Vernon K. Robbins 1984, 114; and, Helmut Koester 1974, 253.

13. Hanfmann, though, interprets the Greek view of personality as still essentially a typical one. He thus has to deal with the problem of how the influence of the typical portraits could arise at all, not to mention have influence, "in an age which unmistakably indicates the rise of individualism" (456). Perhaps Misener's discussion of the rise of individualism in Hellenism supplies the key.

14. P. E. Easterling takes issue with the dictim of G. H. Gellie about characters in Greek tragedies, viz., "These people are different only because their stories are different" (1983, 141). Easterling argues that the impression of individuality for even minor characters who function as types in Sophocles' plays comes not only from the rhetoric of the situation and characterization by style but also from the image that Sophocles had about his characters, from preexisting mythological identities for even minor characters, and from audience-reader imagination at work particularly at ambiguous points, or what I have called "gaps," in the narrative (Easterling, 138-145).

15. Beye, 269. This view, of course, contrasts with the usual interpretation of Aristotle that subordinates character to plot in tragedy and that contends that names only indicate types (1960, 9). For critiques of Aristotle's view of tragedy and its value for interpreting tragedy, see Bilezikan 1977 and the literature cited there. D. D. Raphael concludes his study of tragedy with a typical critique of Aristotle: "I have delayed too long over Aristotle, longer than his theory of tragedy deserves. Little did he dream, poor man, that his scrappy remarks would be taken so seriously by later dramatists and critics. His fate at their hands is indeed unmerited, a fit object for our pity" (1960, 23; cf. 16-24).

16. Stanton 1974, 167-168. I have not discussed the Jewish traditions because they have usually been ignored in any comparison with the presentation of Jesus in the Gospels. Robert Alter, however, has raised the same question for Jewish literature. He asks: "In short, all the indicators of nuanced individuality to which the Western literary tradition has accustomed us . . . would appear to be absent from the Bible. In what way, then, is one to explain how, from these laconic texts, figures like Rebekah . . . emerge [as] characters who, *beyond any archetypal role they may play as bearers of a divine mandate* [italics added], have been etched as indelibly vivid individuals in the imagination of a hundred generations?" (1981, 114; cf. Sternberg 1985, chapters 9-10).

17. Sternberg 1983, 32. Sternberg has argued a similar case for characterization in biblical narrative (1985, 253-254; chapters 9-10).

18. Wolfgang Iser 1980, 282-283; cf. Helene Cixous, 1973-74: 384-385; and, Holland 1975, 273-274.

19. Chapman 138; cf. 117. This is essentially the same way that Barthes reads in *S/Z* (cf. 6-11). For a penetrating discussion of Barthes' reading see Silverman 1983, chapter 6.

20. Barthes, 191; cf. Weinsheimer 1979, 187-188; and, Jonathan Culler 1978, 235-237. For biblical narrative Sternberg is straight to the point. "If for a biblical agent to come on stage nameless is to be declared faceless, then to bear a name is to assume an identity: to become a singular existent, with an assured place in history and a future in the story. It is the naming and dramatization of biblical characters, then, that do duty for the redundant epithets that elsewhere specify character in the interests of realism" (1985, 331).

21. I am following here the excellent critique of Forster by Grahame C. Jones 1983, 115-129.

22. Jones prefers to discuss the transformation in terms of narrative point of view (125-127).

23. It seems that Harvey's notion of ficelles, which is virtually the same as Forster's flat characters, has been used in a similar fashion. Harvey, however, tends to view ficelles on a continuum between type and individual (W. J. Harvey, 1966, 58, 62-73, 147-148, 215-217; cf. Culpepper 1983, 102-103).

24. Thomas Docherty has argued this point for both "readerly" and "writerly" texts. He contends: "It is in the interaction of the writer's language with the positions it affords the reader that the element of the text which we call 'character' is produced" (1983, xiii-xiv).

25. For a fuller reading see my "Characterization in Matthew: Reader Construction of the Disciple Peter" (1987, 13-44).

26. For an excellent summary of this position see Jack Dean Kingsbury 1979, 67-83.

27. Some critics make Peter the dominant character in Matthew. (E.g., Christoph Kaehler 1976-77, 36-58.)
28. Weinsheimer 1979, 187-188. He argues that the reading convention that "so and so is a character in _____ book" did not emerge until the mid-eighteenth century with the rise of the novel. His point is that "character," and the conventions for constructing it, is genre-specific (190).

Alter has argued that biblical scholars have often superimposed methods of modern literary criticism on to biblical texts. These methods usually assume conventions and techniques that are alien to the ancient texts, as, e.g., the notion that characters are only textuality (1981, 15). He seems to follow Auerbach in arguing that a convention of biblical literature is indeterminacy that encourages the reader towards mimesis (27).

29. This seems to distinguish Peter's recognition scene from that of the major characters in tragedies. Recognition in tragedies was integral to the plot (cf. Brereton 1968, 35-37; and Bilezikan 1977, 101). Peter's recognition approximates Aristotle's third type of recognition, which is due to memory and issues in a display of feelings (*Poetics*, 16.8). There is, however, no reversal of the plot, and the discovery (the change from ignorance to knowledge) is only for Peter as a secondary character, not for the main character (Jesus) or the audience (cf. 10.10-11).

30. Although this scene may be the most important one for the characterization of Peter in Matthew, it has been dismissed by form critics as legendary accretions. It is thus removed to the periphery of early Christian proclamation, or in this case the Passion Narrative (e.g., Martin Dibelius n. d, 115, 215). The fruition of this approach is seen, e.g., in the excellent study by Raymond E. Brown, Karl P. Donfried, and John Reumann. They rightly ask: "If all the authority is meant for the body of disciples, why is Peter so often the one singled out by Matthew? A priori, was he not a somewhat unlikely choice since he denied the master publicly? Or did that very fact give Peter a special place not only as a type but as a person?" (1973, 105). They do not deal with the denial scene at all in their exegesis. Form and redaction criticisms have not only removed any interest in the personal to the periphery of proclamation, but they have also posed a false dichotomy of either a type or a person. The former is always integral to early Christian proclamation while the latter is always legendary and peripheral.

31. The reader does not just construct a character by reading sequentially. As I have argued, the reader constructs a *paradigm* of traits *at the story level* from indicators that are strewn along the textual continuum. A great deal of work remains to be done with paradigmatic study of character in biblical narratives. Papers presented to the Society of Biblical Literature Group "Literary Aspects of the Gospels and Acts" have begun the work. See Elizabeth Struthers Malbon, "Disciples/Crowds/Whoever: A Markan Narrative Pattern," (1982); Willem Vorster, "Characterization of Peter in the Gospel of Mark," (1985); and Norman Petersen, "Myth and Characterization in Mark and in John," (1985). In another context James Garvey has proposed a model to help determine whether or not characterization has occurred and to what degree ("Characterization in Narrative," 63-78). His model could work in concert with Chatman's view of characterization since Garvey also rejects the dichotomy of either person of textual function in the reading of character.

JOHN E. STANLEY

B.A., Anderson University; M.Div., Anderson University School of Theology; S.T.M., Lutheran Seminary (Gettysburg, Pa.); Ph.D., Iliff School of Theology/University of Denver.

Assistant Professor of Religion and Chair, Department of Religion, Warner Pacific College (Portland, Oregon). Former student of Dr. Boyce W. Blackwelder.

Chapter 6
Holy Spirit as Empowerer for Ministry in Luke—Acts
by John Stanley

Introduction

My studies under Boyce Blackwelder involved regular discussions of the relationship between Luke's theology and historical events in the life of Jesus and the church. So did my course in Luke at Lutheran Theological Seminary in Gettyburg in 1974. Blackwelder emphasized the historical accuracy of Luke's report[1] whereas my professor at Gettyburg minimized Luke as a historian and stressed Luke's theology.[2]

When I taught Luke-Acts at Warner Pacific College for the first time in 1984, I organized the class around an ongoing debate between a theological or historical approach to Luke-Acts. But the more the class read, debated, and did exegesis, the more we realized that we were engaging in a debate that could not be resolved. In a sense, class members were rehashing their dispositions to favor either a theologial or an historical approach, or a combination of the two. Realizing this caused me to change my methodology. Although many exegetes continue to debate the priority of a theological or historical approach, I now begin with a literary reading of biblical texts. My transition in exegetical approach is paralleled by many other biblical exegetes.[3]

The Ministry of the Holy Spirit in Luke 1-4 and Acts 1-2

My reading of Luke 1-4 and Acts 1-2 has uncovered five theological affirmations concerning the ministry of the Holy Spirit.

1. The promise of the Holy Spirit as power ties Luke-Acts together. At the conclusion of his gospel, Luke has Jesus command the disciples, "You are witnesses of these things. And behold, I am sending forth the promise of My Father upon you; but you are to stay in the city until you are clothed with power from on high"

(Luke 24:48-49, NAS). At the beginning of Acts, Luke reiterates that promise, "but you shall receive power when the Holy Spirit has come upon you; and you shall be My witnesses both in Jerusalem, and in all Judea and Samaria, and even to the remotest part of the earth" (Acts 1:8, NAS). Luke drives home the promise of power to witness by placing the promise in a conspicuous ending and beginning of his two-part narrative. Also, the preface to Acts included the promise of the Holy Spirit (Acts 1:4-5). As G. W. H. Lampe observed, "the connecting thread which runs through both parts of St. Luke's work is the theme of the operation of the Spirit of God" (Lampe 1967, 159).

2. The Holy Spirit prepares persons for the birth of Jesus in Luke's gospel and for the birth of the church in Acts. Two literary devices signal the significance of this theological thrust—pairing and repetition. Three couples are instrumental in the birth and recognition of Jesus. These pairs are Zechariah and Elizabeth, Mary and Joseph, and Simeon and Anna. The Holy Spirit filled Zechariah (Luke 1:67) and Elizabeth (Luke 1:41). The Spirit came upon Mary (Luke 1:35) and Simeon (Luke 2:25). At first glance the Spirit did not appear to move upon Anna. However, the title "prophetess" implies someone on whom the charismatic Spirit had worked as with other prophetic figures of Israel. Thus the Spirit explicitly filled, or moved upon, Zechariah, Elizabeth, and Mary to prepare them for the birth of Jesus. Likewise, the Spirit prepared the aged Simeon and Anna to recognize Jesus when he was brought to the temple.

Why does the text not mention the Spirit visiting Joseph? Being the excellent narrator he was, Luke knew that variety amid repetition makes a story flow better (Alter 1981, 91. Also see Sternburg 1985, 365-440). Luke included Joseph and Mary by virtue of the device of pairing, and Luke enhanced his theological goal of stressing the conception of Jesus by the Holy Spirit by omitting references to the Spirit's ministry in Joseph.

It is possible Simeon and Anna are a pair whose role contrasts with the two young couples. Tannehill correctly described their role of recognizing the Messiah:

> They are old. The promise that he would see the Lord's Messiah is evidently the only thing holding Simeon to life, and a considerable point is made of Anna's age. They are expectantly waiting and have waited long. They represent the long history of an expectant people, nourished by God's promise (Tannehill 1986, 39).

I suggest that Simeon and Anna represent expectant Israel while the two young couples symbolize the emerging new community being birthed by the Spirit. If so, then the elderly couple and the two couples are a pair with the theological significance of waiting and fulfillment.

In Acts, the Spirit prepares persons for the birth of the church. As in the Third Gospel, men and women await the decisive moment in an Upper Room (Acts 1:13-14). Like Simeon and Anna, they anticipate the fulfillment of Israel (Luke 2:25-26, 38; Acts 1:6). The liberation theologian Jose Comblin comprehends the preparatory ministry of the Holy Spirit as follows:

> [Luke] understood that the liberation brought by God was worked in two different stages, each marked by the coming of the Holy Spirit: first on Mary to bring about the incarnation and prepare for the birth of Jesus; then on the community of the disciples in Jerusalem to prepare for the birth of the church.[4]

3. The Holy Spirit descends upon Jesus in Luke's gospel and upon the church in Acts. Again Luke employs the literary technique of repeating significant parallel incidents in both parts of Luke-Acts. What happens to a person in the gospel often, but not always, happens to a people in Acts.

Before the Spirit descended upon Jesus after his baptism, the Spirit had been working in Jesus' life. The Spirit prepared Mary and ministered to the extended family of Jesus. At his dedication in the temple, the Spirit enabled Simeon and Anna to identify the infant Jesus as a

> "light of revelation to the Gentiles,
> And the glory of Thy people Israel" (Luke 2:32, NAS)

Luke's descriptions of Jesus' growth in wisdom, stature, favor, and grace recall the development of young Samuel (Luke 1:40, 52). Despite the steady growth of Jesus, Luke presents the baptism of Jesus as a climactic turning point. Immediately prior to the baptism, John the Baptist functions in the narrative as a prophetic precedent as he announces the imminent coming of an anticipated Christ (Luke 3:1-17). Then Herod imprisoned John (Luke 3:18-20).

Immediately after the baptism, Luke's narrative reminds readers that Jesus "being supposedly the Son of Joseph" (Luke 3:23) actually is the universal Son of God whose lineage can be traced back to Adam. Then Jesus goes into the desert for forty days of temptation (Luke 4:1-13). Between setting the stage through the ministry of John and the emphasis on Jesus as Son of God through the genealogy and temptation, Luke inserts the baptism of Jesus. Luke announces:

Now it came about when all the people were baptized that Jesus also was baptized, and while He was praying, heaven was opened, and the Holy Spirit descended upon Him in bodily form like a dove, and a voice came out of heaven, "Thou are My beloved Son, in Thee I am well-pleased" (Luke 3:21-22, NAS).

After his temptation, Jesus came to Nazareth and preached his inaugural sermon from Isaiah. His actions and words have the force of saying that what had been prophetic expectations now had become present fulfillment because the Spirit was upon him (Luke 4:18, 21). The Spirit transformed messianic promises into present experiences.

The parallel to the descent of the Spirit upon Jesus is the descent of the Spirit upon the church at Pentecost in Acts 2.[5] Luke interprets the Spirit's descent at Pentecost as the fulfillment not only of Joel 2:29-30, but also of Luke 2:49 and Acts 1:8. Acts 2:33 and 2:38 claim that the Spirit is available to the church.

Lampe has elucidated the connection between the Spirit's descent upon Jesus and the church:

> The descent of the dove at the baptism denotes a Messianic activity with the particular divine power necessary for his mission, that is, with the same energy of the Spirit which his followers were to receive at Pentecost for the missionary task to which that had been appointed (Lampe 1967, 168).

Likewise, Tannehill noted:

> This connection between the descent of the Spirit and the beginning of Jesus' mission parallels the course of events at the end of Luke and the beginning of Acts. The risen Jesus connects the beginning of the apostles' mission with the coming of the Spirit upon them (Luke 24:46-49; Acts 1:8) . . . Thus in both Luke and Acts the descent of the Spirit initiates the central sequences of events which dominate these writing (Tannehill 1986, 57).

4. The Spirit empowers Jesus in Luke's gospel and the church in Acts for witness and mission.[6] Luke utilizes the repetition of similar incidents to demonstrate this truth. Luke's narrative shows Jesus and Christians acting as empowered witnesses. Actions, rather then exposition, convey the experience of empowerment. Also, Luke uses the literary devices of back reference and anticipation to illustrate how the empowered church will continue what Jesus began.

Empowerment through the Spirit prepared Jesus for his ministry. At the conclusion of his synagogue sermon in Nazareth, Jesus mentioned two prophetic precedents for the universal ministry that would emerge through him and the church. He told how a Phoenician widow fed and ministered to Elijah. He reminded his Jewish listeners that Elisha healed the Syrian leper Naaman. Luke's readers who had witnessed the coming together of Jew and Gentile in the church read these references as prophetic anticipations of Jesus' eventual ministry to a Roman centurion (Luke 7:1-10) and to a Samaritan leper (Luke 17:11-19). Jesus was able to follow in the prophetic tradition of Elijah because he had been empowered by the Spirit at baptism. Luke 4:33-37 is a miracle story that witnesses to the "authority and power" of Jesus. The Spirit enabled Jesus to minister.

In Acts, the empowered church continues what Jesus began. The seeds of universal mission implicit in the encounters of Jesus with the Roman centurion and the Samaritan leper blossomed with the expansion of the church into Judea, Samaria, Antioch of Syria, and ultimately to Rome. The Pentecost of Acts 2 was paralleled by the Gentile Pentecost of Acts 10:24-48. As Jesus healed, so did the church in Acts (Acts 3:1-10).

Empowerment by the Spirit propelled Christians to witness. Peter testified that "we cannot stop speaking what we have seen and heard" (Acts 4:20). Stephen, full of the Holy Spirit (Acts 7:55), faced death as the first Christian martyr. The list of accomplishments by empowered Christians in Acts could go on. Empowerment was for witness, mission, and service. Thus, Ward Gasque was on target when he maintained:

> It is the Spirit that assures continuity with Jesus and is the source of the vitality of the Christian mission. Hence the theology of Acts is a mission-centered theology: the church exists not for herself but for the world, to bear bold testimony to what God has done and is doing in Jesus (Gasque 127).

Likewise, Talbert submits that Luke narrates the works and words of Jesus "with the intent that they be emulated—not in a mechanical way but with imagination and conviction, and not through one's own strength but through the power of the Holy Spirit (Talberts)."

Comblin, from his pastorate in Brazil, testifies of contemporary Latin American Christians who have experienced "an unexpected transformation" in the Spirit. His portrayal of the empowerment experienced by oppressed people sounds like a chapter in a twentieth century Acts of the Apostles when he writes:

> People feel themselves taken hold of by new strength that makes them do things they had never thought of doing. Individuals and communities that had been downhearted,

lacking in dynamism, resigned to the endless struggle for survival, discover themselves to be protagonists of a history far greater than themselves (Comblin 20).

Although my treatment of Luke's emphasis on empowerment may seem preachy, I remind readers that Boyce Blackwelder, in whose honor I am writing, taught that exegesis is for proclamation.

5. The Holy Spirit produced a new quality of life through Jesus in Luke's gospel and through the Spirit endowed church in Acts. Luke's values and theology become obvious as he repeatedly mentions ministry to a human need. As a narrator Luke could select what he included or excluded from his account of Jesus and the church. Parallels exist between the ministries of Jesus and the ministries of the church to the total needs of persons. What Luke has included we accept as essential to his world view. A literary reading discovers what Luke said and then compares what Luke said with other writers of the day.

To Luke the gospel was universal and available to all persons. The Christmas announcement proclaims a great joy to "all" people (Luke 2:10). When Simeon blessed Jesus he rejoiced,

> "For my eyes have seen Thy salvation,
> Which Thou hast prepared in the presence of all peoples, a light of revelation to the Gentiles, and the glory of Thy people Israel" (Luke 2:30-32, NAS).

Luke traced the genealogy of Jesus back to Adam rather that to Abraham. The three paired couples—Zechariah and Elizabeth, Mary and Joseph, Simeon and Anna—are male and female, young and old. Their inclusion probably is an intentional narrative design of Luke to stress the inclusiveness of the gospel. The missionary outline of Acts 1:8, the mission to the Gentiles, and the ending of Acts in Rome continues the universal mission in Acts.

Luke values poor people and advocates a ministry of mercy to the poor. Mary's Magnificat (Luke 1:46-55) anticipates God's action in behalf of the poor. In the Christmas story Mary and Joseph stay in a stable rather than an inn. They cannot afford to offer the sacrifice prescribed for poor persons in Leviticus 12:8, a pair of turtledoves or pigeons (Luke 2:24). In Acts the Christian community initially shared their property and possessions (Acts 2:44-47; 4:32-37). Later chapters in Acts refer to the deacons who care for widows, and the church in Antioch offering famine relief to the church in Judea (Acts 6:1-7; 11:27-30) (Dayton 264-266).

Women play prominent roles in Luke-Acts. Elizabeth, Mary, and Anna exert key roles in the birth and recognition of Jesus as God's Messiah. Women financially support the travels and preaching of Jesus (Luke 8:1-3). Looking at Luke 24, which functions as a connective seam with Acts, twice Luke mentions the women at the tomb (Luke 24:10, 24). In Acts 1:12-14, Luke makes explicit reference to women being in the Upper Room waiting for the promised Holy Spirit. Later in Acts, Lydia becomes the first convert in Europe and Priscilla functions in a teaching role over Apollos in Corinth (Acts 16:14-15; 18:2, 24-28). Sharon Pearson, in *Called to Minister, Empowered to Serve,* (Leonard 1989) and Donald Dayton implore holiness churches such as the Church of God, Anderson, Indiana, to recover the equality in ministerial roles, functions, and office that used to characterize our ministry (Pearson "Biblical Precedences 13-33; Dayton 304-337). Luke's narrative includes women as equals with men in ministry. His account fulfills the promise of the Spirit being poured out on men and women in Acts 2, as evidenced by his citation of Joel 2:28-29 in Acts 2:17-18.

Luke establishes a contrast between the inclusive visions of Jesus and the church and the divisive limiting environment. Jesus and the church reached out to the poor and the affluent, to women and men, to persons of different racial and ethnic backgrounds. E. R. Dodds attributes the phenomenal growth of Christianity to the inclusiveness practiced by Jesus and the church. Dodds speaks of the feeling of belonging that converts discovered in the church:

> Within the community there was human warmth; someone was interested in them, both here and hereafter. It is therefore not surprising that the earliest and the most striking advances of Christianity were made in the great cities—in Antioch, in Rome, in Alexandria. Christians were in a more than formal sense "members one of another." I think that was a major cause, perhaps the greatest single cause, of the spread of Christianity (Dodds 137-138).

Luke's narrative covers two eras—the time of the Spirit-led Jesus and the times of the Spirit-led church. The Holy Spirit, for Luke, is the power of God empowering and giving people the confidence to witness and serve. The Spirit produces a quality of life together in the church. The Spirit propels the church out in ministries of mercy and compassion with the poor, ethnic groups, and social outcasts.

A Discussion of Exegetical Method

A concern to be clear about one's exegetical method marks contemporary exegesis. My discussion of the ministry of the Holy Spirit in Luke 1-4 and Acts 1-2 utilizes a literary approach. My evolving understanding of a literary approach to Luke-Acts involves six procedural assumptions or operating guidelines. I share these to clarify my method and to introduce some readers to the methodological debate occuring in biblical studies.[7]

First, I am concerned with the finished form of Luke-Acts. I do not do source criticism and try to discover Luke's sources, although I believe Luke used Mark and Q as sources for his gospel. Nor do I do redaction criticism analyzing Luke's use of Mark and Q.[8] Although those are worthy goals, they are not the aims of a literary approach that concentrates on interpreting the text that lies before the reader.[9]

Second, I accept The Gospel of Luke and The Acts of the Apostles as a literary unity. The prefaces in Luke 1:1-4 and Acts 1:1-4 state that the author composed a two volume work.[10]

Third, primarily I investigate the beginning of Luke's gospel and Acts and the connecting seam of Luke 24:44-50. What an author says at the beginning and ending of a work is crucial. Beginnings, connecting seams, and endings often contain emphases and thematic summaries. Tannehill states that "narrators have frequently found it useful to guide readers by allowing them to anticipate certain events in advance and by encouraging them to reflect on them afterwards."[11]

Fourth, I pay attention to Luke's literary devices of pairing and parallelisms. Pairing occurs when an author places two characters or events together such as Zechariah and Elizabeth, Mary and Joseph, Simeon and Anna, and John the Baptist and Jesus in Luke 1-4. Luke used parallel incidents, persons, summaries, and patterns. Talbert's *Literary Patterns, Theological Themes and the Genre of Luke-Acts* lists cycles of similar content, as does his *Reading Luke*. For example, Talbert's analysis of Luke 3-4 uncovers the following structural parallels or what he calls a literary pattern.

	John		Jesus
3:1-6	John's person	3:21-38	Jesus' person
3:7-17	John's mission	4:1-13	Jesus' mission
3:18-20	Summary	4:14-15	Summary

(Talbert 1974, 45.)

Fifth, I study the structure and composition of the early chapters of Luke-Acts to discern a repetition of similar events and themes in the gospel and in Acts. I ask, How has Luke composed his gospel and Acts so that we have a compositional pairing of events and themes? This compositional analysis is not a mere linear search for similar themes.

Instead, it searches for parallel events, paragraphs, conversations, and persons such as the way both books conclude with farewell speeches by key characters Jesus and Paul. Another example is that the four trials of Jesus in Luke's gospel are matched by four trials of

Paul in Acts. Talbert explains how he reads Luke/Acts and seeks the unity of the narrative by noting that "the thrust of this approach is on understanding large thought units and their relationships to Lukan thought as a whole rather than focusing on the individual pieces of the narrative."[12]

Sixth, I read the text to get its theology. As Talbert maintains, the object is "to enter the narrative world of the text and listen to what Luke-Acts wants to say about religious reality. It is the Lukan theological point of view that is sought (Talbert, *Acts*, 4)." At first glance this concern for theology through reading the text might seem obvious and simplistic. However, interpreters of Luke often have approached Luke primarily as a historian or theologian instead of as an author of a narrative that refers to history and states a theology. Advocates of a literary approach believe their method leads to a dialogue with the biblical text, and eventually to the theology of the text, more quickly than the other two methods do. Ward Gasque underscores a common goal of students of Luke when he reminds us that "whether one still considers him to be a historian, thinks of him primarily as a theologian, or stresses his artistic abilities in shaping his narrative, all would agree that the author (Luke) is driven by fundamental theological concerns (Gasque 124)."

Because Christianity is an historical religion emerging from God's action in Jesus and the church, exegesis must eventually relate the biblical text to its historical setting. Otherwise, exegesis is not being true to the nature of biblical faith. Thus, in my emphasis on the inclusive vision of Jesus and the church as portrayed by Luke, I referred to the supportive findings of E. R. Dodds, a historian of the Hellenistic era. But exegesis should begin with a close reading of the biblical text, not with a reconstruction of or defense of the history referred to in the text or with a desire to defend a set of theological propositions one brings to the text.

Luke's emphasis on the ministry of the Holy Spirit can best be discovered through an exegetical method that links Luke's theology to the structure of Luke's narrative.

Endnotes

1. I. Howard Marshall stresses Luke as a faithful historian in *Luke: Historian and Theologian* (Grand Rapids: Zondervan, 1971).

2. Hans Conzelmann offers a theological interpretation of Luke that minimizes the relationship of theology to historical events in *The Theology of St. Luke* (1960).

3. The works of Robert Tannehill and Charles Talbert have informed my study of a literary method, as well as shedding light on Luke-Acts. See Robert C. Tannehill 1986; also, consult Charles H. Talbert 1982; also, see Talbert 1974 and Mikeal Parsons 1987, 687-720.

Beverly Roberts Gaventa notes that "the many successful efforts to separate Luke's theology from its narrative home should convince us that the enterprise is doomed. Lukan theology is intricately and irreversably bound up with the story he tells and cannot be separated from it" (1989, 150.)

4. Jose Comblin, *The Holy Spirit and Liberation*. Translated by Paul Burns (Maryknoll: Orbis Books, 1989). My wife, Susie, referred me to Comblin.

5. Boyce Blackwelder would have agreed with Wayne McCown's interpretation of Acts 2:1-13 in "The Spirit in the Book of Acts," *The Spirit and the New Age*. Edited by Larry Shelton and Alex Deasley (Anderson: Warner Press, 1986), 89-117.

6. Susie Stanley and I have had ongoing discussions on this point. She develops her views in "Empowered Foremothers: Wesleyan Holiness Women Speak to Today's Christian Feminists," *Wesleyan Theological Journal* (forthcoming) and in "What Sanctification Means to Me: Holiness as Power," *Centering in Ministry* (forthcoming).

7. As pointed out by David Bartlett, "Biblical Scholarship Today: A Diversity of New Approaches," (1981, 1090-1094).

Robert Morgan and John Barton, in their excellent analysis of exegetical methods, conclude "that a literary framework, that includes the results of historical and linguistic research, is today more promising for the study of religion and for theology than the historical framework (which includes literary study) that has dominated New Testament studies in particular since the 1830" (1988, 266). Barton's *Reading the Old Testament: Method in Biblical Study* provides a helpful review of exegetical methods.

Contrary to Morgan and Barton, Pauld Hansom delineates the first task of exegesis as the historical task of locating the test "in the world of its origin," followed by the literary "construction" (1988, 40-41).

8. Joseph Fitzmyer does a suberb job of source analysis and redaction criticism in *The Gospel According to Luke (I-IX)* (1981).

9. Robert Alter accuses biblical exegetes of spending more excavating the history behind the biblical text than they do in actually interpreting the passage (1981, 12-14).

10. Robert Wall voices the consensus that "the evangelist's gospel and Acts were written roughly at the same time for a similar life setting" (1989, 17).

11. Tannehill 1986, 10. I developed this finding in a 1976 sermon published as "Stay in the City," *Colloquium* 8 (November-December 1976), 3, 7.

12. Talbert 1982, 2. C. K. Barrett's *The Holy Spirit and the Gospel Tradition* (1966) demonstrates the need for a narrative analysis of Luke-Acts. Barrett begins by elucidating the central role of the Spirit in Acts and in Paul's writings. Then he erroneously suggests "that the Synoptic Gospels, on which alone we can rely for knowledge of the life and teaching of Jesus are almost silent about the Holy Spirit (p. 2). Barrett even has a chapter entitled "Why Do the Gospels Say So Little About the Spirit?" (140-162). His negative conclusions stem from his inadequate method. He merely listed references to the Spirit in the Gospels. Instead, he should have done a compositional analysis of Luke 1:1-4:37. If he had, he would have learned that four of Luke's twenty-four chapters deal with the work of the Holy Spirit in preparing people and Jesus for the Spirit-endowed ministry of Jesus. Barrett should have discerned how Luke built an emphasis on the Spirit's work into his structure of The Third Gospel rather than just seek explicit references to the Holy Spirit.

LYNN SPENCER SPAULDING

B.A., Anderson University; M.Div., Anderson University School of Theology; Doctoral studies, University of St. Andrews.

Assistant Professor of Bible and Religion, Anderson University (Anderson, Indiana). Former student of Dr. Boyce W. Blackwelder.

Chapter 7

The Significance of the Differing Audiences in Galatians and Romans
by Lynn Spencer Spaulding

In spite of his enormous importance in the later development of Christian theology, it is sometimes difficult to understand what Paul's views were. Apparently this is not strictly a modern difficulty but one that was noted in the early church, as 2 Peter 3:15 acknowledges. Part of the difficulty is that Paul was not a systematic theologian. Even so theological an epistle as Romans is not a systematic theological treatise (Sanders 1977, 433).

The Problem of Differences

A number of scholars have noted differences among the Pauline letters that are difficult to account for. Particularly significant are the differences between Galatians and Romans on the subject of the law. In part it is these differences that have prompted some scholars to reconsider Paul's views (Räisänen 1983).

Clearly that there are sizable differences between Galatians and Romans. The tone of Romans is cooperative and conciliatory, but that of Galatians is angry and at times even sarcastic. Galatians has the flavor of battle. Romans is calmer and more studied. Romans lacks the crisis atmosphere of Galatians. The critique of the law in Romans is gentle and the permanent significance of Israel is affirmed. More importantly, the two letters are different in theological emphasis. Romans and Galatians do not seem to have exactly the same view of the Jewish law. How should these difference be viewed?

Hans Hübner in *Das Gesetz bei Paulus* raises the question of whether Paul underwent development in his theology between his first and last letters (Hübner 1980, 47). Hübner believes that Paul's view of the law developed between Galatians and Romans. He thinks that Paul was forced by later circumstances, perhaps severe criticism from the Jerusalem apostles, to reconsider the very negative assessment of the law that he had articulated in Galatians.

John Drane is in agreement with Hübner that development took place in Paul's theology between the writing of Galatians and the writing of Romans. Drane is of the opinion that the events of 1 Corinthians caused Paul to moderate his initial position when he wrote to Rome (Drane 1975, 134).

Other scholars have not been enthusiastic about Hübner and Drane's positions. While it is possible that Paul's theology could change, Paul's mature stature in the faith and the short time between Galatians and Romans make many scholars skeptical about the thesis of theological development. Heikki Räisänen, in his definitive book *Paul and the Law*, goes much further when he argues that no consistent position on the law can be found in Paul (Räisänen 1983, 267). This skepticism, seems excessive, although Räisänen's examination of the data is detailed and provocative.

A more adequate response to the issue of the differences between Galatians and Romans is to be found in a reconsideration of the different audiences to which each letter was addressed. This will serve as the general thesis of this article.

The first section of the article indicates three different factors that have caused some to underestimate the significance of the different audiences of Romans and Galatians. First, the reading of Paul's letters has been determined by too much emphasis on the Reformation reading of Paul, which focuses exclusively on justification by faith and negativity toward the law and ignores alternate readings of Paul. Second, the canonical reading of Galatians and Romans suppresses the differences between the books. Third, previous methodology that focuses on the intention of the author is inadequate to express the full weight of the audience in understanding a text.

In the second section of the article, Reader Response Theory is used to show the significance of the audience in understanding Galatians and Romans. The general setting in each letter is described, followed by assessments of the implied authors and readers.

In the third section, the differences between Romans and Galatians are illustrated by the way Leviticus 18:5 is used in each letter. First, one notes, the Greek form of the quotation is different in each letter. Second, the surrounding quotations are different in each letter. Third, the line of thought developed using Leviticus 18:5 is different in each letter. These differences are shown to be consistent with the different implied audience and implied author of Galatians and Romans. Finally the article suggests further approaches that could be used to explore this proposal.

A common scholarly conclusion is that the letters of Paul are occasional letters (Doty 1973, 26). Romans has sometimes been noted as the exception that proves the rule, although a number of current scholars see even Romans as written in response to a local situation (Kuemmel 1975, 313). It also is commonly understood that because of the occasional nature of the letters, each letter should be given an independent reading.[1] Often Paul's letters have been read not as independent works written at specific times to specific audiences for specific purposes but as one body of integrated material. Passages in one letter are used to interpret passages in another letter even though they did not have that purpose when Paul wrote them.

These difficulties are especially acute in regard to Galatians and Romans. While it is obvious that the two letters were sent to two geographically diverse locations, and while most agree that two distinct audiences were addressed in the two letters and while many would see the dominant issues in each letter as different, few seem to practice exegetically what these insights proclaim. With startling frequency Galatians is used to interpret Romans without any reference to the diverse audiences to which the letters were sent.

Causes for Failure to Recognize the Significance of Audience

Three factors which account for this apparent failure to recognize the implications of the occasional nature of the Pauline letters. The first is Luther's assumption, shared by other reformers, that Galatians and Romans have basically the same center and that center is a forensic understanding of justification by faith.

For Luther, Paul consistently presents justification by faith alone as the only way to God and exhibits a stubborn intransigence toward the Jewish law. In this reading, Paul in fact seems strangely like Luther in position and personality, and Paul's conflicts with the law also ring suspiciously in tune with Luther's perception of the religious legalism of his time. Any other reading of Paul that is more subtle in regard to the law or richer in its imagery of salvation is eliminated *nolo contendere*. Most Protestants read Paul through the filter of the Reformers.[2] The Paul revealed as author in both the letters of Galatians and Romans, however, is much more subtle, richer of image and insight, and more flexible in style and expression than the Paul Luther constructed.

The monolithic view of the relationship of Galatians and Romans has recently come under substantial attack.[3] Specifically, scholars have raised questions in the areas of Paul's understanding of Judaism and the law,[4] and Paul's view of salvation,[5] questions that directly affect the understanding of the relationship of Galatians and Romans.

E. P. Sanders has argued definitively that traditional Reformation views of the Jewish law and the Jewish practice of the first century are incorrect and that Paul's own views do not match those of the Reformers. Sanders' evaluation of Paul and the law is based on his previous work on the nature of Rabbinic Judaism in the First Century and Paul's relationship to it. His book, *Paul and Palestinian Judaism*, has become a classic in the field.[6]

In reaction to the exclusive emphasis on justification by faith that characterizes Luther and the tradition that grows out of him, Sanders again argues that the central theme for Paul is not "justification by faith" but "participation in Christ (Sanders 1977, 434f.)." Paul's view is said to be that God has appointed Christ as Lord and Savior of the world. All who believe in him have the Spirit as the guarantee of future full salvation and are at present considered to participate in Christ's body, to be one Spirit with him. As such, they are to act in accordance with the Spirit, which is also to serve Christ as the Lord to whom they belong (Sanders 1977, 463)." According to Sanders the main key to Paul's view is really participation in Christ rather than justification. While surely no one would maintain that Paul never makes use of forensic understandings of justification, to see justification by faith alone as the sole salvation image in Paul may be unfaithful to the materials Paul left behind. It is even possible to ask with Sanders, Schweitzer and others whether being "in Christ" might not be the more central image for Paul.

Sander's analysis may be open to criticism, but it is sufficient for the purpose here to note that a powerful and convincing reading of Paul is possible that does not assume Luther's understanding of Paul.[7]

A second factor that continues to affect the Christian reading of Romans and Galatians is their canonical status. One does not have to hold with some fundamentalists that God is the direct author of all scriptural materials for this effect to be noted. The presence of canonical status carries a gentle pressure to view the two books as linked in a larger pattern. This pressure may be present even for those who recognize that there is no evidence that Paul saw his letters as part of a larger pattern or even, except in one case where two churches are adjacent, that he had any expectation that his letters would circulate beyond their original destinations.[8] They now are read by Christians as part of a canon, but for Paul and apparently for his first readers they were not part of a canon. Their present canonical status tends to obscure any differences in the two letters for the sake of the larger canonical harmony. It is important to acknowledge how easily one may be caught by the canonical status of these books and encouraged to understand them in a harmonistic manner.

Scholars commonly maintain that Paul's letters should be allowed to speak for themselves. However, this is easier articulated than practiced because the tradition of canonical status is with us all. James A. Sanders has written helpfully in *Canon and Community* of canonical criticism as a way of regaining for the Christian church the relevance of the Bible without losing the gains that have been made by biblical criticism (Sanders 1984).

Building on form and redaction criticism, canonical criticism focuses on the final form of the Bible in the setting of the believing communities where it received its full stature. For Sanders "the Holy Spirit was at work all along the path of the canonical process: from the original speaker, through what was understood by hearers; to what disciples believed was said; to how later editors reshaped the record, oral or written, of what was said; on down to modern hearings and understandings of the texts in current believing communities (xvii)." The history of the canon is a major element of this method that may directly shape interpretations of individual texts (21). For each specific text the long process of canonical development in both Judaism and Christianity needs eventually to be articulated, from the first inklings of the value of the text down to their final form and eventual acceptance as canonical scripture, rather than simply focusing on the end result of the process. Canonical criticism recognizes the multivalent nature of scripture that makes it adaptable through resignification to new situations (22).

This examination of the canonical process is very helpful in some ways. It recognizes the fact that canon affects the reading of the material. Specifically in the case of Galatians and Romans, it can demonstrate that these were separate books with no certain relationship to each other. What Sanders does not adequately explain is that previous views of canon too quickly read the texts on the basis of the reading community near the time of the final canonization of the Bible rather than showing the reading communities that proceeded the ones at the time of canonization. The one ought to be done but the other not left undone.

What ultimately must happen is that the whole process must be laid bare from the author and first readers, to the early Church Fathers, to readers at the time of the formation of the canon, to the Middle Ages, to the Reformation, to the contemporary church. If this is not done the reading of the texts will always be obscured by narrow interests. The text will too easily be captured either by the contemporary church's views or lost to the church in the minutia of the past. This means we must examine Galatians and Romans separately before they are considered canonically.

A third factor is the choosing of the author's intention as the complete locus of meaning. Since Galatians and Romans have the same author, the assumption has been made that the two books must basically have the same meaning. This is bolstered by a piety that fears that any change of view or inconsistency in Paul will weaken the divine authority of the materials.

Increasingly it is evident that knowing the intended meaning of the author is no simple task. The variety of interpretations produced by well informed and sincere readers is one mark of this difficulty. In actual practice meanings are achieved only when there is a frame for their reception in the reader, whatever might have been the intention of the author. No author can guarantee the reception of his intention, nor can any reader guarantee that the meaning the reader gains from the text is the same as the author's intention. What is hoped for is a high degree of correspondence between the author's intention and the reader's understanding.

What is needed is a method of interpretation that better acknowledges how the differing audiences in Galatians and Romans affects the reading of the two letters. A partial answer may be found in Reader Response Theory, a method that may encourage a fresh look at the material.[9]

Help from Reader Response Theory

Reader Response theory in literary studies has made many scholars aware that the meaning of a text may not be found simply in the author's intention (Mailloux 1977, 414). Rather, when the reader appropriates the text the meaning is present (Rimmon-Kenan 1983, 117). The reader in one sense creates the meaning of the text because previous to the reader's engagement with the text it only has the potential for meaning.[10] The insights and understandings of the reading community shape how the reading will be understood (Mailloux 1977, 414-415). Competent authors form their material with the reading community in mind and are themselves in some kind of reading community.[11]

For the purposes of this article four technical terms from Reader Response theory are important. The "actual author" is the literal composer of the letter. The "implied author" is the author who can be inferred by using the letter alone. By using the materials one reconstructs a picture of what characterizes the author for this specific piece of writing. The "actual readers" are in this case the audiences in Galatia and Rome who first received Paul's letters. The implied reading community or "implied audience" is the audience that can be implied from the text itself.

So one might ask, what is the reading community implied by Paul in Galatians? Is it the same reading community as that implied in Romans? It seems certain that the actual author of these two letters is the Apostle Paul, but is the author implied by the material in each letter exactly the same or are there different characteristics for each one? (Rimmon-Kenan 1983, 119). If there is enough difference in the answers to these audience questions one would be well on the way to accounting for the differences in the two letters.

Assuming as a given that the Apostle Paul is the actual author of the two letters and that the actual audience for the Letter to the Galatians is the churches in the District of Galatia and the actual audience for the Letter to the Romans is the church or churches in Rome, one then can ask, what are the audiences implied in the text of Galatians and of Romans and what are the characteristics of the author as implied in each book?

Galatians Overview

To understand the implied audience in Galatians it is necessary first to establish an overview of the situation of the Galatian letter. The letter attempts to counter a problem situation that had developed in the Galatian church. Two groups are implied in the text: the Galatians and Paul's opponents.

The Galatians had either submitted to circumcision or were considering doing so. It may be impossible to determine exactly who Paul's opponents were.[12] But it is possible to say that the Galatians had been influenced by someone, probably from the outside, to add at least circumcision and the observance of Jewish seasonal practices to their understanding of the gospel (See Howard 1979, 19. See also Gunther 1973, 59). There is some indication that some appeal was made to the Galatians that these teachings were a higher form of spiritual experience (Gal. 4:17).[13] Whoever was promulgating this teaching seems also to have been attacking the nature of Paul's apostleship. Some of these attacks seem to have been of a personal nature. The central thrust of the attacks seems to have been that Paul's gospel is derivative, that it comes from human sources, specifically from the Jerusalem apostles, and that Paul had not been faithful to what he had received.

Paul counters with a defense of his apostleship. He argues passionately that if circumcision brings salvation then Christ's death has no significance. Paul maintains that our sharing in Christ's death through faith alone brings salvation to the Jew or the Greek. If the Galatians accept circumcision as necessary to salvation they step outside of Christ's death into a relationship to the law that will never bring them to salvation.

Significantly, no other observances of the law are mentioned in Galatians.[14] If Paul used circumcision as a kind of code word for a Galatian decision to observe all the requirements of the law, as some maintain, then his separate mention of seasonal observances would seem unnecessary (Drane 1975, 11). Paul argues that to accept circumcision means actually taking on the whole burden of the law, but this is directed against the Galatians or his opponents who also may have thought of either partial or symbolic observance of the law.

The structure of the epistle to the Galatians is also significant in understanding the nature of the audience to which the letter is directed. The author logically chooses a form that will be convincing to the situation of the audience. Betz argues that Galatians can best be understood in terms of the "apologetic letter" genre (Betz 1979, 14-25). Brinsmead picks up this idea and uses it as the basis of his understanding of Galatians (Brinsmead 1982, 37ff). Brinsmead outlines the structure of the "apologetic letter" from Greek and Roman rhetorical handbooks as consisting of six parts, some of which may be combined or missing in a particular letter (Betz 1979, 24). They are: (1) introduction or proemium, which attempts to gain the hearers' attention and state the case, (2) the narrative or statement of the facts, which aims to set forth the historical background in a persuasive manner, (3) the divisio (partitio or proposito), which shows what are the agreed matters and what is contested, (4) the proof (probatio or confirmatio), which presents the argument, (5) the refutation (refutatio or confutatio), which aims at the destruction of the adversary, and (6) the peroratio or conclusio which sums up the case with a strong emotional appeal.

While the "apologetic letter" genre provides an overall structure to Paul's letter and adds an element of persuasiveness out of its "court of law" tone, Betz notes correctly that it also presents some drawbacks. First, it is written and so misses the power of an oral delivery. But more importantly it has the problem of rhetorical speech itself that is focused on the arts of persuasion. The concern of ancient rhetoric was less for truth than for persuasion of the audience. The appeal of rhetoric is basically rational, which may not always be persuasive (25).

One may say that Paul has been very successful—as a skilled rhetorician would be expected to be—in disguising his argumentative strategy. In spite of apparent confusion, a clear flow of thought is present. What makes these chapters look so confusing is the frequent interruption of the argumentative sections by dialogue, examples, proverbs, quotations and the like. But this is in conformity with the requirements of Hellenistic rhetoric. For the rhetoricians of Paul's time, nothing could be more boring than a perfect product of rhetorical technology. Therefore the appearance of an argument as a dead system of inescapable and performed syllogisms had to be avoided; instead, the arguments were to be presented in a lively way. Quintilian's advice was to "diversify by a thousand figures." Paradoxically, extremely perfected logic was thought to create suspicion and boredom, not credibility, while a carefully prepared mixture of some logic, some emotional appeal, some wisdom, some beauty, and some entertainment was thought to conform to human nature and to the ways in which human beings accept arguments as true (129). Paul uses the apologetic letter form in a way that is both rational and persuasive.

Using the apologetic letter form, Paul raises again in his letter the arguments that have been raised by his opponents in Galatia. He makes an often spirited defense, reasoning from Scripture, from tradition, from his own experience and from his former teaching in Galatia.

Implied Audience of Galatians

The implied audience in Galatia are faithful groups who have been subverted from what Paul taught them. Paul writes to persuade them. The audience is put in the role of children who must be corrected and persuaded back to the truth. They are Gentiles who may well recognize the apologetic letter form and the rhetorical techniques that it involves. The use of the form implies an audience capable of understanding the form. The personal appeals used in the argument imply that the group had residual positive feelings for Paul. Rhetorically, all this demands that it not be the Galatians themselves who were the source of the problem, but outsiders. The Galatians were victims of external influence. The author may be astonished at their vacillation but ultimately does not see them as perfidious. They are a group oriented around Christ and his gift of the Spirit. Their own spiritual experience in the Spirit runs counter to what they consider espousing.

Implied Author of Galatians

The implied author is one who is comfortable with Hellenistic letter form, in this case the apologetic letter form. The tone is parental and corrective. The author is willing to use anger and other strong emotions rhetorically to persuade his hearers. He is obviously an educated and cultured writer, but he is not above employing shocking language if it accomplishes his purpose. The author asserts his authority by claiming independent apostolic office, by referencing his impeccable Jewish credentials, by illustrating the equality of his apostleship and his gospel with that of the apostles in Jerusalem and by designating himself to be the defender of the Gentile church's freedom in Christ. The author's personal relationship with the Galatians and his personal authority is called on often, even to the extent of a first person proclamation in 5:2. Virtually everything in the letter is turned to the task of persuading the Galatians of the inadequacy of placing themselves under the law. The author seems intent on placing the law in the worst possible light as it relates to the Galatians.

The author evidences little concern for those who are his opponents and he repeatedly separates the Galatians rhetorically from those who trouble them. He counters these opponents; but the audience for his remarks is not the opponents; rather it is the Galatians themselves. Quite possibly the actual Galatian audience could have been one with the opponents, but rhetorically this is never acknowledged. Paul intends not to persuade his opponents but the Galatians, so he may scold the Galatians but uses special harshness for his opponents.

Romans Overview

While the actual author of Romans is the same person as in Galatians, the author implied by the text is somewhat different. Both the actual and the implied audiences in Romans are much different than the actual and implied audiences of Galatians.

Romans is an occasional letter written to introduce Paul to a church he did not found, perhaps with the hope that it would provide help with his work in spreading the gospel farther west and would support him at least morally in his presentation of the collection from the Gentile churches to the poor in Jerusalem. As he does in all his letters, he writes as the Apostle to the Gentiles guiding and encouraging them in response to situations that are either present or potentially present.[15] Specifically in the Roman Church Paul seems to address the relationship of Jewish and Gentile believers in the faith with the apparent aim of defending the value of Judaism to the church generally while avoiding any thought that Gentiles should become Jews.

Noticeably absent is any specific polemic against those who would circumcise Gentile believers, indicating that there was no problem with this issue in the Roman Church. The authenticity of Romans 16 is to be assumed as part of the local setting of the letter.[16] That there were in the church in Rome both Jewish and Gentile Christians should also be assumed.[17] Francis Watson evaluates the relationship of these two groups as one of sharp division into two separate congregations, one Jewish (perhaps including proselytes) and one Gentile (possibly with more liberalized Jews like Paul included). He believes Paul's purpose was to bring together the two congregations into one. He argues particularly for the Gentiles as part of the community of faith (Watson 1986). This may not be the best explanation. It may even be that, in apparent contrast to most of Paul's other letters, Paul is trying to guarantee a proper place for Jewish believers both in the present and in some eschatological future.[18]

Watson's contention that "the social reality which underlies Paul's discussions of Judaism and the law is his creation of Gentile Christian communities in sharp separation from the Jewish community" is really the opposite of Paul's hope for unity and mutual tolerance (Watson 1986, 19). It is most basic to Paul that there be one church in which Gentiles, elect Jews and eventually all Israel are participants. The analysis which Watson presents is fascinating and insightful at points but it seems lacking in sociological subtlety. It is on the right track in seeing the key to understanding the audience in Romans by positing two groups, Jewish believers and Gentile believers. As a result of the Edict of Claudius, Jewish Christians were absent from Rome for a time and barriers had arisen between the two groups. Recognizing the validity of a place for Jewish believers, and in Romans 11 for redeemed Israel, seems very important in the letter. This fits well with Paul's concern for the upcoming offering from the Gentile churches for the poor of Jerusalem.

The structure of Romans is more difficult to determine than that of Galatians and therefore less revealing of the nature of the implied audience. It is not an apologetic letter. Perhaps it is best to view it as an ambassadorial letter.

Implied Audience of Romans

The text implies an audience that is independent of any direct experience with the author. The relationship is ambassadorial. No previous mutualities are assumed except those that come from common commitments to the faith. The conflict situation involves two equal parties. The author is asking for mutual acceptance of each other in the church. No clear winner and loser are expected here. The sides of the argument are finely balanced with an aim to establish a mutually interactive relationship in which both sides are acknowledged as necessary and valuable.

Implied Author of Romans

The implied author is an ambassador of a mutually acknowledged power. He has no previous introduction to the group but has reason to expect a favorable response given his position as apostle to the Gentiles. He wishes to establish cordial relationships of mutual trust so that he can bring his gifts to bear on the situation. If there are tensions within the group, he may mediate them. All this is written with a tone of mutuality and common respect. In contrast to Galatians, the author is practically mellow. The use of emotions to persuade, while not absent, is more subtle and evocative. Little personal data is used. Rationality in the argument is emphasized over the specific experience of the congregation until near the end of the letter. Appeals are made rather than proclamations given. The claim of apostleship to the Gentiles is uncontested in the text's view and might imply that firmer action could be taken; nonetheless gentle action is chosen.

If the implied readers and authors in Galatians and Romans are as identified above, one might expect that actual readings of Galatians and Romans could be interpreted differently. An initial approach would be to examine possible differing interpretations of shared material in Galatians and Romans. If viable but divergent interpretations can be supported, one would be encouraged to examine other text material in Romans and Galatians and to consider examining in greater detail the implications of the actual and implied audiences.

The Example of Leviticus 18:5

The quotation of Leviticus 18:5 in both Galatians and Romans provides an ideal beginning. As one examines Romans 10:5 and Galatians 3:12 where Leviticus 18:5 is quoted, differences become obvious.

First, the actual quotations of Leviticus 18:5 are different. The Galatians text has almost no significant variants. Later manuscripts include *anthrōpos* in the quotation, but early support consistently omits it. Romans 10:5 has many variants that support a quite different reading than that of Galatians.

The Septuagintal form of Leviticus 18:5 in Sinaiticus reads *kai fulaxesthe pavta ta prostagmata mou kai panta ta krimata mou, kai poiēsete auta ha poiēsas anthrōpos zēsetai en autois* (Brooke and MacLean 1909, 366).

Galatians 3:12 reads *ho poiēsas auta zēsetai en autois* in both Nestle/Aland (26th edition) and in Westcott and Hort (1881). Galatians 3:12 is quite close to the reading of Sinaiticus. The reading is an exact match for that of Philo in *De Congressu Quaerendae Eruditionis Gratia* (no. 85-87 in volume IV of the Loeb Classical Library). Philo goes on to quote *egō kurios ho theos*. According to Philo the one who walks in the judgments and ordinances of God is the one who has true life. All this is the opposite of the practices of the godless which bring death. To do them is life; not to do them is death (Philo 1949).

Romans 10:5 presents some interesting textual variants. Nestle/Aland (26th edition) reads: *Mōusēs gar graphei tēn dikaiosunēn tēn ek [tou] vomou hoti ho poiēsas auta anthrōpos zēsetai en autois* (Aland 1979). Westcott and Hort (1881) reads: *Mōuses gar graphei hoti tēn dikaiosunēn tēn ek vomou ho poiēsas anthrōpos zēsetai en autē* (Westcott and Hort 1956).

Looking at Romans 10:5 it is easy to see why a scribe would want to make the quotation conform to either the LXX or to Galatians 3:12. It is difficult to see why the scribe would go the other direction. It is not at all difficult to think that Paul might make the passage conform to his argument either by adapting the passage or by choosing a version that conformed more closely to his needs if such were available. It is even possible that there is a Pauline midrash here that has been missed because of the more obvious midrash in verses 6-8. The very presence of the same verse in Galatians should make us cautious of any facile modern assimilation. Its very difficulty argues for its consideration. With Westcott and Hort, with Nestle/Aland (25th edition) and the bulk of modern editions of the Greek New Testament and against Nestle/Aland (26th), one should favor *hoti* after *graphei* and *en autē* against *auta . . . en autois*.

It is noteworthy that while obviously Paul in Romans 10:5 is quoting Leviticus 8:5, he quotes neither the Hebrew Massoretic text nor the Septuagint as we have them. Paul's version in Romans 10:5 does not even match that which he uses in Galatians 3:12. The main import of this is that while we have the same quotation in Galatians 3:18 and Romans 10:5, the quotation is not in the same form.

Second, while in both cases the quotation of Leviticus 18:5 is surrounded by other quotations of the Old Testament, they are not the same quotations in Romans as in Galatians. Galatians makes use of quotations from Genesis 15:6 and 18:3 (in reference to Abraham), Deuteronomy 27:26 and Habakkuk 2:4 before Leviticus 18:5, with Deuteronomy 21:23 and quotations from Genesis in the verse's following the Leviticus quote. In Romans 10:5, by contrast, Leviticus 18:5 is preceded by Isaiah 28:16 and followed by Deuteronomy 30:11-14, Isaiah 28:16 and Joel 2:32. The difference in quotations reflects a different line of thought in each letter. One would have expected the same surrounding passages if the same meaning was intended.

Third, the line of thought that is developed using Leviticus 18:5 in Galatians 3 is different from the line of thought developed using Leviticus 18:5 in Romans 10. A closer examination of the two chapters will demonstrate this difference.

Galatians 3

In Galatians 3 Paul is quite obviously attempting to establish that the decision the Galatians are making to be circumcised is contrary to their experience with the Spirit, is not supported by Scripture, and misunderstands both the law and their relationship to Christ.

Perhaps this section ought to be seen as a kind of dialogue with the Galatians.[19] The dialogical section which begins chapter 3 would support this. The major mark of the Galatians' inclusion in Christ is the presence of the Holy Spirit who has come to them by faith and not by works of the law. Not the circumcised but the persons of faith are the sons of Abraham and those who receive the blessings of God, i.e., life in its fullness now and in the future. Those who rely on the works of the law are under a curse unless they do all of the law. Not doing all the law results in the promised curse for those who put themselves under the law. Life does come to those who are righteous through faith. Life is promised to those who do the law, but only to those who fulfill all of the law (Betz 1979, , 145-146). In this contest, Leviticus 18:5 seems to be used as a small subset of the argument focused on only one aspect of its meaning.

The larger issue is carried by Deuteronomy 27:26. If Paul's opponents have proposed Deuteronomy 27:26 to persuade the Galatians that they must practice the law, Paul has effectively turned the argument on its head by inserting the word "all." It seems likely too that these Christians were not advocating a complete return to the law (Brinsmead 1982, 119). Certainly any discussion of sacrifice, the ritual system, or food laws are lacking. Paul's response indicates that they are not doing all the law and so fall under the curse rather than avoiding it. The Galatians really were not entering fully into the law. Jews would not forget repentance and sacrifice as part of the structure of the covenant, but the Galatians operated from a different perspective.[20] Probably Jewish sacrifice has already been given up and been reworked in relation to Jesus. Repentance is tied to belief in Christ. The life promised in Leviticus 18:5 cannot be theirs by their doing the law because it would operate apart from faith in Jesus Christ.

It is this doing of the law which Paul combats in his comment on Leviticus 18:5. If Paul has in mind a fuller exegesis of Leviticus 18:5, he does not give it here. He seems to be defusing a real or supposed use of the verse by his opponents, not to be providing a full exegesis of the passage. The Galatians cannot receive life from the law because they will not do all of the law. Paul may understand the problem to be that no one is able to do the whole law, or he may be arguing that the Galatians are really unwilling to attempt the whole law.[21] Paul does not specify what he intends. The focus is finally on the failure of everyone to do the law since everyone is consigned to sin. Life comes not to those who *do*, but to those who *have faith* in Christ.

In the context of Galatians 3:12, Leviticus 18:5 is used to contrast "doing the law," which has not produced life with "having faith in Christ" which has produced life, because Christ has removed the curse of the law. If the Galatians move out of the protective circle of being in Christ to being under the law then the whole curse of the law descends on them.

Romans 10

If one does not begin with the assumption that Romans 10:5 indicates Paul's opposition to the Mosaic law, some interesting interpretative possibilities present themselves. The presence of the *gar* demonstrates that he sees verse 5 and verses 6-8 in addition as explanatory of verse 4 (Cranfield). Käsemann and Wilckens see verse 5 as providing a scriptural proof or justification for verse 4, but it is preferable to see the whole section as explanatory of verse 4, particularly if one does not take verse 5 as a scriptural proof for *telos* as termination.[22] Paul appears to be taking the quotation here initially at face value. Any one who does the righteousness out of the law shall live. Leenhardt's comment, that it would be blasphemous to hold that total obedience to the law would be irrelevant, since then either God or Moses would have deceived Israel, is quite overstated, but it does highlight a basic concern. Would not Paul feel pressure in his argument to indicate some way in which the Scripture might be said to be true in more than a theoretical way? Fitzmyer in "St. Paul and the Law" maintains that Paul actually agrees that those who keep the law will live.[23]

Paul suggests that it is actually possible to gain righteousness through the law, but only for Jesus Christ. Doing the law is not a commonplace, but in fact only has a single representative, Jesus Christ who is the *telos* or goal of the law. Paul would then be said to accept the concept of Leviticus 18:5 that if one fully does the law, life will be the result, but maintains that only Christ has in fact fulfilled the law. As K. Barth in his *Shorter Commentary on Romans* expresses it, "The man of whom Moses says (10:5) that he shall live by the fulfillment of the law, the man who means and wills the law is Christ; he will fulfill the Law by his death and raised from the dead he will live (Barth 1959)."

Cranfield, who follows Barth's reasoning with a closer exegesis of the actual text, speaks of Christ's achievement as "the one man who has done the righteousness which is of the law in His life and above all in His death, in the sense of fulfilling all the law's requirements perfectly and so earning as His right a righteous status before God." Cranfield notes that Christ also makes a righteous status available to those who believe in him.[24] The meaning of Leviticus 18:5 is here understood Christologically as it was interpreted in the Greek and Latin Fathers. Christ is the one who does the law and he receives life, as his resurrection necessarily reveals.

Summary

Leviticus 18:5 in the context of Galatians 3 is used negatively to establish that the law is concerned with doing not with faith. Not doing all the law results in the curse from which only Christ can release us. If the Galatians put themselves under the law by circumcision, they remove themselves from Christ and they are then under the curse that failure to do the whole law brings. This view fits very well with the kind of implied readers and author that were described for Galatians above.

Leviticus 18:5 in the context of Romans 10 is used positively to indicate that Christ is the goal of the law because he does the law and so finds resurrection life and can then give life to those who are in him. This view fits very well with the kind of implied readers and author that were described earlier for the Roman letter.

As expected, even when Galatians and Romans use the same quotation, Leviticus 18:5, they do not use it in the same way but in a manner that is consistent with the implied author and audience in each separate letter.

Conclusion

Paul adapted his materials in Romans and Galatians to the two differing audiences. That adaptation is demonstrable in the text itself. These differing audiences adequately account for at least some of the differences between Galatians and Romans. Reader Response theory is found to be a meaningful methodology to give greater weight to audience in determining the meaning of a Pauline letter. Clearly a heightened sense of the significance of audience has a real effect on the exegesis of specific texts. Recognizing this significance, we may come to see how our own traditions have developed and we can let the whole history of Christian thought, and especially the understanding of those first reading communities that provided the context for the writing and reception of Paul's letters to Rome and Galatia, critique our present views. As we examine our interpretation in light of the interpretation of the past, we may come to better interpretation in our reading communities in the present.

Endnotes

1. The necessity of doing an independent reading of each Pauline letter before comparisons between them are made is not properly emphasized even in so good a student introduction to exegesis as Conzelmann and Linemann 1988.
2. Krister Stendahl in "The Apostle Paul and the Introspective Conscience of the West" (1963, 199-215) explores how Western Christianity through Augustine and Luther have filtered our understanding of Paul's introspection in inappropriate ways. The same principle can be applied to other areas of perception about Paul.
3. E. P. Sanders, Hans Hübner, John Drane, Heikki Räisänen, and others have raised questions about the differences between Galatians and Romans.
4. H. J. Schoeps 1961; W. D. Davies 1948; Samuel Sandmel 1970; and E. P. Sanders 1977 are appropriate beginning points for exploring the discussion of Paul's views on Judaism.

5. A rereading of Albert Schweitzer's views on Paul's understanding of salvation as being "in Christ" found in *The Mysticism of Paul the Apostle* (1956) is overdue in many quarters in Pauline Studies.
6. The page numbers in brackets in this next section are from E. P. Sanders 1977.
7. E. P. Sanders provides a strong alternate reading to Paul, but of course his positions are open to criticism as the lively discussion among Sanders, Hübner and Räisänen amply illustrates.
8. Colossians 4:16 indicates that the letter should also be read in the Laodicean church and their letter read to Colossae.
9. A sketchy introduction to Reader Response Criticism can be obtained from Shlomith Rimmon-Kenan 1993; Steven Mailloux 1978, 83-108; and Steven Mailloux 1977.
10. Mailloux 1979, 100, "Any patterns found are placed not in the text but in the structure of the reader's response."
11. The author may be seen as engaging in manipulation of the reader.
12. Earle Ellis n.d. "Paul and His Opponents"; See introduction to H. Schlier 1971. John H. Schutz 1975, 125; John Gunther 1973, 315-317, believes Paul's opponents were believers whose background were mystic-apocalyptic, ascetic, nonconformist syncretistic Judaism akin to Essenism and who were in the same sense syncretists, gnostics, and pneumatics themselves. Bernard Hungerford Brinsmead (1982, 22) is less sure and call the whole issue problematic.
13. See Brinsmead's description of Paul's opponents as typified by nomistic enthusiasm, 188; Ernest de Witt Burton, 1920, 1920, 158; and Gunther 1973, 82.
14. The mention of Peter and his problem with table fellowship makes the silence of the rest even more startling.
15. A. J. M. Wedderburn's suggestion in "The Purpose and Occasion of Romans Again" 1978, 137-141 that the collection from the Gentile churches for Jerusalem provides part of the occasion for Romans is very helpful at this point.
16. See Harry Gamble 1977 *et al* on the relationship of chapter 16 to the rest of Romans.
17. See C. E. B. Cranfield 1975 for a typical indication of the presence of Jews in Rome.
18. Romans may be written in part as a defense for a continued relationship between Jewish and Gentile Christians and also a continuing relationship between Christianity and Judaism.
19. Hans Dieter Betz (1979, 130) describes it more forcefully as an interrogation of witnesses.
20. The Galatians are already under a covenant as evidenced by the Spirit; see Betz 1978, 133.
21. Much of the commentary material on Romans 10:5 fits potentially better as comment on Galatians 3:12 especially if this verse is seen as implying that doing the law is impossible.
22. Robert Badenas (1985) gives a particularly good summary of the background and use of telos establishing "goal" as its meaning.
23. Fitzmyer (1967, 23) represents a common Roman Catholic opinion that sees Paul's view of the law here as positive.
24. Barrett seems to be interpreting 10:4 somewhat in this same light when he comments, "For Christ by realizing righteousness for every believer proves to be the end of the law."

GENE MILLER

B.A., Anderson University; M.Div., Anderson University School of Theology; Ph.D., Duke University.

Associate Professor of New Testament, Anderson University School of Theology (Anderson, Indiana). Former student of Dr. Boyce W. Blackwelder.

Chapter 8

Teleios as "Mature," "Complete," or "Brought to Completion" in the Pauline Writings
by Gene Miller

Introduction

The term *teleios* is one of a vitally significant family of words in the Greek New Testament. Cognates include two nouns: *telos*—end, consummation (as in 1 Cor. 1:8)[1] and *teleiotes*—completeness (as in Col. 3:14).[2] Along with these substantives, two verbs occur: *teleioo*—to carry out, finish, complete (as in John 19:30, 2 Tim. 4:7);[3] and *teleo*—to complete a requirement, fulfill (as in Rom. 2:27).[4]

A common practice in some theological circles has been to resolve the issue by assigning to the term *teleios* and its cognates such meanings as "perfect love,"[6] "relative perfection,"[7] or "perfect in attitude or intent."[8] At their best, such formulations leave much to be desired in terms of exegetical validity, doctrinal understanding, and application to Christian life and development. Another frequently suggested approach is that the statements are not intended to be taken specifically or practically, but rather as a "goal or ideal" toward which the Christian is to strive continually but can never expect to reach or will reach "only in heaven."[9] Some, on the other hand, have attempted to equate "perfection" with sanctification or holiness.[10]

Accurate translation and interpretation will demonstrate that *teleios* in the New Testament, particularly in the Pauline writings, ordinarily does not refer at all to "perfect" or "perfection'" in the usual sense of those terms, but rather to certain concepts and experiences that are properly related to their basic significance and that bear at some most crucial points upon Christian life and experience. While this study focuses particularly on the Pauline writings in the New Testament, *teleios* and its cognates are employed in other New Testament writings. Reference will be made to such supportive or complementary material at appropriate points in the study.

Three major aspects of the use and significance of *teleios* or its cognates will be examined: *teleios* as mature, fully developed, grown up—especially in terms of spiritual maturity; *teleios* as complete, entire, whole as opposed to partial or incomplete; *teleios* as complete in experience or qualification, brought to completeness or fullness, having full effect. Obviously, these concepts or nuances of meaning are related, sometimes closely; yet at the same time they involve significant differences in emphasis, area of operation, and application.

Unless otherwise noted, all quotations from the New Testament are translated by the author directly from the Greek New Testament. Occurrences of *teleios* and cognates are especially noted whenever they occur in the text.

Teleios As Mature, Fully Developed, Grown Up

One of the key sections at this point is 1 Corinthians 2 and 3, especially 1 Corinthians 2:6 to 3:3. That passage reads:

2:6 Now we speak wisdom among the mature [*teleiois*], but not a wisdom of this age or of the rulers of this age, who are being brought to nothing. 7 But we speak a wisdom of God in a mystery, which has been hidden away, which God decreed before the ages for our glory, 8 which none of the rulers of this age knew; for if they had known, they would not have crucified the Lord of glory. 9 But just as it stands written, "What the eye has not seen, and the ear has not heard; and it has not occurred to the heart of man, what God has prepared for those who love him." 10 But God revealed it to us through the Spirit. For the Spirit searches all things, even the deep things of God. 11 For who of men knows the things of God except the Spirit of God? 12 Now we did not receive the spirit of the world but the Spirit which is from God, that we might know the things freely given to us by God. 13 And what we speak is not in human teachings of human wisdom but in teachings of the Spirit, comparing spiritual things with spiritual things, 14 Now the natural man does not receive the things of the Spirit of God, for they are foolishness to him, and he cannot understand them because they are spiritually discerned. 15 But the spiritual man discerns all things; but he himself is discerned by no one. 16 For who knew the thoughts of the Lord; who will instruct him? But we have the thoughts of Christ. 3:1 Now I, brothers, was not able to speak to you as spiritual persons but as fleshly persons, as babies in Christ. 2 I fed you milk, not solid food, for you were not yet able to receive it. Indeed, neither are you yet now able, 3 for you are still fleshly. For while jealousy and strife are among you, are you not fleshly, and conducting yourselves according to man?

In this section, Paul pointed out that the "mature" or *teleioi* (not "perfect!") are able to understand divine or spiritual wisdom. "Spiritual people" (i.e., spiritually mature people or *teleioi*) can understand and receive "spiritual things"—profound divine truth. They have grown up (spiritually) and no longer need to be fed on "milk," but are ready for "solid food." The spiritually immature ones are still "babies in Christ"; that is why they are "conducting [themselves] according to man." Dr. Boyce Blackwelder expressed the nuance of "spiritual" in these verses: "As for me, brothers, I could not talk to you as to spiritually minded men" (Blackwelder 1971, 46).

In his letter to the Colossian Christians, Paul expressed unequivocally his devotion, as an apostle, to the task of bringing to spiritual maturity all those to whom he ministered:

1:27 To whom God willed to make known what are the riches of the glory of this mystery among the Gentiles [nations], which is Christ among you, the hope of glory; 28 whom we proclaim, admonishing every man and teaching every man with all wisdom, so that we may present every man mature [*teleion*] in Christ, 29 for which I also labor, striving according to his working, which is powerfully at work in me.

The centrality of this concern for Christian pastors and for the body of Christ as a whole is expressed even more fully in Ephesians 11-16:

11 And he gave the apostles, the prophets, the evangelists, the pastors and teachers, 12 for the equipment of the holy people for the work of serving, for building up of the body of Christ, 13 until we all attain to the unity of the faith, and the thorough knowledge of the Son of God, to a mature person, to the measure of the stature of the fullness of Christ, 14 so that we might no longer be babies, tossed back and forth and blown around by every wind of teaching in the craftiness of men, in their cleverness with deceitful plots. 15 But speaking the truth in love, let us grow up into him in all things, who is the Head, Christ, 16 from whom all the body, joined together and knit together through every joint with which it is supplied, according to the proportionate work of each one of

the parts, makes bodily growth for building itself up in love.

Note that *every* Christian—not merely a superspiritual elite—is to grow up into Christ or reach spiritual maturity. Each is to be a "mature person"—*teleios*, not "perfect."

In this equipping and maturing, Christ is the head, the example, and the integrity of it all. Here, Christian pastors and other leaders are specifically assigned the momentous task of equipping the Christians for service, and thus "building up the body of Christ." Spiritual maturity (being *teleios*) is regarded as being closely related to *unity, thorough knowledge of Christ, wisdom,* and *discernment.* The vital relationship between spiritual maturity and wisdom/understanding is especially emphasized by the apostle. He admonished the Corinthian Christians: "Brothers, do not be children in understanding; rather, in evil be babies, but in understanding be mature [teleioi]" (1 Cor. 14:20). The Christian may well be a "baby" (i.e., innocent) where "evil" is concerned, but must be "mature" (*teleios*) in spiritual understanding and responsibility! Furthermore, spiritual maturity involves, at least in some instances, the occurrence and significance of divine revelation: "Therefore, those who are mature [*teleioi*], let us understand this; and if in anything you think otherwise, God will reveal even this to you" (Phil. 3:15).

Teleios As Complete, Entire, Whole, As Opposed to Partial Or Incomplete

An excellent example of *teleios* employed in this capacity is I Corinthians 13:9, 10: "We know in part, and we prophesy in part; but when that which is complete [*teleion*] comes, that which is partial shall be done away with." The partial or incomplete is only temporal; it will be replaced by the whole or complete (*teleios*). In this particular instance, the partiality is applied to personal knowledge, experience, and insight—and even prophecy. Sometimes even those revelations or insights that proceed from divine sources and are declared through a grace-gift of the Spirit are in this life and realm of experience "in part."

Speaking of his own experience as a "soldier of the cross," Paul said, "I have fought the good battle, I have finished (*teteleka*) the race, I have kept the faith; finally the crown of righteousness is laid up for me, which the Lord, the righteous judge, will give to me on that day, and not only to me, but also to all those who have loved his appearing" (2 Tim. 4:7, 8). It is not enough to *begin* the race (the task, the assignment, the commitment); one must *finish* to receive the victor's wreath. Like the writer of Hebrews, Paul was not one of those who "shrink back to destruction" (Heb. 10:39), but rather one of those who keeps the faith and finishes the race (see John 4:34).

In the Pauline writings the concept of completeness or wholeness is related also to the relationship of believers in Christ. Paul exhorted the Christians at Colosse to exhibit and practice compassion, kindness, goodwill, and generosity toward each other, and then added: "And upon all these love, which is the bond of completeness (*teleiotetos*)" (Col. 3:14). The term translated "bond" in this passage is from the Greek *desmos*, often employed to refer to actual chains or fetters, as in Colossians 4:18.[11] The tie, then, between and among believers is a powerful, forceful one—one that brings them together into "completeness" (*teleiotetos*). Only through "love" can the members of the body of Christ be complete in harmony and relationships.

J. L. Houlden stated: "Pagan moral thinkers could use the same word (syndesmos = bond) to express the idea of a principle of unity and cohesiveness in ethics. 'Perfectness' recalls *teleios* in 1:28 (mature), which is the corresponding adjective; the idea will then be that love is the chief characteristic of fully developed Christian life" (Houlden 1977, 207). An excellent comment on this use of *teleios* with reference to partiality as opposed to completeness in Christian life and practice is made by R. V. G. Tasker in his treatment of Matthew 5:48.[12] Followers of Christ are not expected to "be perfect as [the] heavenly Father is perfect," nor to be "perfect in love"; they are expected to be *complete* in their demonstration of love and kindness, not "picking and choosing" but showing kindness to all, even as God makes no exception.

Teleios As Complete In Experience Or Qualification, Brought To Completion Or Fullness

To the Philippian Christians Paul wrote: "That I might know him and the power of his resurrection and the fellowship of His sufferings, being conformed to his death, that somehow I might attain to the resurrection from the dead; not that I have already received this or already been brought to completion [*teteleiomai*], but I pursue it that I might lay hold upon it, just as I was laid hold upon by Christ Jesus" (Phil. 3:10-12). Though the apostle was dramatically and decisively converted, was totally dedicated to the ministry to which he had been called, and was engaged in an all-out effort to win others to Christ at any cost to himself, he realized that he had not yet "been brought to completion" in experience. He had not yet received all that God had in store for him—particularly the resurrection.

Every Christian should understand this thrilling insight. The believer has been saved "in hope"—the blessed hope of resurrection and eternal life with God. This concept is affirmed at several points by other New Testament writers. See, for example, 1 John 4:13-18. *Teleios* or *teleioo* in this connection does not refer in any way to moral, ethical or spiritual lack or transgression, but to a completion or consummation of the experience begun in personal salvation. This concept of completion in experience or qualification was definitely a part of the mission and task of Jesus (see Heb. 2:10 and 5:8,9).

Colossians 4:12 exemplifies a similar use of *teleios*: "Epaphras, one of you, a bondservant of Christ Jesus, greets you, always agonizing in your behalf in his prayers, that you may stand complete (*teleioi*) and fully assured in all the will of God." The believer *can* and *should* stand *teleios* (complete)—fully knowledgeable and "fully assured" or confident—in all of God's will for faith and life. Blackwelder aptly rendered this phrase "in everything regarding God's will" (Blackwelder 1971, 128). The believer's relationship with God ought to be characterized by full realization and stability regarding the divine will, rather than partial understanding and doubt. Second Peter 1:8 expresses this same concern, in slightly different terms: "For if these qualities are yours and are increasing, they constitute you neither unprofitable nor unfruitful in the thorough knowledge of our Lord Jesus Christ."

The will of God is that all believers be *complete* in their experience in terms of knowledge, wisdom, understanding of God's will for them, and assurance—in other words, truly mature Christians.

Implications For Christian Life, Service, and Leadership

Given all of the above, several important implications appear justified. They are crucial for Christian life, service, and leadership.

1. Christians need not labor under the erroneous belief that they are required or expected to be "perfect," or to reach "perfection"—to be absolutely without fault or blemish of any kind. Such will never take place in this life and is not demanded or anticipated in New Testament teaching.[13]

2. Paul (along with other New Testament writers) did indicate beyond question that every believer is to "grow up in Christ"—reach spiritual maturity. Just as it is normal for each individual to grow to maturity physically or humanly speaking in body, mind, and emotions, so it is normal and expected that each believer grow up spiritually and become a knowledgeable, contributing, stable member of the body of Christ.[14]

In common human experience, certain levels of jealousy, competitiveness, self-centeredness, and contention over inconsequential issues on the part of children are not a cause for undue alarm. When people reach adulthood, however, they normally are expected to "put off childish ways," and exercise a modicum at least of wisdom, self-control, and concern for others. Tension, ill-will, and conflict are often generated because of immaturity rather than overt desire to harm others or to create difficulties. The same is true in the realm of *spiritual* development and maturity. Realizing this, pastors and other spiritual leaders need to give the same priority as Paul gave to the effort to "present every person mature in Christ."

3. Believers are to be brought to maturity or completeness in terms of personal experience, relationships with other Christians, and in their service to the Lord. Many a person has made a good start in life, but, because of malnourishment, adverse experiences, accident, indolence, or other factors, has failed to complete the journey to personal maturity in one or more areas of development. Because of immaturity, one person may begin one job, endeavor, or enterprise after another, never carrying through on any. Another may begin marriage and family life, only to abandon it after a short time. Another may determine to make important changes in life, but never take action to implement the resolutions. Another may be unable to establish or maintain lasting, harmonious relationships with others. Another may avow loyalty and faithful service to some cause or ideal, only to lose enthusiasm and "drop out." Many factors may be at work in such cases, but in countless instances immaturity is a major one.

Unfortunately, the same can happen in terms of *spiritual* experience and endeavors. When new "babies" are born into the family of God, they need to be recognized as such, so that they will receive the nourishment, teaching, direction and encouragement necessary to bring them to spiritual maturity. In recent decades much public concern has been expressed regarding "cultural dropouts," "high school dropouts," and "social dropouts." These are indeed serious concerns in society. The church, as God's society, must begin to demonstrate even greater concern for "spiritual dropouts," those who begin the "race," only to quit before it is done; those who gladly respond to the message of salvation, only to lose their enthusiasm and intent; those who are saved, only to be abandoned by the church or left "on their own"; those who have been Christians for some years but have never "grown up in Christ."

4. "Now we speak wisdom among the mature (*teleioi*)" (1 Cor. 2:6); "Therefore, those who are mature (*teleioi*), let us understand this" (Phil. 3:15). Let those who are spiritually mature be thankful to those who have helped them to grow up in Christ and be diligent in helping others to attain maturity. Let those who are spiritually immature acknowledge it and seek those experiences and disciplines that will bring them to adulthood in Christ. Through the Word of God, personal devotion and prayer, obedience, learning, and the guidance of dedicated Christian leaders, every member of the family of God can "attain to the unity of the faith and the thorough knowledge of the Son of God, to a mature man, to the measure of the stature of the fullness of Christ" (Eph. 4:13).

5. God has given to the church spiritual leaders and guides—"apostles, prophets, evangelists, pastors, and teachers"—for the "equipment of the holy people for the work of service, for building up of the body of Christ," to the end that all may reach spiritual maturity. For this divine plan to be fully effective, the following elements are vital:

a) *Challenging* young Christians with the possibilities and potentialities of a call to full-time Christian ministry and leadership;

b) *Alertness* on the part of the church and its leaders to the working of the Holy Spirit in calling and inspiring individuals to Christian ministry;

c) *Openness* and *responsiveness* on the part of individual Christians to the particular call of God to spiritual leadership and service;

d) *Diligence* on the part of pastors and other Christian leaders in identifying, encouraging, and training those who are called to spiritual leadership and ministry;

e) *Willingness* on the part of the church to grow and mature under the guidance of capable leaders and teachers.

f) *Support*, at every level from local congregation and family to national agency and institution, to provide and continue high-caliber preparation and training for those who are called to leadership and ministry in the church. If the church does not encourage, teach, and train leaders for its own work, the task may be done inadequately by others—or not at all.

The quest and the call, then, according to Paul, are not to perfection, but to spiritual maturity and completeness of experience. How the church in every generation needs and must find profound spiritual understanding and wisdom, genuine unity, discernment, courage, and integrity! How those who profess Christ need to demonstrate the very kindness and love of God himself! How the people of God need to rejoice in, proclaim, and reaffirm the blessed Christian hope of resurrection and eternal life! How believers need to know God's will for them and to have the dedication to carry it out at any cost! How the church needs to reproduce itself—over and over again! High aspirations indeed, but no more than the Lord of the church demands and expects from his bondservants who are truly *teleioi*—mature citizens of the kingdom in Christ.

Endnotes

1. "[Our Lord Jesus Christ] . . . also will confirm you blameless to the end (*telous*) on the day of our Lord Jesus Christ."

2. "And upon all these love, which is the bond of completeness (*teleiotetos*)."

3. "Then when he had taken the sour wine, Jesus said, "It is finished (*tetelestai*), and having bowed his head, he gave up his spirit" (John 19:30).
"I have fought the good battle, I have finished (*teteleka*) the race, I have kept the faith" (2 Tim. 4:7).
4. "And the one who is physically uncircumcised, having fulfilled (*telousa*) the law, will condemn you, who through the letter of the law and circumcision transgress the law."
5. "One of the most distinctive Wesleyan terms is *perfection*. It is a word that has been variously interpreted and as a consequence widely misunderstood" (Wynkoop 1972, 268).
"The man of faith who takes seriously the clearly defined ideal of holiness in the New Testament is most vulnerable to this crucial threat. He needs to understand how a man can be holy and yet human. Such an understanding must begin with a clear insight into what the New Testament, and specifically Paul, teaches about the ideal. It is most unfortunate that the Christian ideal is identified, by all too many, with a totally nonbiblical concept of holiness and perfection" (Howard 1975, 214).
6. "The resultant life of Christian holiness is known as perfect love or Christian perfection" (Carter 1983, 521.) Carter further elaborates, "'Perfect love' is a favorite synonym for 'Christian perfection.' Neither expression implies perfect judgment, complete wisdom, or full maturity of skills or perfection in performance. But both do imply a heart cleansed from sin and filled with the Holy Spirit" (532).
7. "We do well to inquire what Christian perfection is not. The older apologists for this doctrine would say that it is not the perfection of angels, nor of God, nor absolute perfection, but a relative perfection appropriate for man in his present condition" (Turner 1977, 79.)
"The Thessalonian epistles have been analyzed as intentionally and thematically developed to lead young Christians into the experience and life of holiness for the relative perfection of life here and with a view to Christ's appearing" (Carter 1983, 562.)
"This points up the more explicit observation that there is an absolute and a relative meaning to evangelical perfection" (Wynkoop 1972, 296).
"What is Paul's concept of perfection? The first and most important thing to understand about Paul's—and the entire New Testament's idea of perfection is to recognize that *it is a relative concept* . . . All perfection, in its New Testament sense, is relative (Howard 1975, 215).
8. "God looks on this inner perfection and remembers that the outer man is fallible and faulty. . . . Christian perfection is a matter of the heart—of love, attitude, and relationship" (Carter 1983, 537).
Regarding Matthew 5:48, Wynkoop says: "The general tone of the whole passage emphasizes right attitudes as being acceptable to God rather than simply right conduct. It is a characteristic or quality, not a degree of accomplishment" (1972, 285).
9. "The ministration of the New Testament was that of the 'Spirit which giveth life'—a Spirit, not only promised, but actually conferred; which should both enable Christians now to live unto God, and fulfill precepts even more spiritual than the former; and restore them hereafter to perfect life, after the ruins of sin and death" (John Wesley qtd. in Carter 1983, 526).
10. But see, on the other hand, Wynkoop 1972, 297: "Evangelical perfection has no meaning scripturally apart from an understanding of its "this-life" relevance. No

exegesis can find textual warrant for deferring the biblical teaching of perfection to another life. Its terms, or the norms which determine it, have to do with the powers, relationships, and provisions of grace encountered in "this present world."

"Perfection has been interpreted in terms of crisis or process according to the whole background of presuppositions brought to the subject. Some equate sanctification wholly with the crisis/perfection syndrome. Others, with a totally different concept of possibility, relate process and perfection, either distinguishing between sanctification and perfection so as to preserve crisis in relation to sanctification, or equating sanctification and perfection and dismissing crisis as a viable theological category, making all progress gradual and natural." (Wynkoop 1972, 269). "The writer to the Hebrews issues the call to perfection (6:1, KJV) and says that without this sanctification no one will see the Lord (12:14). Sanctification and perfection are the very essence of the Christian fulfillment (12:23; 13:12)" (Carter 1983, 524).

"The heart of the doctrine of entire sanctification as the purification and perfection of the believer is intact as Wesley believed and taught it" (526). "For Wesley, to reject the concept of Christian perfection would be to reject holiness, because "it is only another term for holiness. They are two names for the same thing. Thus everyone that is holy is, in the Scripture sense, 'perfect' " (539).

11. "The greeting by my own hand—Paul. Remember my bonds [*desmon*]. Grace be with you."

12. "Perfect is here a misleading translation of *teleios*, and is largely responsible for the erroneous doctrine of 'perfectionism.' Men can never be perfect as God is perfect; and Jesus himself taught that at best, when men have done everything possible, they are unprofitable servants, who have only done their duty (see Luke xvii, 10). Torrey would seem right in supposing that the underlying Aramaic word was active in sense, and that the meaning here is 'all-including (in your good will) even as your Father includes all.' 'Be therefore perfect,' he writes, 'would be mere nonsense, even if it were not wholly unprepared for in this context. Nothing here leads up to the idea of perfection—to say nothing of equalling the perfection of God Himself.' In this paragraph the disciples are taught that they must show kindness to all men, just as the heavenly Father makes no exception" (Tasker 1961, 70).

13. "This does not mean that there will not be moments of 'sin improperly so-called' or perhaps even of 'sin properly so-called,' when in a moment of physical and psychical weakness, carelessness, anxiety, ego-threat or spiritual leanness, that we will not fail of the Christlikeness of attitude and behavior that we so much desire" (Carver 19).

14. "We may safely conclude, then, that the doctrine of perfect love emerged both from a scriptural study and from the certainty Wesley felt about the genuineness of the faith of his converts. Holiness of heart seemed to him, as it has ever since to his followers, what every person who is truly saved by faith will long for. He was convinced that this 'great salvation from sin' would be sent down, 'as at the day of Pentecost' unto 'all generations, into the hearts of all true believers' and that the promise was 'to all them that are afar off, even as many as the Lord shall call' " (Smith 1986, 142).

KENNETH E. JONES

B.Th., Anderson University; B.D., Oberlin Graduate School of Theology; M. Th., Winona Lake School of Theology; Ph. D., International Institute for Advanced Studies; D.D., Warner Pacific College.

Retired Dean and Professor of Theology and Biblical Studies, Mid-America Bible College (Oklahoma City, Oklahoma). Long-term ministerial and teaching colleague of Dr. Boyce W. Blackwelder.

Chapter 9

Babylon and the New Jerusalem: Interpreting the Book of Revelation

by Kenneth E. Jones

B iblical hermeneutics is not a simple subject in any case, but it finds one of its most difficult tests in the Book of Revelation (Feuillet 1962, 7; Guthrie 1987, 11-12). The form of the book and the bizarre symbols with which it is filled give the book a fascination that attracts and yet confuses readers. Although there are almost as many interpretations of the book as there are interpreters, practically all can be classified into five broad categories: preterist, futurist, historicist, idealist, and theological.[1] Our objective in this paper is to examine these approaches to Revelation as illustrated in their understandings of Babylon. Our first task is to review these broad categories of interpretations.

Preterist Interpretation

The Preterist interpretation is also called *Zeitgeschictlich* or contemporary-historical. One form of this method of interpretation—the prevailing approach among historico-critical scholars—views Revelation as a product of its time and seeks to interpret the book in its own historical setting (Ladd). To comprehend the original historical setting of any book is, of course, the initial consideration of a scholar who wishes to understand that book. In a general sense, therefore, we should all begin as preterists.

Probably the most extreme preterist position is that of J. Stuart Russell (Russell 1983), who insisted that the whole of the New Testament, including Revelation, was both written and completely fulfilled before 70 A.D. He meant that the Second Advent took place at that time, and that all the symbols of Revelation had their full meaning in the events leading up to the destruction of Jerusalem. He has few followers.

However, the term preterist is often applied to scholars who not only begin with the historical setting of Revelation, but who also insist that it had no application to any historical period but the first and second centuries. Convinced that there is no such thing as miracle or prediction, they concentrate on the application of Revelation to the first century for this reason (See Summers 1951, 44). They believe that since there can be no prediction, John was necessarily writing about his own time.

Preterists insist that John was writing to the church of his own time, to encourage them to be true in spite of the troubled times facing them. In this they are bound to be correct, but we then have to ask what meaning the book has for all those in the centuries since then. If its meaning was truly exhausted in the first century, why should it have been preserved for us? To begin our study with the first century, which is the time of composition of the book, is the only way in which to come to an understanding of the writer's meaning and purpose. But if the book is to have relevance for today, we must go further.

At the same time, we recognize that the preterist viewpoint has much good to offer one who truly aspires to understand the book, since it is true to the historical background of the writing. This method makes the book meaningful to the first readers in the first century, as some other methods do not, and this is significant. For if it had no meaning to the first readers, but only to people of a much later time, they would hardly have had reason to preserve it as inspired writing. In this it is like the prophecies of the Old Testament. Even when the prophets were speaking of the Messiah who would come centuries after their own time, they gave the message in such a way that it had clear application to their own generation. That this is true can be seen by looking at the context of any of the great Messianic passages in the Old Testament.

To see the Book of Revelation from the preterist point of view is to see that John was writing to encourage the Christians at the end of the first century to be true and to persevere in their faith in Christ in spite of the troubles and persecution that buffeted them. Persecution would increase, but God would keep those who were faithful and true and in the end God would win the complete victory for the faithful.

Otto F. Linn, who was widely recognized as a leading New Testament scholar, was a firm believer in the inspiration and authority of the whole Bible and wrote a commentary on Revelation from the preterist point of view. He insisted that "the first thing we must understand is that apocalyptic literature rose out of contemporary and local circumstances which made it intelligible to the people of that time."[2] In this he was surely correct. We must begin with the first century, but we must not limit our study to the author's own time. We must seek to find meaning for later generations.

Futurist Interpretation

The futurist (*endgeschichtlich*) interpretation takes most of the book as applying only to events that are still future and having little or no relevance to our own age or any previous age, except that we know that certain great events will occur sometime in the future. The clearest example of the futurist interpretation is that type of premillennialism that we can all dispensationalism, represented by Darby and Scofield, and which has been popularized by the three versions of the Scofield Bible and by the recent books of Hal Lindsey.[3] Although one has difficulty in saying much about their teaching with which all dispensationalists would concur, agreement among them is rather general that chapters 1-3 bring us down to the present time, and that beginning with chapter 4 we find predictions of events that are yet future, but not now far in the future.[4] In some fashion Revelation 4:1 represents the secret rapture of the church, which is to take place shortly, removing all Christians from the earth before the events occur that we find described in the rest of the book.[5]

Such an interpretation is the very opposite of the preterist position. Instead of saying that it is fulfilled in the first century, when it was written, most of it is declared to pertain only to the end of history, after the return of Christ.[6]

A major objection to this futurist interpretation of Revelation is that it would remove the book from relevance to the churches to which it was addressed (See Summers 1951, 33-34). If we are to understand what any prophet meant, we must begin with the times in which the author wrote and the circumstance in which the first readers were involved. When we look at the churches at the end of the first century we see the difficulty they faced, the persecution, and can understand their need for a prophetic word. We need not know whether or not there was general persecution of Christians by Rome under Domitian, for we know that some in Asia Minor were being caused much suffering (Rev. 1:9), and this is the problem addressed by John in the book. What good would it do to tell them that in a few thousand years all the nations would gather together in the valley of Megiddo, and Jesus would bring an army and destroy their enemies? Would that encourage them to be patient a little longer?

A second problem with this interpretation is that it implies that nations that have long ceased to exist will be resurrected so that Jesus will overcome them in a final great battle. For example, there is the role of the Roman Empire in the book. Dispensationalists disagree concerning whether or not the Roman Empire will be raised up again, but most see that as a distinct necessity if the predictions are to be fulfilled literally.[7] Others indicate that the

Roman Empire still exists.[8] This seems most strange to any student of history. It seems just as strange to think of the ancient city of Babylon and the Babylonian Empire as being resurrected after these millennia and again becoming a world power to be defeated by Christ.

The futurist position has other problems, especially in the usual forms of dispensationalism, but they are better discussed elsewhere.[9]

Historicist Interpretation

The Historicist, Continuous-historical, or Church-historical classification of interpretations is a collection of different approaches to Revelation, but they can all be called historicist since they think of the Book of Revelation as predicting events covering all the history from the time of John to the Second Advent of Christ.

The Historicist interpretation is usually traced to Joachim of Floris (died in 1201) (Ladd 1972). What Joachim did was to find in the symbols and figures of Revelation the events and hopes of the twelfth century. For him, "the Beast from the sea is Islam, wounded to the death by the Crusades; the False Prophet is identified with the heretical sects of the age; Babylon is Rome, no longer pagan, but worldly and vice-ridden nevertheless. Of the seven heads of the Beast the fifth is the Emperor Frederick I, and the sixth Saladin" (Swete 1951, ccxii). Joachim was loyal to the Roman church, but others quickly turned the method of interpretation against the church and considered the papacy to be the Antichrist. From then to the present this interpretation, in various forms, has been a dominant one and led to the adoption of a form of it by the Protestant reformers. By that time it was becoming common to see in the book, not secular history, but primarily the history of the church—hence the term church-historical (Swete). Six problems with Historicism should be noted.

1. It requires continuous reinterpretations.[10] Amazing ingenuity has been expended by historicists to fit the symbols of the book into the facts of history. But each of them has concluded that he or she was living in the very last days before the Second Advent and has fitted the symbols into the history up to that point, speculating about the historical events still to come. Herein lies the failure of the view. One who studies the history of the interpretation of Revelation can see the problem more and more clearly, as it is noted how each interpreter has seen only up to that time, yet has fitted all the symbols of the book into that history. So there have been many applications of some of the pictures in Revelation.

Each century has been seen by some interpreters as the very last before the coming of Christ and the end of the world. Many such predictions of the end of the world, based on Revelation and Daniel, have been made in the last century, and some of these have been very specific. Recently I heard of another such person predicting the end of the world in the next few weeks. This would mean that there is no sense completing this writing, since the book will not have time to be published! But I have heard many such positive predictions in my lifetime and have been able to list one such prediction for almost every century since the first. To me, this is a clear indication that something is wrong with the method itself.

2. The method has produced no lasting consensus. Though a great variety of interpretations can be classified as historicist, almost as many varieties as interpreters, all of them have much in common, especially since the twelfth century. A strong emphasis has been placed on chronology and thus on mathematics. F. F. Bruce points out:

> No important contribution to the exegesis of Revelation was made by those who concentrated on its numerics—whether J. A. Bengel in Germany or Joseph Mede, Sir Isaac Newton and William Whiston in England—eminent as these exegetes were in other fields of study. The book itself has suffered in its reputation from the extravagances of some of its interpreters, who have treated it as if it were a table of mathematical conundrums or a divinely inspired *Old Moore's Almanac* (Bruce 1986, 1595).

3. The method is not based on sound exegesis. The subjective nature of the historicist interpretation is seen in the wide variety of them. Each interpreter feels free to make her or his own calculations and applications of symbols to history. What uniformity there is can be attributed to the fact that some of them investigate works already published and make the changes felt to be beneficial. Thus some of the symbols have been interpreted in the same general manner since the sixteenth-century Reformation. Yet, the time span covered has stretched out as time has gone on, and the consequence is an infinite variety of interpretations and chronologies. Further, some have gloried in finding in Revelation fancied references to atomic bombs, airplanes, and army tanks.[11] Once one begins this kind of search for modern things, there is nothing to check the imagination in its free roaming quest for coincidences in spelling or sound. But since there are no rules guiding such an inquiry, one cannot feel free to follow it or to accept the conclusions of one who does.

4. It is based on the equation of a day and a year. All those who seek to calculate the time of the end of the age through the continuous-historical method seek to locate the times of events by the year/day method (Summers 1951, 39-41). In prophecy, it is said, a day is equal to one year. Three and a half days are then three and a half years. Hence, 1260 days are taken as 1260 years. This method

of calculation is usually supported by reference to Numbers 14:34, Ezekiel 4:4-6, and Daniel 9:25. However, none of these presents a general rule, and all of them together are negated by other passages in which a day is not a year, and a year is not a day.[12] Further, this method has repeatedly led to predictions of the end that have been proven wrong by failure.

5. It is not exegetically sound. An explanation of Revelation in terms of the history of the church and the world is not in any sense an exegesis of the text. Instead it is an "application" of the text to certain events and situations in history. Just as futuristic dispensationalism is based, not on sound exegesis of the New Testament, but on a theology based on an unusual interpretation of certain Old Testament passages, so historicist explanations are based on an unproven method of deriving dates and periods of time from the few indications of time in Revelation. This method is based on a particular interpretation of Daniel, which in turn is based on the unproven year-day principle.

6. It results in distortion of Scripture and history. This search for coincidences has led many of the historicists to read history in the quest for new applications of the details of some vision to a particular date or period.[13] This has resulted in some bizarre interpretations of certain visions and to much distortion of history. Since the Reformation, the Roman Catholics have written their own interpretations in answer to those of the Protestants, but even if we look only at those of the Protestants, there has been an amazing variety.

During the American Revolution, some Colonial preachers declared that Britain was the beast from the sea (Rev. 13), and that the Church of England was part of the Roman Catholic beast from the land. After the war this interpretation held no more interest, but room had to be made somehow for the French Revolution. Samuel F. B. Morse wrote a series of articles declaring his conviction that the Roman Catholic nations of Europe were conspiring to undermine American liberties (See Patterson 1988, 448).

The Russian revolution of 1917 brought that nation to the attention of historicist interpreters, and this interest has continued to the present. Russia is often identified with the "power of the North" of Ezekiel 38-39, and in various ways with the antichristian powers of Revelation 12-20.

Certain symbols in Revelation which have long fascinated historicists and caused them to search history for some way to identify their fulfillments. They include the two beasts of chapter 13, the number of the second beast (666), the battle of Armageddon (although no battle is mentioned), and Babylon.[14] The second beast, from the land, is often called "Antichrist," though that term does not occur in this Book, but only in First and Second John. For most of these two thousand years, minds great and small have pointed to one or another historical persons as "The Antichrist."[15] Swete pointed up the folly of this method of revising interpretations with the progress of events (Swete 1951, ccxv). By the nineteenth century, some were turning away from the continuous-historical method to some form of futurism. And in Germany there was arising a new way of looking at the book as simply a noncanonical apocalypse, which could best be studied by searching for pagan sources. Both futurism and source criticism are still being used to interpret Revelation by some of those who reject the continuous-historical interpretation.

Idealist or Philosophy of History Interpretation

Another method of interpretation for those who reject the Preterist, Futurist, and Historicist approaches is one that has a number of forms and names. Such writers as Leon Morris and Merrill Tenney call it "Idealist," since it stresses ideas rather than historic events. Both writers like some aspects of this interpretation but feel that it mostly ignores the historical background of the book. This criticism was more true of some of the earlier forms than of writers of the present.

Merrill Tenney, who was head of the graduate school at Wheaton, also called it "spiritualist" since he said it interpreted the whole book "spiritually" rather than "literally (Tenney 1957, 143)." However, both of these terms are used in such different ways that to decide exactly what a writer means when one of them is used is difficult. Although Tenney was not a dispensationalist, he was enough of a futurist to be fond of seeking a "literal interpretation" of each part of Revelation. Probably the most enlightening discussion of the meaning of "literal interpretation" is that by Vern S. Poythress, Professor of New Testament Interpretation at Westminister Theological Seminary (Poythress 1987). He concluded his discussion by writing that "literal interpretation is a confusing term, capable of being used to beg many of the questions at stake in the interpretation of the Bible (96)." The same can be said about the term "spiritual interpretation."

Dr. Mounce of Whitworth College refers to this interpretation as "idealist or timeless symbolic (1977,43)." The latter term refers to the idea that the Book of Revelation does not describe specific dates or events to take place in the future but rather presents the principles on which God works in all history. He refers to William Milligan, of the late nineteenth century, as a pioneer of this view. Raymond Calkins wrote in the same manner a few decades later.[16]

The idea of "principles of history" leads to the term that is now much preferred: "philosophy of history." Those who use this term today do begin with the first century background of Revelation and know that there is no way to understand the book without seeing it in that historical setting. But they deny that the author predicted that certain events would occur at specific dates in the future. They insist instead that the book sets forth the principles that govern history.

Such an approach to the book has the value of beginning properly with the historical situation of the author. It sees the whole book against its own background, just as we should look at any other biblical book. So it recognizes that the book had meaning to the earliest readers. This interpretation avoids the problems of the historicist and futurist approaches. It gets from the book some encouragement for every Christian and faith in the providence of God. This is an important aspect of the study of Revelation, since the book has been chiefly a closed book to all except a few.

Yet dangers in this method have misled some interpreters. It would be possible to think of the philosophy of history as working itself out in some impersonal fashion, forgetting that it is God who is at work. On the other hand, some have presented history as a continual struggle of good and evil, with no denouement in view.[17] While scholars who have used this term for their method of interpretation have generally avoided this pitfall and have presented a Christian philosophy of history, there is value in using a different and more accurate term. We do not differ with those who speak of a "philosophy of history" interpretation of Revelation, but suggest that "theology of history" more accurately describes what the best of them have done.

Theological Interpretation

If one takes the idealist view and avoids the problems that may attend it, the result can be close to a true theology of history. This biblical theology of history is the foundation for all prophecy in both the Old Testament and the New.

Prophecy is not so much concerned with predicting future events, though it may include that, as in throwing the light of eternity on human lives. The Old Testament prophets made some specific predictions of events (almost all of them concerned with the Messiah, or the preservation of the people through whom the Messiah would come), but the bulk of their preaching was the message that (1) God is holy; (2) sin separates from God and brings punishment; (3) God is merciful and wants to save; and (4) God has a plan for forgiveness and salvation from sin.

This method recognizes that God is Lord of history and that all history is thus moving toward the fulfillment of God's will and purpose.

Five times John declares emphatically that his book is a prophecy. (1:3, 27:7, 10, 18, 19) and that it must not be altered or ignored. We are then justified in treating it like other books of prophecy. The prophet always speaks to his or her own time, but speaks in the light of eternal truths about the ways of God, and those truths apply to every age, as well as to the one immediately at hand. Thus we are justified in considering Revelation to be presenting a theology of the way in which God deals with humans throughout history. The difference between a philosophy of history[18] and a theology may be primarily a difference in emphasis. Theology puts the emphasis on God, while the philosophy may tend to emphasize history. Fiorenza is at her best when she declares Revelation to be a "theology of justice and judgment."[19] This is clearly seen in the cry of the martyrs for justice to be done, and in the plight of the woman in chapter 12, and of the camp of the saints in chapter 16.

The theological interpretation of Revelation is what Fiorenza and some others call "Eschatological." But they are using the term in a technical sense different from that of the futurists who use it to mean those events that will immediately precede the second advent of Christ. Fiorenza uses it to mean something like "God-breaking-into-history" or the way God assures justice and judgment in spite of history. One way to see the difference between the two views is to see how they treat the passage about "Armageddon" (16:16). Futurists put great stress on the coming "Battle of Armageddon," even though no such battle is described. All that is said is that the forces of evil gather together at "Armageddon" for battle. But the worst the forces of evil could do was to prepare to fight; without a battle, the Lord overcame! God brings victory in his own way, without the help of human beings, and without any of us God will bring an end to history. Eschatology has to do with the work of God, rather than the course of history.[20] Thus the Book of Revelation is concerned with the work of God, not the course of historical events.

With this view of the various methods of interpretation, we can turn to see what the book says about "Babylon."

Description of Babylon in Revelation

The name *Babylon* is used six times in Revelation (14:8; 16:19; 17:5; 18:2, 10, 21). In each case it is called "the great city," or "Babylon the great," in ironic reference to Daniel 4:30 where Nebuchadnezzar looked out over the city in pride and exclaimed, "Is not this Babylon the great which I have built?" (translated from the Septuagint, where we find the same expression as in Revelation). The term "Babylon the Great" is used nowhere else in the Old Testament. It is used in Revelation as an ironic reference to the pride of Nebuchadnezzar, which went before his fall (Beale 1984, 249ff). Seven times we find the term "the great city" without the name "Babylon" (16:19a; 17:18; 18:10, 16, 18, 19).[21] Twice the city is referred to as "the great harlot" (17:1; 19:2). In each case the word "great" is clearly an ironic reference to human pride. This human pride would come to the mind of John's first readers as they thought of Babylon the great and the ancient Tower of Babel. The tower had been a monument to human's desire to be as great as God, and Nebuchednezzar had gloried in the great city that he himself had built for his own exaltation. It seems fitting therefore for John to speak of Rome as "Babylon, the great city." "Babylon," then, though it primarily refers to the city of Rome (Ellul, 189), stands for the tendency of humankind to self-worship (Morris 1969, 180).

J. Massyngberde Ford insists that "Babylon" refers to Jerusalem. She does this because it is consonant with her theory that the bulk of the book was written by John the Baptist and his disciples, and was not originally a Christian book. Christian editors and writers added the first three chapters and the last three and radically edited some of the rest (1975, 28-56). We may assert against this that Babylon is in Revelation never referred to as "adultress" (*moicheia*), but always as "harlot" (porn). Ford then points out that Israel is referred to as a "harlot" in such passages as Hosea 2:5, 3:3, 4:15, Isaiah 1:21, and Jeremiah 5:7. This only shows that the meaning of the term must not be decided on the basis of etymology or Old Testament usage, but by a study of the context and manner of usage in Revelation. The description of Babylon and its fall in 17 and 18 can hardly be applied to Jerusalem. Also the contrast between Babylon "the great city" and the New Jerusalem "the holy city" helps to make the meaning clear. If "the holy city" is all the people of God, it makes sense to think of Babylon, which the world likes to call "the great city," as all other people, under the ultimate control of Satan.

The term *Babylon* is used also in a much-discussed passage in 1 Peter 5:13, but without the expression "the Great." Since Peter directed his book to the "the exiles of the Dispersion" (1:1), it is natural to think that he was reminding them that Christians live in the world as exiles just as the Jews once lived as exiles in Babylon.[22]

The first actual use of the name "Babylon" is in 14:8, where we read, "It is fallen! It is fallen! Babylon the great."[23] This proleptic announcement of the fall of Babylon is typical of the author of Revelation,[24] and the actual fall is not described until chapter 18. This verse then is one of the clear indications that the Book of Revelation is not presented in chronological form.[25]

In 16:19 there is first a statement about "the great city" being torn into three parts by an earthquake,[26] which also destroyed "the cities of the gentiles," and then a parallel statement about "Babylon the great" being "remembered by God." Thus John indicates that though punishment for sin is long in coming, it is sure, because God is the one who sends it (Fiorenza 1985, 6). This, too, is a preliminary announcement of the judgment of Babylon, but the judgment to come is almost present.

In Chapter 17 we see the way in which John was shown a vision of Babylon the great. She was a harlot sitting on the beast. It was natural for John to see Babylon as a woman, since cities were always thought of as feminine, just as they are today.[27] In this chapter we find the harlot in stark contrast with the woman in chapter 12. This contrast, indeed, is one of the surest clues to the identity and meaning of Babylon. As the woman in 12 was representative of the faithful people of God, so this harlot in 17 represents all who rebel against God. John and his readers would think immediately of Rome as being the epitome of opposition to the will and purposes of God (cf. Rist 1957, 471; Bowman 1955, 91, 113).

John is first told that he will be shown the "judgment of the great harlot who is sitting on many waters," and he is shown the woman sitting on the beast of chapter 13. The "many waters" reflects the reference to ancient Babylon in Jeremiah 51:13, and sitting on the beast shows her close connection with the forces of evil.[28] As John looks he sees that on her forehead is a name written, which is a name of "mystery," meaning that it is something revealed (as in 1:20).[29] As the woman in chapter 12 is the mother of the church, so this harlot (metropolis = mother-city)[30] is the mother of harlots, "the source and fountain-head of its impurities (Swete 1951, 217)." This natural suggestion of the meaning of the expression "mother of harlots" is much better than some historicist applications.[31]

In 17:7 the angel begins to explain to John some of the meaning of what has been seen. Note that the angel says that the beast on which the woman sits "was, and is not, and is about to come up from the abyss and to go into destruction." This is in conscious contrast to God "who is and who was and who is to come" (1:4, 8). God is eternal; evil beings will come to a final end. This is a basic part of the message of Revelation.

The explanations of the angel do not remove all difficulties. In verses 9 and 10 we see that the heads are seven hills, which clearly points to Rome, and then that the heads are also seven kings, or emperors. Scholars who have tried have always failed to identify with certainty a particular seven of whom John may have been speaking. But John centers attention on the eighth. The double significance of the heads points out the fluidity of the symbolism, and the impossibility of working out a sure chronological interpretation. John was more interested in the theological concepts of God and his victory over evil. John's primary purpose here is to show that the horns will turn against the harlot they have been supporting and punish her as Oholibah was punished in Ezekiel 23:25-29, 47. A comparison of the two passages shows that John was saying that just as Jerusalem was punished for her sin, so much more will Rome be punished. There is no cohesion in evil, and the house divided against itself will fall, and this fall is in the plan of God (Rev. 17:17). The closing verse of this chapter identifies the woman as "the great city" and as the one who "reigns over the king of the earth" (verse 18, NAS). Thus the fall of Babylon is described briefly but with finality in 17:16-17.

Chapter 18 is a series of songs about the fall of Babylon, in which John has drawn on the concepts and expressions found in the Old Testament prophecies against Babylon in Isaiah 13 and Jeremiah 51, along with prophecies against Edom in Isaiah and Nineveh in Nahum 3. "Babylon" is named only in verses 2 and 21, but is referred to in verses 16 and 18 as "the great city."

The jubilant rejoicing evident in chapter 18 has been labeled subchristian by such commentators as Moffatt, who postulated a pagan source (Expositor's Greek Testament v, 455-456). However, this is nothing other than a call for justice and judgment on evil people and evil forces, such as are found in the Old Testament psalms and prophets. Fiorenza compares the chapter to a courtroom scene, with a class action suit against Babylon (Rome) for murder, with the plaintiffs being all martyred Christians, such as the ones under the altar in chapters 6 and 20 (Fiorenza 1981, 171-172). The point of these two chapters with reference to the fall of Babylon is that Babylon is receiving a just reward, which God has promised to all sinners. The concept of justice is strained for some by verse 6, which in the central command calls for Babylon to receive "double" for all she has done. Meredith Kline has made a strong case for translating this "equivalent" here and in all similar passages (Kline n.d. 177-178) Doing so would lessen the contrast with the first part of verse 6, and would stress justice more adequately.

Identification of Babylon

Babylon is one of five enemies of Christ and the church as described by John. These enemies are: Dragon (12); Beast from the sea (13:1-10); Beast from the land (13:11-18); Scarlet woman (17); and Babylon (17—18). John makes clear that the dragon is in charge of all the other four. They do his work in the world, and all their authority and power is given to them by the dragon. So it is fitting that he describes all five of them as going to the same doom in the lake of fire. John also clearly states that they are all overcome "by the blood of the Lamb" and not by human warfare.

Undoubtedly the first readers identified Babylon in their own minds as Rome and the Roman empire, which found its center in Rome. This would be the view of all preterists, who see no other interpretation than that of the first century. This is the correct place to begin to understand any book—in its own historical setting. Yet this book is prophecy and, as the New Testament clearly teaches about the Old Testament prophecies, they have relevance beyond their own time. This is true partly because God does not change his ways of dealing with people, so when God reveals his ways to the prophets we can know God will continue to act in those ways in all generations.

John used the Old Testament prophecies in just this way as he took wordings and ideas from prophecies that had been directed against other cities and applied them to the punishment and destruction of Babylon/Rome of his own day. This fact gives us room to look for new applications of John's prophecies to the enemies of God in our day, rather than limiting their relevance to his century. Thus the preterist view is insufficient.

The futurist skips over the intervening centuries or millennia and interprets Babylon to mean the resurrected and rebuilt city and empire of ancient Babylon. Each futurist of the last two centuries has assumed that he or she was living in the last days—in the days when the end was imminent and has therefore assumed that ancient cities and nations were being rebuilt, or were about to be. All have so far been proven wrong. Why believe in those now proclaiming such a concept?

Ralph Earle denies the futuristic dispensational concept that calls for a rebuilt Babylon to be destroyed, but is not far from it when he judges that the four enemies of God under the power and direction of Satan are various federations of world power that will come about just before the end (Earle n.d., 598-599).

Historicists since the pre-Reformation period have thought of Babylon as the Roman Catholic Church. This would leave the first centuries with nothing but puzzles in Revelation. If the world stands long enough, this application also will be outgrown as others have been in the past. Already changes in the world situation make such an application less relevant than in the sixteenth century.

As we have pointed out previously, Linn insisted that Babylon must not be equated with the Roman Catholic Church, and that it is wrong to make Protestant churches the reference in 17:5—as F. G. Smith did in his historicist interpretation. Linn gave strong reasons against this understanding.[32] We should also point out that Linn was not the only Church of God scholar protesting against the historicist interpretation of Revelation. C. E. Brown also argued against it. Though Brown did not write an exposition of Revelation, he taught in his college classes something akin to a theology of justice/judgment. He made clear that the book was a "tract for hard times" and that any thoughtful Christian, without a detailed knowledge of the course of church history, ought to be able to read the book and receive comfort and strength from that reading.[33]

F. G. Smith once said to me: "If I were proven to be wrong in my interpretation of Revelation, it would not change my faith in the church. I saw the church before I began the study of Daniel and Revelation." This remark, being made in the most sober manner, made a deep impression on me. I knew then that he was not only conscious of the criticism others made of his interpretative approach, but that he was determined to follow truth wherever it led.

In discussing the harlot of chapter 17, Otto F. Linn once wrote:

> By some queer method of reasoning some people have explained this profligate woman as the papacy and her daughters as the Protestant denominations. In the first place this cannot be true, for John uses the present tense in 17:18, the woman was then reigning "over the kings of the earth." In the second place his obvious use of contrast makes this impossible. The children of the first woman are explained as the converts of the church, how then could the children of the second woman who stands in contrast with this righteous woman be institutions, denominations? The children of the first woman are definitely declared to be those "that keep the commandments of God, and hold the testimony of Jesus," which would indicate that in the contrasting symbol the daughters would be those who do not keep the commandments of God or the testimony of Jesus (Linn 1942, 135).

This comment has been quoted in full because this concept is one that has been used widely in the Church of God reformation movement (Anderson, Indiana) to show the place of the movement in prophecy. Yet it is not built on a strong exegetical foundation, for John said nothing about the "daughters" except to call the woman "mother of harlots." This expression simply amplifies the nature of the woman herself. Nothing is made of any children of the woman in the book, and they play no part in the picture at all. Yet the "denominations" that are supposed to be their antitype have been important for centuries. Surely if that were John's intention, he would have said more.

Conclusion

Can Babylon have a wider application today than in the first century? When we speak, not of exegesis, but of application, we realize that we need to understand what the Book of Revelation has to say to us today. In exegesis we must deal with the first century. But in application we can deal with our own time.

We have already seen that there are no dates in Revelation, and that only two main time periods are mentioned, three and one-half days/times/years and one thousand years. The first is the time for the dominance of evil in this world, and the second is the time for the reigning of the saints. The relative length of these two time periods is what is important. John was not concerned with chronological predictions, but with presenting the theological position that God is truly in charge of the destiny of the world and everything in it. Once we see that, we see that there are no predictions of specific historical events of future eras.

We then find relevance for every age. We see that Satan is a defeated enemy, and that the four enemies under Satan are defeated as well, and will receive their doom from the hand of God, and that it will be the same as Satan's.

Babylon is then a type of all human opposition to God and his kingdom.[34] Revelation views human evil, suffering, and salvation from the viewpoint of eternity, and from this viewpoint all human opposition to God is, like Babylon, under the control and direction of Satan and is leading to the same end.

The Book of Revelation was clearly written as a "tract for hard times." The church was facing persecution, and some thought its very existence was threatened. It needed the kind of encouragement and exhortation to stand firm that John gave them by his writing. F. F. Bruce, in his introduction to a commentary on Revelation, pointed out that "the book has always spoken its message most clearly to readers who were involved in the same kind of situation as those to whom it was first addressed" (Bruce 1986, 1593).

Endnotes

1. For another way of classifying the interpretations, see George Ladd 1988, 171-177. See also Ray Summers 1951. For a historical survey of methods of interpretation since the second century, see Henry B. Swete 1919, 318-336.

2. Otto F. Linn 1942. This book was volume 4 of a set, and the first three were printed by the Gospel Trumpet Company (now Warner Press, Inc.), but because of the opposition of F. G. Smith, who had been long known for his "Church-historical" view of Revelation, the company would not put their imprint on the book. They printed it for the author with the imprint of their commercial press. (For details, see Harold L. Phillips 1979, 249. Yet Linn, who had previously done a master's thesis on Revelation, was a good scholar, and deserves our attention.

3. *The Late Great Planet Earth*, 1970. His other books are simply variations on the same theme, that Revelation 4-20, and most of the Old Testament, consists of predictions of the period between the "Secret Rapture" of the saints, and the "Tribulation."

4. This position is usually called futurist, although it is in fact a special kind of historicist interpretation, since the letters in chapters two and three are taken as an outline of all of church history between the first century and the secret rapture, which begins the final events of the world. But it is called futurist since the bulk of the book is applied to the last-age of the earth, and is therefore still future.

5. Besides the notes in the Scofield Bible, see also J. Dwight Pentecost 1958; John F. Walvoord 1966; Vern S. Poythress 1987.

6. John Walvoord 1966; Tim LaHaye n.d., in *Revelation Illustrated* arguing against the extreme futurist or dispensational position, calls it "a dispensational scheme of redemptive history [that] posits two different people of God—Israel and the Church—and therefore two programs of prophecy. Accordingly, in Revelation the seven letters to the seven churches . . . have usually been seen as an outline of a seven-stage church era. . . . This view is based not on an inductive study of Revelation but on a system of theology drawn largely from the O. T., literally interpreted."

7. Dwight J. Pentecost 1958, 318-326. In the pages following this passage, Pentecost presents the common dispensational concept that Russia, which did not exist until centuries after John wrote, is described as a major participant in the final struggle at the Second Advent.

8. G. H. N. Peters n.d., 643. Peters gave long chapters to his proof that the Roman Empire did not cease to exist in the fifth century but is still in existence today. He is quoted with apparent approval by Pentecost.

9. Vern S. Poythress n.d. This recent study is unique in its irenic criticism of dispensationalism, which is the most common form of futurist interpretation and will well repay careful study. See also Kenneth E. Jones 1981, 333-341.

10. G. C. Berkouwer, in his book, *The Return of Christ* (1972, 274ff.) uses the term "continuous reinterpretation," but not in a historicizing sense. His method results in a view close to the "philosophy of history" view later described.

11. Bruce, F. F. 1986, 1595. This kind of imaginative applications that caused G. K. Chesterton to write that "though John saw many strange monsters in his vision, he saw no creature so wild as one of his own commentators" 1908, 29. Qtd. by Eugene H. Peterson 1988, xiii.

12. Isaiah 7:8; 16:14; 23:15; Jeremiah 29:10; Daniel 9:2; and Matthew 20:19.

13. See Fiorenza 1985, 46: "The proponents of this interpretation seek to trace in the sequence of visions a continuous or dialectical line of history. That John wanted to portray the temporal course of events of the end time is even maintained by the *endgeschichtlich* interpretation. However, previous attempts to explain the sequence of visions or the total composition of Rev. either by a linear or cyclic understanding of time have not succeeded in presenting a convincing interpretation, as a quick glance at the variety and multiplicity of proposed solutions can reveal. The central apocalyptic section (4:1—22:5), in particular, creates difficulties for these successive temporal interpretations, because here the author mixes together past, present, and future elements of time. His doublets and his repetition of an entire cycle of visions cannot be satisfactorily explained as a temporal or historical sequence."

14. In discussing Babylon in Revelation 17, Dr. Otto Linn remarks: "By some queer method of reasoning some people have explained this profligate woman as the papacy and her daughters as the Protestant denominations" (1942).

15. Persons identified in this way have included certain ancient Roman Caesars, popes, British kings, various conspiratorial groups (real or imagined), Kaiser Wilhelm, Hitler, Mussolini, Haile Selasse, and various current world leaders.

16. Raymond Calkins, *The Social Message of the Book of Revelation*, New York: The Woman's Press, 1920. Referred to by Merrill Tenney, *Interpreting Revelation*, page 143.

17. Such writers as Mounce, Summers, and Ladd criticize the idealist view because they think it leaves no room for any predicted events, which they feel are a major part of the eschatological purpose of Revelation.
18. Feuillet is one of those who advocates a philosophy of history as the best approach to Revelation.
19. Elizabeth Schussler Fiorenza, 1985, page 24: "The main concern of the author is not the interpretation of history but the issue of power. The focal point of the 'already' and 'not yet' of eschatological salvation is not history but the kingdom of God and the rule of Christ. Therefore the main symbol of Revelation is the image of the throne and its main motif that of kingship." Also on page 6: "The Book of [Revelation] is written for those 'who hunger and thirst for justice' in a socio-political situation that is characterized by injustice, suffering and dehumanizing power. In ever-new contrast images the rhetoric of [Revelation] elaborates the opposition between the life-giving power of God and the death-dealing power of Rome without falling prey to a total metaphysical or ethical dualism. Power is 'given' to the anti-divine forces for a 'short time.'
20. Fiorenza 1985, 46: "If [Revelation] is not structured according to a 'temporal-historical' sequence, then the question arises: are not its contents instead thematically ordered? Hence, I would argue that the main concern of [Revelation] is not [salvation] history, but eschatological, that is, the breaking-in of God's kingdom and the destruction of the hostile godless powers. The author of [Revelation] is, indeed, aware of time, but he knows only a 'short time' before the eschaton. The eschatology of [Revelation] is, therefore, not dependent on or legitimated by a certain course of historical events. Rather, time and history have significance only insofar as they constitute the 'little while' before the end. This means that in [Revelation] 'history' is completely subordinated to eschatology and receives its significance from the future. Thus it is necessary to analyze the eschatological understanding underlying [Revelation] and its composition and to explicate how this eschatological understanding is related to the central purpose of the book, which is to strengthen and to encourage the Christian communities of Asia Minor."
21. In 11:8 there is another reference to "the great city," which many commentators take to mean Jerusalem, primarily because of the statement "where their Lord was crucified," but which is a proleptic reference to "Babylon the great city." In the same verse it is called "spiritually" or "analogically" "Sodom" and "Egypt." It is true that Isaiah compared the people of Jerusalem once to Sodom, but the city was never called Sodom and was certainly never referred to as "Egypt." Yet Rome could be compared to both because Egypt represented bondage, and Sodom represented evil. (Cf. also the note by Rist in IB, Vol. 12, 447).
22. H. Seebas, "Babylon" in *New International Dictionary of New Testament Theology*, Vol. I, 141. Rome was also called Babylon in 2 Bar. 11:1 and Sib. Or. 5:143ff. For a strong contradictory argument that Babylon is Jerusalem, see J. Massyngberde Ford, *Revelation*, Garden City: Doubleday, 1975, 282-288.
23. Cf. Isaiah 21:9, where the Septuagint uses a different form of the verb and does not add the words "the great."
24. John sometimes brings a character on stage very abruptly, without previous preparation (great city, 11:8; Beast, 11:2; Harlot, 16:19).
25. This fact, and the author's pattern of intercalation, have led historicists to speak of some kind of historical parallelism. But this has in turn led to the problem of fitting the progressive events of history into the Procrustean bed of John's

outline, and we have to wonder if John would recognize any of the multitude of outlines formed by his interpreters!

26. Cf. with Zech. 14:4, which is applied to Jerusalem.

27. Fiorenza 1981, 161. As she further pointed out, the Old Testament prophets regularly spoke of cities as feminine, and developed the idea of the bride or wife of God, and of the harlot as unfaithful.

28. John does not seek to show us logically consistent pictures but to reveal theological truths that can strengthen our faith in God and clarify our vision of the world as seen by God.

29. Translators have used three different ways of punctuating around the word since the Greek is ambiguous. The basic question is, Is mystery part of the name of the harlot, or part of the description of it? Here we have taken it to be descriptive. It is a name with a meaning to be revealed, as it is in v. 7ff.

30. Beckwith points to the fitness of this suggestion (1922, 693), and Swete agrees (1951, 217).

31. F. G. Smith's application of the "harlot daughters" to the protestant churches seems to be making too much of a simple phase and also ignores the parallel statement "[mother of] the abominations of the earth."

32. In discussing the harlot of chapter 17, Linn states: "By some queer method of reasoning some people have explained this profligate woman as the papacy and her daughters as the Protestant denominations. In the first place this cannot be true for John uses the present tense in 17:18, the woman was then reigning 'over the kings of the earth.' In the second place his obvious use of the contrast makes this impossible. The children of the first woman are explained as the converts of the church, how then could the children of the second woman who stands in contrast with this righteous woman be institutions, denominations? The children of the first woman are definitely declared to be those 'that keep the commandments of God, and hold the testimony of Jesus,' which would indicate that in the contrasting symbol the daughters would be those who do not keep the commandments of God or the testimony of Jesus" (Linn 135). He continues on the next page with two more reasons.

33. Other similar statements are Thomas F. Torrance, The *Apocalypse Today*, 115; Leon Morris, *Revelation of St. John*, 213; Robert H. Mounce, *The Book of Revelation*, 320; F. F. Bruce, "Revelation," *International Bible Commentary*, 1622.

JAMES EARL MASSEY

B.R.E., B.Th., Detroit Bible College; M.A., Oberlin Graduate School of Theology; D.D., Asbury Theological Seminary.

Dean and Professor of New Testament and Preaching, Anderson University School of Theology (Anderson, Indiana). Long-term ministerial and teaching colleague of Dr. Boyce W. Blackwelder.

Chapter **10**

Ministerial Authority in Biblical Perspective
by James Earl Massey

Ministerial authority, as the New Testament illustrates it, must be understood as the privileged right to serve some spiritual end *for* and *within* a communal setting; the welfare of the ones being served is the chief motivating factor. The right so to serve is derived from Christ (Matt. 28:18), but that right is practically exercised by consent of the community and for its best interests (see 1 Cor. 12:4-7).

Understood thusly, ministerial authority is a derived authority. It is an authority disciplined by a motivating love (Gal. 5:13b). It is an authority for which the minister is accountable to the church (Matt. 18:15-20), to other ministers (1 Cor. 3:8-9; 1 Pet. 5:5b), and to God (Heb. 13:17). All of these passages help the reader of the New Testament to understand that ministerial authority must always be viewed in context. According to the New Testament writings, the power, right, or privilege to do something as a minister is exercised in a communal setting and usually requires that community's consent.[1]

I

Among the many passages in the New Testament regarding ministry, there is an understood relation between those who minister and the community that is being served. The salutation of Paul when writing to the Philippian believers addressed "all the saints in Christ Jesus who are at Philippi, with the bishops and deacons" (1:1), clearly recognizing the understood relationship between the house-churches and their stated officers or leaders.[2] The term "bishop," from *episkopos*, means someone who has oversight within the fellowship, while the latter term "deacon," from *diakonos*, points to someone in an appointed category who is presumably subservient in role. In 1 Timothy 3:8-13, some basic qualifications are stated for those chosen to serve as deacons, but that passage does not detail their task.

The New Testament does not explain the range of responsibilities that could devolve upon a deacon, but it does offer a rather full statement of the expected duties of a bishop. According to 1 Timothy 3:1-7, a bishop was expected to be an official teacher of the faith and a care-manager within the church. That word "care-manager" is translated from *epimeleomai* (3:5) and means to care for; the term is found only here and in Luke's account of the Good Samaritan Parable (Luke 10:25-37), in which the Samaritan's attentiveness to the ailing man who had been robbed, wounded, and left for dead is highlighted as caring concern. The accent in 1 Timothy 3:1-5 is upon the bishop's diligent and detailed exercise of concerned caring for the people.[3] Given this accent on concerned caring, it is increasingly clear about the kind of loving relationship the minister must nurture as a "bishop," i.e., as one entrusted to oversee the affairs of a local church.

The common understanding is that "bishops and deacons" were two different groups of church leaders.[4] It appears that both exercised an authority both by divine order and congregational regard. Paul's use of the plural in addressing the leaders suggests that separate house-churches were being addressed, but one should not overlook that he wrote to them all as a single congregation; his use of the singular for "church" in Philippians 4:15 makes this quite clear.[5]

The leadership pattern reflected in Philippians 1:1 and elsewhere in the New Testament writings reflects models of social organization known in other social groupings within Judaism. For example, the Pharisees were a religious group guided by its responsible *mebaqqer*, "supervisor," who served as spiritual leader and caring shepherd. So it was with the Essenes, some aspects of whose organizational pattern no doubt influenced that chosen by the early Christian believers.[6] In his highly informative treatment of this result, Joachim Jeremias also traced how "the title *mebaqqer* [supervisor] corresponds literally with the Greek *epikopos*" (1982, 261).

Paul's word to the ministerial leaders from Ephesus, gathered to his call at Miletus, was to remind them about their understood service to the churches:

> Take heed to yourselves and to all the flock, in [*en*, "within"] which the Holy Spirit has made you guardians, [*episkopous*], to feed the church of the Lord which he obtained with his own blood (Acts 20:28).

It should be underscored that those leaders being addressed were being reminded that they were *part* of the flock called the church, that they were made (literally "placed" as) guardians *within* the same community to which they belonged and to which they were to give service. The authority of the "bishop," the supervisor, the overseer, the pastor, falls within the province of the given duties known and regarded by the congregation; that authority does not exist separate from a given relationship between leader and group.

The concept should be kept in mind that ministry in the early church had the model of Jesus to influence the way its granted authority was to be handled. According to Mark 10:43, Jesus taught his disciples that "whoever would be first among you must be slave of all." The focus in this stricture is plainly against any spirit of self-serving as a leader within the church.

In 1 Corinthians 12:28 Paul explained that "God has appointed in the church first apostles, second prophets, third teachers, then workers of miracles, then healers, helpers, administrators." This extended statement moves from foundational ministries known when the church began to functions that would be needed in local settings as the church continued its life and work. Interestingly, those who are gifted in the "helpers" [*antilempseis*] category are actually close in service description to those who are the *diakonoi*, the "serving helpers." Likewise, a correspondence should be drawn between those who are *episcopoi*, "bishops, guardians," and those gifted to serve as administrator-directors [*kuberneseis*].

II

When the question is asked about how the deacon's role came to be, the passage in Acts 6:1-6 is usually cited. That passage is Luke's report about the appointment of The Seven, a group called into being to handle the daily distribution of foodstuffs and finances for needy members in the Jerusalem church. The apostles themselves for a time had been managing this service, making distribution from the proceeds of what had been sold and given to their handling to meet needs, as Acts 4:34-35 reports.

But this service had become too time-demanding for them, preventing a needed concentration on "prayer and . . . the ministry of the word" (Acts 6:4), thus the suggestion to the gathered church to appoint other hands for "serving tables" and the congregational choice of The Seven.[7] Although the seven persons selected are not called "deacons" in the narrative, the title has since been used for them, thus identifying them with a role that retained this same description in the churches of the Gentiles. That this early account of appointing persons for specific services was viewed as foundational can be sensed because even later in Acts (21:8) the group is referred to as "The Seven."

It is also interesting to note that when The Twelve made the suggestion that they be replaced in the service of distributing to the needy, the group of believers acted upon that suggestion as a concerned community; it was "the body of the disciples" (6:2), "the whole multitude" (6:5) that responded positively and chose the persons to replace them in this work.

Then The Twelve "laid their hands upon them" (6:6) and transferred this responsibility and authority to The Seven. This *seminkhah* ceremony would be repeated in other places as the gospel message spread and new congregations were established (Acts 13:3; 14:23), and in each instance some appointments to distinct service-roles were involved. The imposition of hands in each instance was more than a symbolic way to indicate appointment; it also associated the appointed persons with authorizing leaders. In time the church began to make formal distinctions between "bishops" and "deacons," between "those who labor in preaching and teaching" (1 Tim. 5:17) and persons appointed "to serve tables"—however widely or narrowly those services were expected to range.

This distinguishing between such service roles was never intended to suggest inequality among ministers before God. A full study of the New Testament descriptions of "ministry" will show that all believers are gifted and responsible for some service to each other and the communal group. Interestingly, in 1 Corinthians, which is largely defensive about his apostleship, Paul equates Apollos and himself as "servants through whom you believed, as the Lord assigned to each. I planted, Apollos watered, but God gave the growth. So neither he who plants nor he who waters is anything, but only God who gives the growth. He who plants and he who waters are equal, and each shall receive his wages according to his labor" (1 Cor. 3:5-8). This equality despite distinctions in service-roles is mentioned again in 1 Corinthians 12:4-7, where Paul explains:

> Now there are varieties of gifts, but the same Spirit; and there are varieties of service [*diakonion*], but the same Lord; and there are varieties of working, but it is the same God who inspires them all in every one. To each is given the manifestation of the Spirit for the common good.

Although those "who labor in preaching and teaching" are traditionally labeled as ministers, the fact is that the New Testament insists that all believers are involved in a stewardship, with each member responsible for some service *to* and *for* the other members of "the household of faith."

This point is also quite clear in Ephesians 4:7, 11-12, where it is stated:

> But grace was given to each of us according to the measure

of Christ's gift . . . And his gifts were that some should be apostles, some prophets, some evangelists, some pastors and teachers, to equip the saints for the work of ministry, for building up the body of Christ.

The words "for the work of ministry," *eis ergon diakonias*, can help us to correct the way we have mistakenly restricted this term *ministry* to but one set of servants in the church, namely those who labor as preachers and teachers of the Word. Although those who labor as preachers and teachers are surely distinguished within the congregations being served, they are at the same time equal sharers in a common fellowship of faith with all others in their communal groups.

The Petrine witness carries this emphasis to a still sharper point of focus. In 1 Peter 5:1-5 a passage is given to remind the elders, the *presbuteroi*, the local church leaders, about the importance of humility and the spirit of true service in relating to the church. The admonition is clear and forceful:

Tend the flock of God that is your charge, not by constraint but willingly, not for shameful gain but eagerly, not as domineering over those in your charge but being examples to the flock (vs. 2-3).

This exhortation is a reminder that all believers have rights that must be regarded and all must share in a relationship that should be honored out of a loyal love.

The spirit of sharing is stressed by Paul and Peter, and both of these chief apostles distinguished between kinds of services rendered within and to the group. The Pauline words in Corinthians and Ephesians have been noted above. A second passage from 1 Peter makes clear how he distinguished between the service-roles: In 4:10-11, he wrote:

As each has received a gift, employ it for one another, as good stewards of God's varied grace: whoever speaks, as one who utters oracles of God; whoever renders service [*diakonei*], as one who renders it by the strength which God supplies; in order that in everything God may be glorified through Jesus Christ.

Whatever one's service-role and means for sharing, that service and sharing must be done with each other's good in view and the glory of God as the motivation. Please note that the division between "words" and "deeds" is highlighted, indicating a distinction between those who labor using the medium of words—preachers and teachers, and those who serve in other ways. But whether the one or the other, a gift is being employed in the interest of benefiting others. Here, again, mutuality is underscored and a sense of equality and harmony encouraged.

Also instructive to observe is the way Paul dealt with those who served in ministry with him, those who were part of his travel and service team. Interestingly, although Timothy was considered by Paul as his "true child [*teknon*] "in the faith" (1 Tim. 1:2; 2 Tim. 1:2), that younger man was always honored by him as an able associate and "brother" (2 Cor. 1:1); although a known subordinate who followed the apostle's instructions and was given assignments from him, Timothy was respected by Paul as a worthy "staff member" and partner.[8]

What we see as indicative of Paul's regard for his associates is most instructive for relationships among those we now refer to as multiple ministry staff members. Although not much has been done in scholarly literature regarding the interpersonal relationship between Paul and Timothy, it is possible to trace in their sixteen-year association—and the literature that treats their teamwork —a mutual concern to grant enablement to each other for a more effective service.[9] Paul paid a high tribute to his younger associate when he wrote so expressively to the believers at Philippi: "I have no one like him, who will be genuinely anxious for your welfare. They all look after their own interests, not those of Jesus Christ. But Timothy's worth you know, how as a son with a father he has served with me in the gospel" (Philippians 2:20-22). Please note that Paul's tribute about Timothy accented Timothy's service in the gospel "with [*sun*] me," not "*for* me." Small wonder, then, that their association was so long, so rich, and so durable.

III

A brief word at this point about "prophets" is in order. The New Testament writings at times highlight this authority-figure as one whose words were Spirit-inspired, resulting in revelation, advance warning, and needed caution or clarification, benefits resulting from an "immediacy" not ordinarily available through a teacher or preacher occupied with a traditional handling of the gospel message. A case in point was the prophet Agabus, possibly of Jerusalem, mentioned twice in Acts. Acts 11:27-30 gives his prophecy about "a great famine over all the world" which took place, the narrator explains, in the days of Claudius. The local assembly of believers acted to prepare for the event, forearmed by the informing word through the Spirit's use of Agabus. Another prediction is credited to Agabus in Acts 21:10, a word about the coming persecution of Paul upon his arrival in Jerusalem.

Note that in the case of Agabus, the predictive element is highlighted, a feature of ministry that must be separated from the preacher's function of speaking spiritual truths as a forth-teller. The New Testament suggests that there is a certain exclusiveness to this kind of prophetic ministry; that even though the prophet works within the framework of some congregation as a member, he or she is honored not so much for the *preparation* of statements for the church, as a preacher or pastor, but for inspired utterance to the church. The factor of immediate inspiration must be said to attend the prophet, separating this role-order from that of the preacher or teacher. According to 1 Corinthians 14:29, all utterances were to be weighed by the group, each listener exercising judgment in doing so, but the special opening for such speaking was recognized as belonging to those who could thus speak, and verse 30 explains this as a Pauline rule (See Hawthorne 1987, esp. 119, 122-124). Those who had this kind of ministry gave oracles about problems in which the church or its members would be involved, offering the *mind* of the living Lord about the matter at hand or soon to come. Those who had this ministry, as did Agabus, seemed to have had it as a continuing rather than as an occasional one (See Ellis 1970, 55-56). The prophet took no claim for what was said, while those who preached sermons were largely responsible for the way the traditional message was handled. The prophets' authority rested in the fact, readily perceived, that they were "inspired spokesmen for the ultimate authority" (Aune 1983, 204). The prophet did not create his or her own role, it was a result of giftedness through the Spirit, and the service prophets rendered as the living Lord's speaking representatives was so perceived by the group as belonging to God's Spirit and their need. While their message could be "weighed," i.e., evaluated in light of known dominical teachings and biblical truths, the hearers were expected to honor that word in faith and action (219-222).

IV

The authority of the preacher, teacher, or administrator rests initially in a confirmed call from God to serve by sharing truth and a caring heart.

The accent here is upon a "confirmed call." Other believers can witness to confirmation at several levels. There is the level of one's grasp and statement of the truth and how that truth is in line with what the Lord of the Church and his declared apostles taught. One might refer to this in our time as *what is biblically-based*. There is also the level of perceived servanthood, that attitude of the minister by which others sense a basic motivation to honor God and help them. Even Jesus once explained, "My teaching is not mine, but his who sent me" (John 7:16), underscoring his relationship to God and the purpose he was sent to serve. There is also the level of perceived anointing to do what one is sent to do for God, and yet again, the level of moral and spiritual integrity that confirms one's conversion and character as godly.

Much is to be said about the importance of moral and spiritual integrity as elements of authority in one's work. As for the necessity to be persons of integrity, the New Testament highlights this as basic for the minister. First Timothy 3:1-7 is an adequate passage to show this. Even Jesus needed specific affirming from God for his ministry, and that affirmation came, the Gospels tell us, in connection with instances when he was obedient to the claim of God upon his life.[10] It was not enough that Jesus had his roots in divinity (as incarnate Son); he had to maintain and exemplify his true character in the real encounters with life as they impacted him. This is no less a demand upon those who seek to minister in his name.

The moral authority of the minister is largely dependent upon his or her steady compliance to a code of ethics as a professional; that is to say, being accountable to a set of values that determine his or her being and behavior as a Christian. Certification of one's life by God demands the cultivation of spirituality, a spirituality that is tested and exercised in life encounters. The ordination vows involve a public statement of declared accountability, not only to an expected faith-stance but also to a behavioral demand.[11] For an authority as minister, one's character must undergird competence, and it must remain a steady ally of a caring heart.

The person who has a divine call upon his or her life for specific service roles in the Christian community must understand himself or herself as an enabler, which demands on one's part competence, a responsible bearing, and a known code of ethics.

The integrity demanded of those who so serve must include such matters as honesty, self-control, confidentiality, the handling of debts, and being above low motives (out of which attempts to manipulate or exploit others usually issue).

All of what is stated here is crucial for gaining and maintaining credibility, for becoming accepted and regarded within the Christian community. The status that is conferred upon one by ordination grants an authorization, a right to be of service. Certified knowledge and expertise strengthen one's position as a competent servant, while one's character and experience keep that status qualitative and appealing. Knowledge, expertise, character, experience, and concern accent one's "right" or authority to be active in ministry.

V

The Corinthian correspondence of Paul is filled with references to his authority as a minister and apostle. The Apostle was on the defensive in both letters.[12] Not only was he dealing with specific problems of factionalism (1 Cor. 1:10-13; 3:3-4, 21; 4:6) and faulty teaching (I Cor. 6:12-13; Chapter 15), to name only two, but he did so with constant reference to his right to deal with these matters: "Am I not an apostle? Have I not seen Jesus our Lord?" he asked (1 Cor. 9:1b), while in 2 Corinthians 12:12 he asserted that his calling and authority had been clearly established through showing "the signs of a true apostle . . . in all patience, with signs and wonders and mighty works."

Then in 2 Corinthians 13:10 Paul explains his approach as one concerned that "I may not have to be severe in my use of the authority [*exousia*] which the Lord has given me for building up and not for tearing down." All of this was plainly defensive, written with concern to reassert his rightful authority against the opposing claims of others who considered their own status and mission primary. Paul appealed to certain legitimating criteria: along with a claim of "call" from God and Christ in his life were certifying evidences of doctrinal clarity, a Spirit-infused persona, integrity of character, exemplary experiences, unselfish service, and the spirit of humility. As Ralph P. Martin has put it, "Paul's counter-arguments may all be summed up in the contrast between a *theologia gloriae* and Paul's adhering to an embodiment of a *theologia crucis*" (Martin 1987, 286).

True authority, then, is seen in the minister's spirit of service and sacrificial surrender to the experience of the cross—this being proof positive that the servant's life is modeled after his or her Lord. The *imitatio Christi* has always been, and remains, the context for ministerial competence and the required validation for ministerial authority. As E. Earle Ellis has explained it, "the Christ who manifests God's wisdom and God's power is the one who in his exaltation remains Christ crucified, the serving and the sacrificing one. And this exalted Christ manifests these divine gifts among his followers only under the sign of the cross" (Ellis 1978, 79).

Endnotes

1. On the Greek meanings of "authority," see W. Foerster's article on *exousia* and related terms (1964, esp. 566-575).
2. House-churches seem implied by Paul's use of the plural in addressing such leaders as "bishops and deacons." It is interesting, however, that the Apostle does not address the believers as distinct congregations but as a unified fellowship. How different it was when addressing the Galatians, where at 1:2, 22 he used the plural in dealing with the distinct congregational groupings in their separate locales in the Galatia Province.
3. This accent on concerned caring is found also in Luke 15:8, where the related term *epimelos*, "diligently, carefully," appears. Joachim Jeremias has called attention to Luke's use of the *epimel*-wordgroup. See 1980, 192.
4. Interestingly, this listing, "bishops and deacons," does not appear in other Pauline lists about church governance. There is that enumeration in 1 Corinthians 12:28 about apostles, prophets, teachers, helpers, and administrators, and the list in Ephesians 4:11 is almost the same; but in neither listing does the designation "bishop" nor that of "deacon" appear. It might well be that the duties and responsibilities of both positions are assumed under other designations in those listings, i.e., pastor = bishop, helper = deacon, "server."

5. It is instructive to observe Paul's use of the singular and plural of the term "church" in his writings to local congregations. On this, see Rom. 16:1, 4, 5, 16, 23; 1 Cor. 1:2; 4:17; 7:17; 11:16, 18; chapter 14 *passim*; the majority of uses of the term in 2 Cor. reflect the plural. In Ephesians, the singular use of "church" reflects Paul's understanding of the entire body of believers universally. Colossians reflects the same understanding, except for the local use of the term in 4:15, 16. No attempt has been made here to give an exhaustive listing on this matter in the Pauline writings.

6. See the extended discussion of how the organization within the Pharisaic and Essenic communities can be traced back to that among the *hasidim* of Maccabean times, in Joachim Jeremias 1962, 259-262. See also F. F. Bruce 1956, esp. 124-126, 134; B. E. Thiering 1981, 59-74.

7. The wording at Acts 6:2b, "to serve tables [*diakonein trapezais*]" suggests that finance might well have been involved. Among the texts which use *trapeza* in connection with the handling of money, see Matt. 21:12; Mark 11:15, and John 2:15. See also F. F. Bruce 1952, 152.

8. E. Earle Ellis comments that "Although St. Paul had no disciples, no *mathetai*, he did have many associates." (1978, 3). While Timothy's discipleship under Paul appears to be alluded to in 2 Tim. 3:10, 14, Ellis's point is nevertheless quite clear that the Apostle honored his younger associate as a colleague rather than as a disciple.

9. For one brief study on this, see Edwin V. Hayden 1978, 42-49.

10. See especially Matthew 3:13-17; Mark 1:9-11; Luke 3:21-22; John 1:29-34.

11. Denominational recognition of the need for professional codes of ethics for ministers was formalized by the late 1920s. See a brief but pointed discussion of this by Arthur H. Becker 1987, 69-77. See also a rather basic study by Daniel Reeck 1982.

12. On the continuing questions about the nature of the opposition Paul experienced at Corinth, see E. Earle Ellis 1978, chapter 6, 80-115. See also Ralph P. Martin n.d., 279-289.

Bibliography

Aland, Kurt and Barbara. 1979. *Novum Testamentum Graece* 26. Stuttgart: Deutsche Bibelstiftung.
Alford, Henry. 1958. *The Greek Testament*, Vol. IV. Chicago: Moody.
Alter, Robert. 1981. *The Art of Biblical Narrative*. New York: Basic Books.
Anderson, Graham. 1984. *Ancient Fiction: The Novel in the Graeco-Roman World*. London: Croom Helm.
Aristotle. 1960. *The Poetics*. Cambridge, MA: Harvard University.
Auerbach, Erich. 1953. *Mimesis: The Representation of Reality in Western Literature*. Princeton: Princeton University.
Aune, David E. 1983. *Prophecy in Early Christianity and the Ancient Mediterranean World*. Grand Rapids: Eerdmans.

Barrett, C. K. 1966. *The Holy Spirit and the Gospel Tradition*. London: S. P. C. K.
Bartlett, Gene E. Bartlett. 1963. "And Gave Us the Ministry." *The Alumni Bulletin of Bangor Theological Seminary* XXXVIII, No. 2. April.
Bartlett, David. 1981. "Biblical Scholarship Today: A Diversity of New Approaches." *The Christian Century* 98.
Beale, G. K. 1984. *The Use of Daniel in Jewish Apocalyptic Literature and in the Revelation of St. John*. Lanham, MD: University Press of America.
Beasley and Murray. 1974. *Book of Revelation*. London: Oliphants.
Becker, Arthur H. 1987. "Professional Ethics For Ministry." *Trinity Seminary Review* 9. Fall. No. 2: 69-77.
Beckwith, Ibson T. 1922. *The Apocalypse of John*. New York: Macmillan.
Beegle, Dewey. 1978. *Prophecy and Prediction*. Ann Arbor, MI: Pryor Pettengill, Publisher.
Bengel, J. A. 1971. "Word Studies in Revelation." Lewis and Vincent, eds., *N. T. Word Studies*. Grand Rapids: Kregel.
Berkouwer, G. C. 1972. *The Return of Christ*. Grand Rapids: Eerdmans.
Beye, Charles R. 1975. *Ancient Greek Literature and Society*. Garden City, NY.
Bilezikan, Gilbert G. 1977. *The Liberated Gospel: A Comparison of the Gospel of Mark and Greek Tragedy*. Grand Rapids: Baker Books.
Blackwelder, Boyce W. 1958. *Light from the Greek New Testament*. Anderson, IN: Warner Press.
_____. 1971. *Letters From Paul, An Exegetical Translation*. Anderson, IN: Warner Press.
Blaney, J. S. 1966. "Revelation." *Wesleyan Bible Commentary*. Grand Rapids: Eerdmans.
Bornkamm, Guenther. 1960. *Jesus of Nazareth*. New York: Harper & Row.
Bousset, Wilhelm. 1906. *Die Offenbarung Johannis*. Gottingen: Vandenhoeck & Co.
Brereton, Geoffrey. 1968. *Principles of Tragedy: A Rational Examination of the Tragic Concept in Life and Literature*. Coral Gables, FL: University of Miami.
Bright, John. 1967. *The Authority of the Old Testament*. Nashville: Abingdon Press.
Brinsmead, Bernard Hungerford. 1982. *Dialogical Response to Opponents*. Chico, CA: Scholars Press.
Brooke and MacLean. 1909. *The Old Testament in Greek*. Cambridge: Cambridge University.
Brown, C. E. 1939. "Women Preachers." *Gospel Trumpet*. May 27: 5, 13.
Brown, Raymond, Karl P. Donfried and John Reumann. 1973. *Peter in the New*

Testament. New York: Paulist; Minneapolis: Augsburg.
_____. 1952. *The Acts of the Apostles: The Greek Text with Introduction and Commentary.* Grand Rapids: Eerdmans.
Bruce F. F. 1956. *Second Thoughts on the Dead Sea Scrolls.* Grand Rapids: Eerdmans.
_____. 1973. *The Epistle to the Galatians.* Grand Rapids MI: Eerdmans.
_____. 1977. *Paul, Apostle of the Heart Set Free.* Grand Rapids, MI: Eerdmans.
_____. 1986. Bruce, Ellison, Howley, eds. "Revelation." *The International Bible Commentary.* Grand Rapids: Zondervan.
Bultmann, Rudolf. 1968. *The History of the Synoptic Tradition* rev. ed. New York: Harper & Row.
Burnett, Fred W. 1987. "Characterization in Matthew: Reader Construction of the Disciple Peter." *McKendree Pastoral Review* 4: 13-44.
Burton, Earnest de Witt. 1920. *A Critical and Exegetical Commentary on the Epistle to the Galatians.* New York: Charles Scribner's Sons.
Byrum, Russell R. 1982. *Christian Theology,* revised edition. Anderson, IN: Warner Press.

Caird, G. B. 1966. *Commentary on the Revelation of St. John.* New York: Harper and Row.
Carter, Charles W., ed. 1983. *A Contemporary Wesleyan Theology.* Vol. 1. Grand Rapids, MI: Zondervan Corporation.
Carver, Frank C. 1987. "Biblical Foundation for the Secondness." *Wesleyan Theological Journal* 22, no. 2.
Case, Shirley J. 1919. *Revelation of John.* Chicago: University of Chicago.
Cassuto, U. 1961. *A Commentary on the Book of Genesis,* Israel Abrahams, trans. Jerusalem: Magnes Press, The Hebrew University.
Charles, R. H. 1920. *Revelation of St. John.* Edinburgh: T&T Clark.
Chatman, Seymour. 1972. "On the Formalist-Structuralist Theory of Character." *Journal of Literary Semantics* 1: 78.
_____. 1978. *Story and Discourse: Narrative Structure in Fiction and Film.* Ithaca, NY: Cornell University Press.
_____. 1983. *Narrative Fiction: Contemporary Poetics.* New York: Meuthen, 31-32.
Chesterton, G. K. 1908. *Orthodoxy.* New York: John Lane Co.
Collins, Yarbro. 1986. "Reading Revelation in the Twentieth Century." *Interpretation.*
Comblin, Jose. 1989. *The Holy Spirit and Liberation.* Trans. Paul Burns. Maryknoll: Orbis Books.
Conzelmann, Hans. 1960. *The Theology of St. Luke.* Trans. Geoffrey Boswell. London: Faber and Faber.
_____. 1973. *Jesus.* Philadelphia: Fortress.
Conzelman, Hans and Andreas Lineman. 1988. *Interpreting the New Testament: An Introduction to the Principles of N. T. Exegesis.* Peabody, Massachusetts: Hendrickson.
"Council on Biblical Manhood and Womanhood, The Danvers Statement." 1989. *Christianity Today* 33. January 13: 40-41.
Cranfield, C. E. B. 1975. *Romans* I. Edinburgh: T&T Clark Ltd.
Crownfield, Frederick C. 1945. "The Singular Problem of the Dual Galatians." *Journal of Biblical Literature* 64: 494-495.
Culler, Jonathan. 1978. *Structuralist Poetics: Structuralism, Linguistics, and the Study of Literature.* Ithaca, NY: Cornell University.
Culpepper, Alan. 1983. *Anatomy of the Fourth Gospel: A Study in Literary*

Design. Philadelphia: Fortress.
_____. 1988. *Interpreting the New Testament: An Introduction to the Principles of N. T. Exegesis*. Peabody, Massachusetts: Hendrickson.
Dana, H. E. and Julius R. Mantey. 1957. *A Manual Grammar of the Greek New Testament*. New York: The Macmillan Company.
Dayton, Donald. 1986. "Historical Background of Pneumatalogical Issues in the Holiness Movement." Larry Shelton and Alex Deasley, eds. *Spirit and the New Age*. Anderson, IN: Warner Press.
_____. 1987. "Historical Hermeneutic for Women in Ministry" in "Alma White: Holiness Preacher with a Feminist Message." Ph. D. dissertation. Denver: 304-337.
Dentan, Robert C. 1951. "The Unity of the Old Testament." *Interpretation* 5: 154.
Dibelius, Martin. n. d. *From Tradition to Gospel*. New York: Schribners.
Dihle, Albrecht. 1956. *Studien Zur Griechischen Biographie*. Gottingen: Vandenhoeck & Ruprecht.
_____. n. d. "Die Evangeliem und die grieschische Biographie." Peter Stuhlmacher, ed. *Das Evangelium und die Evangelien*, 383-411.
Docherty, Thomas. 1983. *Reading [Absent] Character: Towards a Theory of Characterization in Fiction*. Oxford: Clarendon.
Dodd, C. H. 1974. *The Meaning of Paul For Today*. New York: World Publishing Co. New American Library.
Dodds. E. R. 1970. *Pagan & Christian in the Age of Anxiety*. New York: W. W. Norton.
Doty, William G. 1973. *Letters in Primitive Christianity*. Philadelphia: Fortress.
Drake, John. 1975. *Paul: Libertine or Legalist*. London: SCM Press.

Earle, Ralph. n.d. "The Revelation." *Beacon Bible Commentary*. Vol. 10.
Easterling, P. E. 1972. *Sophocles: A Reading*. Melbourne.
_____. 1983. "Character in Sophocles." *Greek Tragedy: Modern Essays in Criticism*. Erich Segal, ed. New York: Harper & Row: 141.
Eissfeldt, Otto. 1965. *The Old Testament: An Introduction*. New York: Harper and Row.
Ellis, Earle E. 1952. *The Acts of the Apostles: The Greek Text with Introduction and Commentary*. Grand Rapids: Eerdmans.
_____. 1970. "The Role of the Christian Prophet in Acts." *Apostolic History and the Gospel: Biblical and Historical Essays presented to F. F. Bruce*. W. Ward Gasque and Ralph P. Martin, eds. Grand Rapids: Eerdmans.
_____. 1971: "Paul and His Opponents." *Christianity, Judaism, and Other Greco-Roman Cults: Studies for Morton Smith at Sixty*. J. Neusner, ed.
_____. 1978. *Prophecy and Hermeneutic in Early Christianity*. Grand Rapids: Eerdmans, 80-115.
_____. 1978. *Prophecy and Hermeneutic in Early Christianity: New Testament Essays*. Grand Rapids: Eerdmans.
Ellul. n.d. *Book of Revelation*.
Erdman, Charles. 1936. *Revelation of John*. Philadelphia: Westminster.
Evans, Elizabeth C. 1948. "Literary Portraiture in Ancient Epic." *Harvard Studies in Classical Philology* 48-49: 189-217.

Feuillet, Andre. 1962. *L'Apocalypse, Etat de la question*. Paris: Bruges.
_____. 1963. *L'Apoc: Etat de la question*. Paris: Brugge.

Fiorenza, Elizabeth Schussler. 1981. *Invitation to the Book of Revelation.* Garden City, NY: Image Books, Doubleday.
———. 1985. *The Book of Revelation: Justice and Judgment.* Philadelphia: Fortress Press.
———. 1986. "Early Christian Apocalypticism." A. Yarbro Collins, ed. *Semeia*, 36.
Fitzmyer, Joseph. 1981. *The Gospel According to Luke (I-IX): The Anchor Bible.* Garden City: Doubleday.
Foerster, W. 1964. *Theological Dictionary of the New Testament* II. Gerhard Kittel, ed. Geoffrey W. Bromiley, trans. Grand Rapids, MI: Eerdmans: 566-575.
Fokkelman, J. P. 1975. *Narrative Art in Genesis.* Assen: Van Gorcum.
Ford, J. Massyngberde. 1975. *Revelation.* Garden City, NY: Doubleday. Anchor Bible.
Forster, E. M. 1927. *Aspects of the Novel.* New York: Harcourt, Brace.
Freedman, R. David. 1983. "Woman, A Power Equal to Man." *Biblical Archaeology Review* 9.
Furnisn, Victor P. 1979. *The Moral Teaching of Paul.* Nashville, TN: Abingdon Press.
Gamble, Harry. 1977. *The Textual History of the Letter to the Romans.* Grand Rapids MI: Eerdmans.

Garvey, James. 1978. "Characterization in Narrative." *Poetics* 7:63.
Gasque, Ward. 1988. "A Fruitful Field: Recent Studies of the Acts of the Apostles. *Interpretation* 42: 127.
Gaventa, Beverly Roberts. 1989. "Toward a Theology of Acts: Reading and Rereading." *Interpretation* 42:150.
Gill, Christopher. 1983. "The Question of Character Development: Plutarch and Tacitus." *Classical Quarterly* 33: 471.
Glasson, T. F. 1965. *Revelation of John.* Cambridge: University Press.
Guelich, Robert. 1983. "The Gospel Genre." *Das Evangelium and die Evangelien.* Peter Stuhlmacher, ed. Tuebingen: J. C. B. Mohr: 183-219.
Gunther, John. 1973. *St. Paul's Opponents and Their Background.* Leiden: E. J. Brill.
Guthrie, Donald. 1987. *The Relevance of John's Apocalypse.* Grand Rapids: Eerdmans.

Haegg, Thomas. n. d. *The Novel in Antiquity.* Berkeley: University of California.
Hanfmann, George M. 1952. "Observations on Roman Portraiture." *Latomus* 11: 454-455.
Hansom, Pauld. 1988. "Biblical Interpretation: Meeting Place of Jews and Christians." *Canon, Theology, and Old Testament Interpretation.* Gene Tucker, David Petersen, and Robert Wilson, eds. Philadelphia: Fortress: 40-41.
Hanson, Paul. 1987. *Old Testament Apocalyptic.* Nashville: Abingdon Press.
Harvey, W. J. 1966. *Character and the Novel.* Ithaca, NY: Cornell University.
Hasel, Gerhard F. 1975. *Old Testament Theology, Basic Issues in the Current Debate*, rev. ed. Grand Rapids, Michigan: William B. Eerdmans Publishing Company.
Hawthorne, Gerald F. 1987. "The Role of Christian Prophets in the Gospel Tradition." *Tradition and Interpretation in the New Testament: Essays in Honor of E. Earle Ellis.* Gerald F. Hawthorne with Otto Betz, eds. Grand Rapids: Eerdmans: 122-124.
Hayden, Edwin V. 1978. "Paul and Timothy: A Scriptural Study of a Multiple Ministry." *Essays on New Testament Christianity: A Festschrift in Honor of*

Dean E. Walker. C. Robert Wetzel, ed. Cincinnati: Standard Publishing Co.: 42-49.
Hayter, Mary. 1987. *The New Eve in Christ*. Grand Rapids, MI: William B. Eerdmans Publishing Company.
Hendriksen, William. 1944. *More Than Conquerors*. Grand Rapids: Baker.
Henry, Carl F. H. 1960. *Christianity Today* V. No. 4. Wheaton, IL: Christianity Today, Inc. November 21.
Heschel, Abraham. 1969. "What Manner of Man is the Prophet?" *The Prophets*. Harper Torchbooks. New York: Harper and Row.
Holland, Norman N. 1975. *Dynamics of Literary Response*. New York: W. W. Norton.
Houlden, J. L. 1977. *Paul's Letters From Prison*. Philadelphia, PA: Westminster Press.
Howard, George. 1973. *Paul: Crisis in Galatia: A Study in Early Christian Theology*. Cambridge: University Press.
Howard, Richard E. 1975. *Newness of Life*. Grand Rapids, MI: Baker Book House.
Hubner, Hans. 1980. *Das Gesetz bei Paulus*. Goettingen: Vandenhoeck & Ruprecht.
Hynson, Leon O., ed. 1978. *The Development of Wesleyan Holiness Theology*. Marion, IN: Wesleyan Theological Society.

Iser, Wolfgang. 1980. *The Implied Reader. Patterns of Communication in Prose Fiction from Bunyan to Beckett*. Baltimore: Johns Hopkins.

Jeremias, Joachim. 1980. *Die Sprache des Lukasevangeliums: Redaktion und Tradition im Nicht-Markusstoff des dritten Evangeliums*. Goettingen: Vandenhoeck & Euprecht.
———. 1962. *Jerusalem in the Time of Jesus: An Investigation into Economic and Social Conditions during the New Testament Period*. F. H. and C. H. Cave, eds. Philadelphia: Fortress Press.
Jeske, Richard L. and David L. Barr, reviewers. 1988. "The Study of the Apocalypse Today." *Religious Studies Review*. 14:4. October.
Jewett, Paul K. 1975. *Man as Male and Female*. Grand Rapids: William B. Eerdmans Publishing Company.
Jones, Grahame C. 1983. " 'Flat' and 'Round' Characters, The Example of Stendhal." *Australian Journal of French Studies* 20: 115-129.
Jones, Kenneth E. 1981. "An Amillennial Reply to Peters." *Journal of Evangelical Theological Society*. 24/4. December: 333-341.

Kaehler, Christoph 1976-77. "Zur Formund Traditions-geschichte von Matth. XVI.17-19." *New Testament Studies* 23: 36-58.
Keck, Leander. 1986. "Toward the Renewal of New Testament Christology." *New Testament Studies* 32: 362-377.
Kennedy, George A. 1984. *New Testament Interpretation through Rhetorical Criticism*. Chapel Hill: University of North Carolina: 1-33.
Kepler, Thomas J. 1957. *Book of Revelation*. New York: Oxford University Press.
Kermode, Frank. 1979. *The Genesis of Secrecy: On the Interpretation of Narrative*. Cambridge, MA: Harvard University.
Kiddle, Martin. 1940. *Revelation of St. John*. Moffatt New Testament Commentaries. London: Hodder and Stoughton.
Kierkegaard, Soren. 1966. *The Concept of Dread*. Qtd. by Bernard Ramm in *A*

Handbook of Contemporary Theology. Grand Rapids, MI: Eerdmans.
Kingsbury, Jack Dean. 1979. "The Figure of Peter in Matthew's Gospel As a Theological Problem." *Journal of Biblical Literature* 98: 67-83.
Kitto, H. D. F. 1950. *Greek Tragedy: A Literary Study.* 2nd ed. London: Methuen.
Kline. n.d. "Double Trouble." *Journal of Evangelical Theological Society.*
Knierim, Rolf. 1973. "Old Testament Form Criticism Reconsidered." *Interpretation* 27: 435-467.
Koch, Klaus. 1969. *The Growth of the Biblical Tradition: The Form-Critical Method.* New York: Charles Scribner's.
Koester, Helmut. 1974. "Physis." *Theological Dictionary of the New Testament.* G. Friedrich, ed. Grand Rapids: *Eerdmans.* 9: 253.
Korfmacher, William C. 1934. "Three Phases of Classical Type Characterization." *The Classical Weekly* 26: 85.
Kraft, Heinrich. 1974. *Die Offenbarung des Johannes.* Tubingen: J. C. B. Mohr.
Kuemmel, Werner. 1972. *The New Testament: The History of the Investigation of Its Problems.* Nashville: Abingdon.
_____. 1975. *Introduction to the New Testament.* London: SCM Press.
Kufeldt, George. 1984. James Massey, ed. "Context and Meaning." *Education for Service.* Anderson, IN: Warner Press.
Kuhn, G. H. 1975. "Antichrist." "Babylon." *Theological Dictionary of the New Testament.* Colin Brown, ed. Grand Rapids: Zondervan.
Kuyper, Abraham. 1972. *Revelation of St. John.* Trans. Hendrik de Vries. Grand Rapids: Eerdmans.

Ladd, George. 1988. "Revelation, Book of." *International Standard Bible Encyclopedia*, revised. Grand Rapids: Eerdmans [1915] Vol. 4.
Lahaye, Tim. n.d. *Revelation Illustrated and Made Plain.* Grand Rapids: Zondervan.
Lampe, G. W. H. 1967. "The Holy Spirit in the Writings of St. Luke." *Studies in the Gospels: Essays in Memory of R. H. Lightfoot.* D. E. Nineham, ed. Oxford: Basil Blackwell: 159.
Lattimore, Richard A. 1965. *Story Patterns in Greek Tragedy.* Ann Arbor, MI: University of Michigan.
Lenski, R. C. H. 1943. *Interpretation of St. John's Revelation.* Minneapolis: Augsburg.
Leonard, George B. Jr. 1961. *The Student Writer.* December.
Leonard, Juanita, ed. 1989. *Called to Minister, Empowered to Serve.* Anderson, IN: Warner Press.
Lindsey, Hal, 1970. *Late Great Planet Earth.* Grand Rapids: Zondervan.
Linn, Otto F. 1942. *Studies in the New Testament (Hebrews to Revelation).* Anderson, IN: The Commercial Service Company.

Macauley, Robie and George Lanning. 1964. *Techniques in Fiction.* New York: Harper & Row.
Mailloux, Steven. 1979. "Learning to Read: Interpretation and Reader-Response Criticism." *Studies in the Literary Imagination* 12. Genre. Spring.
_____. 1977. "Reader Response Criticism?" *Genre.* Fall: 414-415.
Malbone, Elizabeth Struthers. 1982. "Disciples/Crowds Whoever: A Markan Narrative Pattern." Paper presented to *Society of Biblical Literature* on "Literary Aspects of the Gospels and Acts."
Mandelkern, Solomon. 1986. *Veteris Testamenti Concordantiae, Hebraicae atque Chaldaicae.* Lipsiae: Veit et Comp.

Marshall, I. Howard. 1971. *Luke: Historian and Theologian*. Grand Rapids: MI: Zondervan.
Martin, Ralph P. n.d. "The Opponents of Paul in 2 Corinthians: An Old Issue Revisited." *Tradition and Interpretation in the New Testament: Essays in Honor of E. Earle Ellis*. Gerald F. Hawthorne and Otto Betz, eds.: 279-289.
Marxsen, Willi. 1968. *Introduction to the New Testament*. Philadelphia: Fortress.
McCarthy, Mary. 1961. "Characters in Fiction." *Partisan Review* 28: 173.
McCown, Wayne. 1986. "The Spirit in the Book of Acts." *The Spirit and the New Age*. Larry Shelton and Alex Deasley, eds. Anderson, IN: Warner Press.
McKane, William. 1979. *Studies in Patriarchal Narratives*. Edinburgh: Handsel.
Merritt, John G. 1987. "Dialogue Within a Tradition: John Wesley and Gregory of Nyssa Discuss Christian Perfection." *Wesleyan Theological Journal* 22, no. 2. Wilmore, KY. Weslyan Theological Society.
Metz, Donald S. 1971. *Studies in Biblical Holiness*. Kansas City, MO: Beacon Hill Press.
Miller, Gene. 1976. *God's Saving Power* (formerly *The Power of God for Salvation*). Anderson, IN: Warner Press.
Miller, Stuart. 1967. *The Picaresque Novel*. Cleveland: Case Western Reserve.
Milton, John P. 1963. *Prophecy Interpreted*. Minneapolis: Augsburg Publishing House.
Misener, G. "Iconistic Portraits." 1924. *Classical Philology* 19.
Moffatt, James. 1951. *Revelation of St. John the Divine*. Nicoll. W. Robertson. (Expositors Greek Testament). Grand Rapids: Eerdmans.
Morris, Leon. 1969. *The Revelation of St. John*. Grand Rapids: Eerdmans.
Morton, Robert and John Barton. 1988. *Biblical Interpretation*. Oxford: Oxford University Press.
Muilenburg, James. 1969. "Form Criticism and Beyond." *Journal of Biblical Literature* 88: 213.
Murdick, Marvin. 1960-1961. "Character and Event in Fiction." *The Yale Review* 50: 213.
Murray, George. 1948. *Millennial Studies: A Search for Truth*. Grand Rapids, MI: Baker Book House.

Neusner, Jacob. 1984. *Judaism in the Beginning of Christianity*. Philadelphia: Fortress.

Osley, A. S. 1946. "Greek Biography Before Plutarch." *Greece and Roman* 15: 20.

Parsons, Mikeal. 1987. "Reading Talbert: New Perspectives on Luke-Acts," *Society of Biblical Literature Seminar Papers*. Atlanta: Scholars Press.
Patterson, James Alan. 1988. "Changing Images of the Beast: Apocalyptic Conspiracy Theories in American History." *Journal of Evangelical Theological Society*. 31/4. December.
Pearson Sharon C. 1989. Juanita Leonard, ed. "Biblical Precedents for Women in Ministry." *Called to Minister, Empowered to Serve*. Anderson, IN: Warner Press. 13-33.
_____. 1989. "Women in Ministry." *Vital Christianity* 6. June: 32-36.
Pentecost, J. Dwight. 1958. *Things to Come*. Grand Rapids: Zondervan.
Peters, G. H. N. n.d. *Theocratic Kingdom*, II.
Peterson, Eugene H. 1988. *Reversed Thunder, the Revelation of John and the Praying Imagination*. San Francisco: Harper and Row.
Peterson, Norman. 1985. "Myth and Characterization in Mark and in John."

Paper presented to the *Society of Biblical Literature Group* on "Literary Aspects of the Gospels."
Phillips, Harold L. 1979. *Miracle of Survival*. Anderson, IN: Warner Press.
Philo. 1949. *De Congressu Quaerendae Eruditionis*. Loeb.
Porter, Calvin L. 1964. "Biblical Studies." *The Encounter* XXV, No. 3. Summer.
Poythress, Vern S. 1987. *Understanding Dispensationalists*. Grand Rapids: Zondervans Academie Books.
Purkiser, W. T. 1983. *Exploring Christian Holiness*. Vol. 1. Kansas City, MO: Beacon Hill Press.

Raisenen, Heikki. 1983. *Paul and the Law*. Tubingen.
Raphael, D. D. 1960. *The Paradox of Tragedy*. Bloomington, IN: Indiana University: 16-24.
Redford, D. B. 1970. *Study of the Biblical Story of Joseph*. Leiden: Brill.
Reeck, Daniel. 1982. *Ethics for the Professions*. Minneapolis: Augsburg Publishing House.
Rimmon-Kenan, Schlomith. 1978. On the Formalist-Structuralist Theory of Character." *Journal of Literary Semantics*. 1: 78.
———. 1983. *Narrative Fiction: Contemporary Poetics*. New York: Meuthen; Routledge, Chapman & Hall.
Rist, Martin. 1957. "Revelation." *Interpreters Bible*. Vol 12. New York: Abingdon.
Robbins, Vernon K. 1984. *Jesus the Teacher: A Socio-Rhetorical Interpretation of Mark*. Philadelphia: Fortress.
Russell, D. A. 1976. "On Reading Plutarch's Lives." *Greece and Rome* 13: 139-154.
Russell, D. S. 1986. *Apocalyptic: Ancient and Modern*. Philadelphia: Fortress Press.
Russell, J. Stuart. 1983. *The Parousia: A Critical Inquiry into the New Testament Doctrine of Our Lord's Second Coming*. Grand Rapids: Baker Book House. [1887.]
Ryrie, Charles Caldwell. 1958. *The Role of Women in the Church*. Chicago: Moody Press.

Sanders, E. P. 1977. *Paul and Palestinian Judaism: A Comparison of Patterns of Religion*. London: SCM.
Sanders, James A. 1984. *Canon and Community: A Guide to Canonical Criticism*. Philadelphia: Fortress.
Sawyer, Sharon. 1976. "Women Pastors in the Church of God." *Colloquim* 8. July/August: 1, 2, 7.
Scanzoni, Letha and Nancy Hardesty. 1974. *All We're Meant To Be*. Waco, Texas: Word Books Publishers.
Schoeps, Hans J. 1961. *Paul: The Theology of the Apostle in the Light of Jewish Religious History*. London, Westminster: John Knox.
Scholes, Robert. 1968. *Elements of Fiction*. New York: Oxford University, 17.
Scholes, Robert and Robert Kellogg. 1968. *The Nature of Narrative*. New York: Oxford University.
Schultz, John H. 1975. *Authority*. Cambridge: University Press.
Schweitzer, Albert. 1956. *The Mysticism of Paul the Apostle*. London: Adams & Charles Black.
Seebas, H. n. d. "Babylon." *New International Dictionary of New Testament Theology*. Vol. I.
Seiss, Joseph A. 1957. *The Apocalypse*. Grand Rapids: Zondervan.
Shuler, Philip L. 1982. *A Genre for the Gospels. The Biographical Character of*

Matthew. Philadelphia: Fortress.
Silverman, Kaja. 1983. *Subject of Semiotics*. New York: Oxford University.
Smith, F. G. 1914. *What the Bible Teaches*. Anderson, IN: Gospel Trumpet Company. (Reprint Guthrie, OKlahoma: Faith Publishing House, 1973.)
Smith, Timothy L. 1986. "John Wesley and the Second Blessing." *Wesleyan Theological Journal* 21, no. 2. Wilmore KY: Wesleyan Theological Society.
Stanley, John. 1975. "Women's Liberation & Christianity." *Colloquim* 7. November/December: 2, 6.
Stanley, John. 1976. "Stay in the City." *Colloquium* 8. November-December: 3, 7.
Stanley, Susie. (Forthcoming). "Empowered Foremothers: Wesleyan Holiness Women Speak to Today's Christian Feminists." *Wesleyan Theological Journal*.
———. (Forthcoming.) "What Sanctification Means to Me: Holiness as Power." *Centering in Ministry*.
Stanton, G. S. 1974. *Jesus of Nazareth in New Testament Preaching*. New York: Cambridge University.
Stendahl, Krister. 1963. "The Apostle Paul and the Introspective Conscience of the West." *Harvard Theological Review*: 199-215.
Sternberg, Meir. 1985. *The Poetics of Biblical Narrative: Ideological Literature and the Drama of Reading*. Bloomington: Indiana University.
Stewart, James. n.d. *A Man in Christ*. New York: Harper & Row.
Strong, Marie. 1978. "One Christian's Views of Women's Rights." *Colloquim* 10. May/June 1978: 4-6.
Summers, Ray. 1951. *Worthy is the Lamb*. Nashville: Broadman Press.
Swete, Henry B. 1919. *The Apocalypse of St John*. Grand Rapids: Eerdmans [1908]. New York: Macmillan.

Talbert, Charles H. 1977. *What Is a Gospel? The Genre of the Canonical Gospels*. Philadelphia: Fortress.
———. 1974. *Literary Patterns: Theological Themes and the Genre of Luke-Acts*. Missoula, MT: Scholars Press.
———. 1982. *Reading Luke: A Literary and Theological Commentary on the Third Gospel*. New York: Crossroad.
———. 1984. *Acts: Knox Preaching Guide*. Atlanta: John Knox.
Tannehill, Robert C. 1986. *The Narrative Unity of Luke-Acts: A Literary Interpretation. Vol. 1: The Gospel According to Luke*. Philadelphia: Fortress.
Tasker, R. V. G. 1961. *The Gospel According to St. Matthew*, Grand Rapids, MI: Eerdmans.
Tenney, Merrill C. 1957. *Interpreting Revelation*. Grand Rapids: Eerdmans.
Thiering, B. E. 1981. "*Mebaqqer* and *Episkopos* in the Light of the Temple Scroll." *Journal of Biblical Literature* 100: 59-74.
Todorov, Tzvetan. n.d. "Reading as Construction." *The Reader in the Text: Essays on Audience and Interpretation*. Susie R. Suleiman, ed. Princeton: Princeton University: 77.
Turner, George A. 1977. *Christian Holiness in Scripture, in History, and in Life*. Kansas City, MO: Beacon Hill Press.

Vawter, Bruce. 1965. *Introduction to the Prophetical Books*. Old Testament Reading Guide No. 14. Collegeville, MN: Liturgi Press.
Vermes, Geza. 1984. *Jesus and the World of Judaism*. Philadelphia: Fortress .
Von Rad, Gerhard. 1961. *Genesis, A Commentary*. John H. Marks, trans. Philadelphia: Westminster Press.

Vorster, Willem. 1985. "Characterization of Peter in the Gospel of Mark." Paper presented to the *Society of Biblical Literature Group* on "Literary Aspects of the Gospels."

Wall, Robert. 1989. "The Acts of the Apostles in Canonical Context." *Biblical Theology Bulletin* 18.

Walvoord, John F. 1966. *The Revelation of Jesus Christ*. Chicago: Moody Press.

Watson, Francis. 1986. *Paul, Judaism and the Gentiles: a Sociological Approach*. Society for N.T. Studies. Monographs No. 56. Cambridge: University Press.

Wedderburn, A. J. M. 1979. "The Purpose and Occasion of Romans Again." *Expository Times* 90: 5.

Weinsheimer, Joel. 1979. "Theory of Character: Emma." *Poetics Today* 1: 195.

Westcott, Brooke Foss and Fenton John Anthony Hort, eds. *The New Testament in the Original Greek*. London.

Westermann, Claus. 1984. *Genesis 1-11, A Commentary*, John J. Scullion S.J., trans. Minneapolis: Augsburg Publishing House.

Whiteley, D. E. H. 1964. *The Theology of St. Paul*. Oxford: Basil Blackwell.

Wynkoop, Mildred B. 1972. *A Theology of Love*. Kansas City, MO: Beacon Hill Press.